New Israel / New E

NEW ISRAEL / NEW ENGLAND

Jews and Puritans in Early America

MICHAEL HOBERMAN

UNIVERSITY OF MASSACHUSETTS PRESS

Amherst and Boston

LC 2011032775
ISBN 978-1-55849-920-1 (paper); ISBN 978-1-55849-906-5 (cloth)

Designed by Sally Nichols
Set in Adobe Quaadrat
Printed and bound by Thomson-Shore, Inc.

Library of Congress Cataloging-in-Publication Data

Hoberman, Michael.
New Israel/New England : Jews and Puritans in early America / Michael Hoberman.
p. cm.
Includes bibliographical references and index.
ISBN 978-1-55849-920-1 (pbk. : alk. paper) — ISBN 978-1-55849-906-5 (library
cloth : alk. paper) 1. Jews—New England—History—17th century. 2. Jews—New
England—History—18th century. 3. Puritans—New England—History—17th century.
4. Puritans—New England—History—18th century. 5. United States—History—Colonial
period, ca. 1600–1775. 6. New England—Ethnic relations. I. Title.
F15.J5H64 2011
973.2—dc23
2011032775

British Library Cataloguing in Publication data are available.

This book is dedicated to my mother, Milka Burstein,
whose passion, wisdom, and love know no bounds.

CONTENTS

ILLUSTRATIONS

PREFACE

Like Judaism, Puritanism was a profoundly discursive faith, and its practitioners were never more themselves than when they debated each other. In their own writing about and interaction with actual Jews, Puritans could be at once harshly judgmental and strangely admiring. Although their high regard for the Hebrew Bible was more often than not an instrument with which they sought to chastise those religious outliers who were courageous or foolish enough to enter their territories from the mid-seventeenth century until the Revolution itself, Puritans fashioned a complex and multifaceted religious heritage out of that same Bible fixation. No Puritan worthy of the name was willing to sanction the tolerance of errant peoples or believers, but Puritans themselves were so intrinsically unsettled in their own faith that their internal debates and long-standing ambivalence concerning the sovereignty of God, the proper exercise of human agency, and the role of the church community forced them into creating a society which championed the rights of dissenters over the will of an established church. The tensions that informed their spiritual beliefs and institutions were too powerful to be ignored, and their fascination with Jews and with Jewish history was a primary means by which they articulated both their aspirations and their misgivings.

Puritan discourse on the history of the Jews, as well as the experiences of actual Jews who came to New England during the colonial era, also spoke to the facts of life on the farther edge of the Atlantic world, where religious missions and spiritual intentions frequently proved less powerful than economic expediency and political practicality. Both the Puritans who settled permanently in New England and the Sephardic Jews who occasionally visited and traded with them there were profoundly mobile peoples whose ties on both sides of the Atlantic precluded isolation or insularity. Theirs was no mutual admiration society, but neither was it a doomed encounter between bitter enemies. The complex history of their interactions forms a foundational episode in the development of America's vaunted Judeo-Christian tradition and helps account as well for its more recent embrace of an ecumenical equivalency among the three Abrahamic faiths.

I could not have undertaken the research or writing for this book without the generous assistance of several institutions and individuals. To begin, the funding and support I received from a National Endowment for the Humanities/Massachusetts Historical Society Long Term Fellowship made it possible for me to devote an entire academic year (2008–2009) to working on this project. The grant afforded me the luxury of not having to divide my time between research and teaching that year. I should like to take this opportunity to thank Conrad Wright, the director of research programs at the MHS, for having helped to orchestrate my year there. The fellowship brought with it all manner of additional perks, including the opportunities it afforded me to meet dozens of other scholars in early American and New England history both in the course of my daily interactions and as a result of several weekly seminars and presentations hosted by the MHS. The fellowship also provided access to Harvard's Widener Library stacks, which I came to rely on weekly. Had I not been fortunate enough to receive this fellowship, I suppose I might just about now be at the point of drafting the book's early chapters, if I had taken the project on at all.

I would like as well to thank Fitchburg State University for granting me a full year's leave of absence so that I could benefit from the NEH fellowship. Patrice Gray, Michael Fiorentino, and Robert Antonucci all very kindly and enthusiastically supported my request for the extra time and helped me to manage the necessary health insurance logistics. As my colleagues in the English department at Fitchburg found themselves having to fill various sorts of gaps brought about by my year's absence, I would like as well to thank them for their graciousness in not trying to make me feel guilty for being gone for an entire year at their partial expense.

When it came time for me to shepherd the book through its final stages of preparation and revision, I was also assisted by the Fulbright Program, which offered me a guest professorship (with lighter teaching responsibilities than my usual ones) at Utrecht University in the Netherlands during the winter and spring of 2010. Marcel Oomen and Linda Pietersen of the Fulbright Center in Amsterdam were kind, welcoming, and brimming with practical advice and assistance. My friends and colleagues in the American Studies program in Utrecht, Jaap Verheul and Derek Rubin, offered encouragement and good humor, and helped in every way to make this, my *fourth* Dutch sojourn, possible. Their enthusiasm for this project and for the teaching possibilities that it inspired helped to ensure the success of my Fulbright proposal.

As my first go at conducting archival research, the preparation of this book took me beyond my ordinary parameters. Without the guidance and assistance of several knowledgeable individuals, not to mention the resources of the libraries where they work, I would not have come this far. At the Massachusetts Historical Society, I received frequent and smiling assistance from Peter Drummey, Jeremy Dibbell, Elaine Grublin, Tracy Potter, Anna Cook, Caitlin Corless, and Heather Merrill. Burt Lippencott III provided help at the Newport Historical Society, which I visited in October 2008. Staff members at the American Jewish Historical Society (in New York) assisted me during my visits there. In addition, the American Jewish Archives (Cincinnati), the Virginia Historical Society, and the Beinecke Library at Yale kindly provided me with photocopies of archival materials when I requested them. I conducted additional research at the Widener, Lamont, and Houghton Libraries at Harvard, as well as at Amherst College's Robert Frost Library and the University of Massachusetts Amherst's W. E. B. Du Bois Library.

In part because I am not a formally trained historiographer, I relied heavily as well on the helpful advice of several scholars who were more than willing—on several occasions—to review portions of my chapter drafts. Francis Bremer, Richard Cogley, Meredith Neumann, William Pencak, Reiner Smolinski, Conrad Wright, and one anonymous reader for the *Massachusetts Historical Review* all read bits and pieces of the book in its earliest stages and offered me substantive commentary each time they did so. When the manuscript was complete, Bill Pencak and Reiner Smolinski went to work once again as official reviewers for the publisher. The responses I received from these experts were invaluable to me at every stage in the book's preparation. In addition, I would like to thank several individuals who read the original grant proposal, book prospectus, or some other small portion of the project and were more than willing to share their thoughts with me. These people include Bornali Bhandari, Sean Goodlett, Aruna Krishnamurthy, Ben Railton, and Ian Williams (who also supplied me with a title for the book), all colleagues of mine at Fitchburg State University; Laura Leibman (Reed College); Jonathan Sarna (Brandeis University); and Graham Warder (Keene State College). Brendan McConnville (Boston University), a fellow Reedie and participant in the Boston Area Early American History seminar, offered helpful bibliographic guidance, as did Abe Peck (University of Southern Maine). Finally, I am eager to acknowledge the encouragement, advice, and graciousness of my editor, Clark Dougan, who has helped me at every stage, from conception to completion.

The professional help I received from the people and institutions I've named was accompanied all along by practical and moral support from several friends and family members. Patrick Jackson helped me by transcribing several pages worth of Cotton Mather's nearly unreadable scrawl and Moses Michael Hays's correspondence. Simone Gugliotta kindly translated several sermons by Jehoshua da Silva from the original Portuguese into English. Philippe Simon, my fellow goat-milker, chicken-feeder, and dog-walker here in Buckland, has always made himself available to do farm chores when I've needed to be away, including when I left for Holland *just when the goats were about to kid.* I would also like to thank Joan and Dick Benjamin for their warm hospitality to me during my residency in Boston; I would not have been able to spend such a productive year at the MHS without their having so kindly offered their guest bedroom to me for several nights a week for an entire year. My stepmother, Dr. Hilda Hoberman, offered me a place to stay, delicious home-cooked meals, and a family welcome whenever I needed to visit the AJHS in New York. My wife Janice, daughter Della, and son Lang have all done their part to encourage and inspire me in the production of this, my third "best-selling" academic monograph in a dozen or so years. My mother, Milka Burstein, has given me cheering encouragement all along, and was also generous enough to offer me kind assistance with the preparation of the book's index.

New Israel / New England

"WE SHALL BE FRIENDS"

The European Background for Puritan Judeocentrism

IN THE SEVENTEENTH CENTURY two European peoples sought safe haven, both in Holland and in the New World, from the imperial influence of the Roman Catholic Church. These two peoples shared a reverence for the Hebrew Bible, and they both sought spiritual edification through their careful study of the language in which that Bible had been written. Leaving aside such affinities, however, Sephardic Jews and Puritans could hardly have been more distinct from each other in their geographical origins, ethnic lineage, folkways, linguistic background, or central religious tenets. From their standpoint as a people whose exile had been forced upon them, Jews would have had little reason to view Puritans, who wished only for their conversion, as anything but allies of expediency.

Puritans, on the other hand, thought and wrote about the Chosen People with great frequency and fervor, even as they chafed at the Jews' apostasy. Puritans were fascinated by the Jews' genealogical link to the biblical People of Israel, impressed by their expertise in Hebrew, and thrilled by the central role they were destined to play in the coming millennium. In numerous debates about the meaning of the Jewish historical legacy and the significance of actual Jews, New England Puritans expressed to one another their conflicting ideas regarding the proper balances between individual piety and communal order, covenantal precedent and divine grace, and faith and human action. The Puritans' interest in Jewish subject-matter, which was occasionally stimulated by their encounters with actual Jews in the emergent transatlantic economy, also reflected their struggle to achieve equilibrium in their devotion to both orthodoxy and commerce.

When scholars of Puritan theology and historians of the Jewish American experience have explored the convergence of colonial-era Jews and Puritanism, they have generally read in it either of two opposite meanings. In his pioneering treatment of the Protestant work ethic, Max Weber offered culturally astute, if historically inaccurate judgment. "Puritanism always felt its inner similarity to Judaism," Weber wrote in *The Sociology of Religion*, stating that "the Jews who were actually welcomed by Puritan nations, especially the Americans . . . were at first welcomed without any ado whatsoever."[1] More recently, in 2006, David Gelernter, the Yale professor of computer science and outspoken neo-conservative, stated that a strong affinity for Judaic heritage formed the basis for the Puritans' pioneering experiments in the exercise of representative democracy.[2] At the opposite extreme and commanding more historical authority (while limited by his reluctance to be too wishful, or wistful in his thinking), Arthur Hertzberg asserted unequivocally in his book *The Jews in America* (1989) that any apparent similarities between the Jews and Puritans were insignificant in the face of the facts. "Essays without number," Hertzberg wrote, "argue that the Puritan theocracy, which was so self-consciously modeled on Biblical Judaism, created a pro-Jewish core to the American intellectual and political tradition." Citing general evidence for the Puritans' religious intolerance and early American Jews' indifference to Christian theology, Hertzberg dismissed such arguments as, simply, "wrong."[3]

Because my central claim here is that attention to Puritan encounters with Judaism and Jews is of primary historical value for the insights it affords into the vexing curiosities and contradictions inherent in the Puritan worldview, this book avoids making extravagant and anachronistic generalizations about a "natural" affinity between Puritans and Jews who, for the most part, cared little for each other. At the same time, my focus on Puritanism—a worldview which proves time and again to have been subject to all manner of internal rifts and outside pressures—allows for a fuller consideration of how practicing and professing Jews, both in Europe and in the New World, were able through their mere existence (and occasional physical presence) to help shape the religious discourse of New England during the colonial era. I argue here that both the "wishful thinking" and the skeptical view of the Jewish/Puritan relationship are undermined not only by their authors' lack of historical specificity but by their narrow understanding of a complex Puritan worldview. One view superimposes latter-day cultural affinities between achievement-driven Jews and success-seeking WASPs over a Puritanism that, in its heyday, was not nearly as free of prejudicial thinking as we may wish it to have been. Historians who dismiss the significance of any Jewish/Puritan convergence as a pure fantasy may be more firmly grounded in the discrete facts of colonial history, but because they treat Puritanism as a univocal theology, they fail to account for its practitioners' multifaceted pursuit of Judaic subject-matter.

While *New Israel / New England* does, where it is feasible to do so, recount the lives and adventures of Jews who happened to wander into the New England colonies between the mid-seventeenth and late eighteenth centuries, its primary purpose is to explore the implications of what I refer to as the Jewish legacy as a driving force in *Puritan* discourse. If Jews had settled in larger numbers in colonial New England, or if they had produced more of a documentary record of their sojournings there, perhaps a sustained study of their presence and even impact upon the history of New England would be achievable or warranted. The impact that actual Jews were able to exercise upon the entire history of colonial America, however, was minimal. At most, on the eve of the Revolutionary War, all of the thirteen colonies combined had no more than two and a half thousand Jewish residents, or one tenth of one percent of an overall population of nearly two and a half million. Moreover, Newport, Rhode Island, which was home to nearly all of New England's Jews prior to the mid-nineteenth century, never had more than two hundred resident Jews. The story of Jewish lives and experiences in colonial America is worth telling, but several historians have already completed that task successfully.[4] Instead of seeking to improve upon what scarcely calls for improvement, this book explores another avenue of interest. For while historians have in passing addressed the Puritans' interest in Judaism and Jews, none has offered a sustained treatment of that subject as a centralizing influence upon the Puritans' own evolving theology and shifting sense of identity within the framework of transatlantic cultural politics. Because, as Jorge Canizares-Esguerra has written, "the Atlantic world [was] . . . a space of porous imperial boundaries," readings of Jewish history frequently offered Puritans, as well as other European colonizers "prefigurations [of] their involvement in the

Americas" that often influenced their actions.[5] For Puritans, Jewish history evolved into "a particularly effective way of understanding the two worlds' encounters across time and space."[6] Accordingly, this book's focus on New England, which had far fewer Jews than any of the other areas of the thirteen colonies, follows from my particular interest in the relationship between the Judaic legacy and the evolution of Puritan theology.

Following the book's introductory treatment of the European background for Puritan Judeocentrism,[7] each of the central chapters addresses one phenomenon or episode within the broader history of early New Englanders' interest in Jews. The first three chapters focus on how the Puritans' interest in Judaism served their efforts to define a proper relationship between the covenantal and pietistic aspects of their faith. When a group of Massachusetts Bay's leaders sought, in the immediate aftermath of their settlement of New England, to explore possibilities for adapting sections of "Judaical," or Mosaic law as a basis for their own legal code, the debate that ensued ushered in the opening phase of a split that would result in the founding of Rhode Island as an oasis of relative religious tolerance (and a place where, ironically, Jews would create their first long-term settlement in New England). Second- and third-generation Puritans who, for the first time, encountered actual Jews in Boston at the turn of the eighteenth century also parted ways when it came to choosing a proper application of Jewish precedent and an appropriate stance toward the prospect of Jewish conversion. The contrast between Samuel Sewall's and Cotton Mather's attitudes toward two Sephardic men who traded in Boston between 1695 and 1705 spoke to the long-standing discrepancy between the Puritans' adherence to a patient and private piety, on the one hand, and a more activist approach to helping ensure the achievement of God's purpose. By the early 1720s, when Harvard recruited and helped to oversee the conversion of a Jewish-born instructor of Hebrew, the Judaic legacy had evolved into a vehicle for the renewal of an all but obsolete covenantal faith in a land whose religious life was becoming increasingly diverse, and not every New Englander could be convinced that such a renewal was even called for.

The three chapters that comprise the second half of the book all coincide with the development of a fixed Jewish congregational presence in mid- and late eighteenth-century Rhode Island. This section marks out the rise of a more economically and politically charged engagement of the Jewish legacy on the part of colonial New Englanders. Although the founding of the Jewish community in Newport in the late 1750s occurred in the aftermath and well outside of the immediate influence of the Great Awakening, the congregation's internationalism, as well as its members' ties to a newly mobile and speculative wealth and their pursuit of the trappings of a newly Anglicized "refinement," was in large part a product of the same cultural conflicts that had led to the Protestant revivals of the 1740s. Shortly afterwards, at the height of the Newport Jews' congregational achievement immediately before the outbreak of the Revolution, the "amoris intellectualis" that developed between that city's most prominent Congregationalist leader and a visiting Jewish scholar highlighted the increasing influence of political and even pluralistic interests within the evolution of New England's theological discourse. The revolutionary years saw the permanent settlement of a New York–born practicing and affiliating Jew in Boston itself. The rise of Moses Michael Hays from a debtor's prison in New York to financial and personal success in the birthplace of the Revolution mirrored the evolution of a new civic religion of personal virtue where, a hundred years earlier, the pronouncements of a predominating orthodoxy had rendered all human "works" susceptible to Calvinist critique. Only in the aftermath of the Revolutionary War, as the adoption of federal and state constitutions began, albeit slowly, to institutionalize the United States' vaunted church/state separation, did interest in Jews and Judaism cease to be a subject for almost purely abstract speculation. The book's conclusion addresses the increasingly visible presence of Jews as vocal participants in the life of the new republic, as well as their continued utility as subjects of its theological and political discourse.

The story of the relationship between Puritanism and Judaism begins in Europe and, more particularly, in Holland and England, where the Protestant Reformation and the Sephardic diaspora came into fairly frequent contact. Reformist theologians had a long history not only of Hebraism (that is, a scholarly interest in the Hebrew language), but of exposure to what they called "Judaizing" tendencies, which one recent historian defines as the "borrowing of Jewish practices or doctrines and mingling them into Christianity"[8] Although London would evolve by the mid-to-late seventeenth century into a center for Puritan encounters with Jews, Amsterdam provided a more likely stage for such interactions earlier still. As "the most cosmopolitan city of northern Europe,"[9] the Dutch seaport was host not only to traders from throughout the Atlantic and Mediterranean worlds but to a myriad assortment of religious practitioners of many faiths from diverse cultural backgrounds. At the Amsterdam Stock Exchange, which happened to be the world's first market of its kind, seven or eight languages were spoken, including not only northern European tongues but Greek and Arabic as well.[10] Amsterdam's centrality to the burgeoning of trans-oceanic trade, as well as the Netherlands' already religiously mixed population of Protestants and Catholics, had made the city into a haven for religious tolerance of a kind that had not been seen for centuries.

Mid-seventeenth-century Amsterdam, with a population of 185,000, was "the greatest trading centre in the world," in part because its "broad canals, excavated in concentric circles in such a way as to form building plots, encouraged merchants to put up houses and shops along their banks."[11] The city, as one chronicler has it, "was the emporium of seventeenth-century Europe," whose people, instead of being corrupted by sudden wealth, were "characterized by sobriety of behavior and a distaste for both superstition and any pretension of nobility."[12] Since Judaism and Puritanism alike rejected material and ceremonial excess, their adherents could find comfort in the Dutch capital. By the same token, as both peoples sought economic advancement and self-sufficiency they had, by necessity, to look across the Atlantic for trading opportunities. Amsterdam was ideally situated for nautical enterprises of all types, and its location also made it easily accessible to people from throughout Europe and Britain. By the early seventeenth century, its embrace of a pluralistic and seafaring livelihood had also resulted in its development into a center of intellectual and religious activity and reform. English Puritans who wished to meet and preach outside the immediate parameters set by the Church of England, which many of them considered to be a mere adjunct of the Catholic Church itself, found a hospitable reception in Holland, whose leaders had learned that relative religious tolerance was not only good for business but an expedient to social harmony. Particularly in the aftermath of the Treaty of Utrecht in 1579, which guaranteed freedom of worship to Protestants, Amsterdam and other Dutch municipalities began to attract English dissenters in significant numbers.

The majority of the Jews who filtered into Amsterdam during this period were Iberian *marranos*, whose continued existence in Iberia had become increasingly precarious. Even those "New Christians" who eagerly embraced the conversions that the Inquisition had imposed were subject to widespread discrimination, persecution, and death on the basis of their Jewish ancestry. While Jews could and did live "safely" in the ghettoes of Italy and France, the attractions of a still freer existence in lands where the Protestant Reformation had made inroads began to interest them by the turn of the seventeenth century. By 1639, over one thousand Sephardim were living in Amsterdam where, as one writer puts it, they "could be seen entering and leaving the public synagogue they had built, burying their dead at the cemetery they had established just outside the city, and negotiating on the Stock Exchange floor."[13] Less than forty years later, their numbers had more than doubled, and the number of synagogues had increased to three. Because of its location at the crossroads of Nordic and Mediterranean Europe, Amsterdam also attracted Ashkenazim from Germany. The city gained renown as a center for Jewish worship, scholarship, and disputation. Its Jewish printers soon supplanted those of Venice in their prolific output of, among others, "apologetic and ethical works, guides to Jewish practice, and translations of classic Jewish texts."[14]

Owing to their proximity to so many lands of the greater Diaspora, Amsterdam's Jews played a transformative role on the stage of world Jewry. At the same time, the Jewish community of Amsterdam soon began to exercise an influence upon another stage—that of the Protestant Reformation itself. As increasing numbers of reformers interacted with the *conversos*, the convergence of Jews and Protestant reformers in Amsterdam helped to shape Puritan Judeocentrism. If radical Protestants sought to distinguish their theology from that of the Roman church, no better means for them to do so existed than their reinvestment of the Hebrew Bible with new meaning and spiritual significance as divine sanction. "Judaical" precedent, with all of its lessons on the proper and strict maintenance of congregational life, its emphasis on reifying God's commandments, and the model it supplied of the sort of unmediated relationship to God that the prophets had known, offered English dissenters access to the rigorous Christianity they wished to implement. This covenantal Protestantism, as one historian writes, "was never far in its self-image from its Hebraic roots."[15] Although only a small minority of the English Puritans and Separatists sojourning in Holland merited the title of "Judaizers," the subject of Jewish precedent and Jewish teaching absorbed widespread attention on the part of the would-be purifiers of a corrupted church. In its more extreme form, Jewish teaching and tradition could and did entice at least a few English Protestants away from doctrinaire Christianity and into Judaism itself. Such may have been the case for Hamlet Jackson, a born-Christian whose adherence to Saturday sabbatarianism, kosher dietary laws, and other Judaic practices led directly to his imprisonment in London in the 1630s. Unlike the most famous of the English Judaizers, John Traske (1585–1636), who is often cited as a father of the modern-day Seventh-Day movement, Jackson would actually undergo a formal conversion to Judaism (including the required adult circumcision); he left London for Amsterdam in order to do so.[16]

For all of the exposure that Amsterdam afforded them to a broader religious eclecticism, English dissenters understood that the Jews offered a novel form of exposure. Proximity to actual Jews offered English dissenters in Holland an occasion not for outright apostasy but for the direct engagement of Judaic teaching, particularly on matters concerning the Hebrew language, the kabbalah (whose mysteries, as is the case today, attracted their share of non-Jewish proselytes), and the proper translation of the Hebrew Bible itself. Protestant theologians recognized the scholarly expertise that the Jewish community could supply toward their inquiries into the "original" language of God whose use in the Torah, as the kabbalah instructed them, could be understood to "be [a] configuration of divine light."[17] In part because its many printing houses offered them such wide opportunities for publication, Christian Hebraists, including Englishmen Henry Ainsworth (1571–1622), and Hugh Broughton (1549–1612), found their way to Amsterdam at the turn of the seventeenth century, where they encountered practicing and professing Jews on a regular basis. Broughton, who bore nothing but contempt for Judaism itself, was more than willing, at least on one occasion, to debate a Jew. In 1608, he and David Farar, a Jewish physician and scholar, argued over the validity of the New Testament in a formally staged disputation held at the Latin school in Dordrecht that was administered by Broughton's fellow English Hebraist, Matthew Slade. Although Farar's side of the debate has been lost, Broughton's own recounting indicates that Farar had been the instigator of the exchange;

he had evidently taken offense at Broughton's effort, in a recent pamphlet he had published in Hebrew, to win over Jewish converts.[18] If nothing else, the United Provinces offered a relatively safe venue in which a Jew might propose such an event without fear of being prosecuted or victimized. Interestingly, as the Sephardic presence in Amsterdam increased (the Broughton/Farar debate had occurred in advance of the formal establishment of the Portuguese synagogue there), both the municipal authorities and the city's Jews imposed restrictions on such daring acts as Farar's. In 1616, the burgomasters of Amsterdam expressly forbade Jews from criticizing Christianity, converting Christians, or marrying non-Jews. For their part, in their own eagerness to avoid offense to their Calvinist hosts, the synagogue's officers imposed similar rules from within the community itself. Their situation was tenuous, at best—only the cities of Amsterdam, Rotterdam, and the Hague permitted their presence, and Jews were not accorded the rights of Dutch citizens until the close of the eighteenth century, when the Napoleonic emancipation decrees went into effect.[19]

A short distance across the North Sea in England itself, Jews attracted notice as a result of the same burgeoning of Hebraic and Judaical interests that had affected the English dissenters exiled in Holland. Even as outright Judaization was rare among Puritans, scholarly interest in Jewish learning grew with the ascendancy of Protestant Reform and the ferment that would lead, by the 1640s, to civil war. English Hebraism began to be fortified in the sixteenth century; in 1540, both Oxford and Cambridge created the Regius Chair in Hebrew, which could easily be filled from the growing ranks of Christian Hebraists.[20] Before long, Jewish apostates such as the Polish-born Philip Ferdinand (1555–1598) would become the most sought-out sources of Hebrew knowledge in England. Similar economic forces to the ones that were attracting Spanish and Portuguese *conversos* to Holland drew Sephardic merchants to seek asylum in England, which had officially banned all Jews in 1290. Between 1520 and 1600, according to one historian of Anglo-Jewish history, nearly a hundred New Christian merchants settled in London.[21] Initially, their outward profession of Catholicism was an expedient to their residency in a kingdom that had long since banned all Jews. By the mid-seventeenth century, however, as the cause of Protestant reform and dissent gained the upper hand, the superficial Catholicism that had enabled crypto Jews to gain entrance into England could be utterly dispensed with. If nothing else, the Jews' long history of persecution at the hands of inquisitorial authority in Spain and Portugal rendered them all the more likely to be dependable trading agents and partners in England, which sought to minimize Iberian mercantile influence, especially in the emergent transatlantic context.

English advocates for the readmission of the Jews, who would before long include among them none other than Oliver Cromwell himself, argued their cause on several fronts. While economic interest alone could offer sufficient pretext for admitting Spanish- and Portuguese-speaking enemies of the Iberian states into Protestant England, the prevailing voices in the ensuing debates over allowing Jews into England were those whose underpinnings were religious in nature. As David Katz points out, the intriguing public practices of Christian Judaizers and the growth of interest in Hebrew had already "helped to put Jews in a favourable light" among Protestant Reformers.[22] As millenarian interests gained strength, however, and growing numbers of English dissenters equated Jewish readmission with the furtherance of God's divine will, efforts to secure official sanction for Jews to live and worship freely in England received a still wider hearing and attention. Simply described, the millenarian case for Jewish readmission argued that a necessary precursor for the Second Coming of Christ, as it had been outlined in Revelations, was to be the complete dispersal of Jews into every corner of the world. As long as Jews were forbidden to live openly in England, the argument went, their dispersal would be incomplete and the fulfillment of the prophecy impossible. Once achieved, on the other hand, the restoration of Jews to England would accelerate progress toward the ultimate precursor of Christ's return: the massive return of all the world's Jews to the Holy Land. In 1649 Johanna Cartwright and her son Ebenezer, whose own residency in Amsterdam had brought them into that city's Jewish circuit, introduced a petition into Parliament to allow for readmission in order to "appease God's wrath towards England."[23] The Cartwrights' plea gained insufficient attention and support to succeed, but it proved all the same to be an important precursor to eventual readmission.

Less than ten years later, with the staging of the momentous Whitehall Conference in December 1656, in which a proposal to readmit Jews into England was formally taken up (and rejected) by the English Parliament,

Cromwell himself would bring the subject to the forefront. Official readmission was held up owing in part to the strong objections of several leaders who feared the prospect of Jewish economic domination, and Cromwell himself elected on that basis to dissolve the session before it had a chance to reach any final resolution on the matter. Nonetheless, the number of openly professing Jews in London began to increase significantly in the 1650s even in the absence of official sanction. In December 1656, exactly coincident with the Whitehall conference, the primary emissary from the Amsterdam Jews in London, Menasseh Ben Israel, requested that a Torah be sent from Holland to England to accommodate the needs of a gathering minyan there. At roughly the same time, the London Jews began their rental of a dwelling on Creechurch Lane which they would use as a house of worship until they established a more permanent synagogue at Bevis Marks (in 1701). In February 1657, the group arranged the purchase of a burial ground at Mile End. By the end of the seventeenth century, there would be nearly five hundred Jews resident in London. Their settlement there had been the direct result not only of England's economic interest in maximizing its trading advantages over its European rivals but of a theologically informed Puritan philo-Semitism.

Few English philo-Semites were advocates of outright religious tolerance, and even those who were (Roger Williams, for instance) had little interest in promoting religious equality for non-Christians. The idea of tolerance for Jews (or for "Turks," "pagans," and other "anti Christians") was more of a rhetorical device than a realistic policy—a line of argumentation whose primary purpose it was to promote the dissenting Protestant sects in their effort to dislodge the Church of England (and for James II, a practicing Catholic, a means by which tolerance for Catholicism might also be secured). When Englishmen expressed sympathy for Jews, they did so in order to advance the greater cause of Jewish conversion. If an inadvertent result of such sympathy would prove to be the actual admission of practicing Jews into England, the greatest advocates of such a policy could and did plead their primary interest as having been in winning over the souls of those Jews to Christ. Many Reformed Protestants trusted firmly in their eventual success at such an endeavor because of their conviction that Sephardic Jews in particular, who constituted the majority of the nearly five hundred Jews resident in London in 1699,[24] would be especially

Menasseh ben Israel (1604–1657). From a seventeenth-century engraving by Salmon Italia. Courtesy of the Bibliotecha Rosenthalania Special Collections at the University of Amsterdam.

receptive to the Puritan critique of the Catholic emphasis on ornate iconography and lavish ritual. If the Jews might only see Christianity at its
true and primitive core, free of all fetishized impediments to their stalwart
monotheism, they would be all the more willing to accept Christ as their
own humble messiah.

As events would prove, readmission was less of an expedient to Jewish
conversion than its millenarian advocates had hoped it would be. With the
Restoration of the Church under Charles II in 1660 and the consequent
weakening of Puritan initiative, pragmatism would soon replace eschatology as the primary shaping force behind English policy toward religious
minorities. Although interest in their conversion never waned entirely,
Jewish residents of England began to gain recognition as an alien but
increasingly influential mercantile interest. Their own worship and autonomy flourished with minimal infringement on the part of proselytizing
Puritans. For all of their hopes that Jewish readmission would usher in a
"national" conversion, Puritan philo-Semites were aware that, in terms of
sheer numbers, their efforts could not possibly attract a sufficient number
of Jews to instigate such a momentous result (nor would the population of
England support or sanction the entry of a massive influx of aliens).

As Puritans reached the height of their political power, during the years
leading up to and including the Civil War, an entirely different population
of "Jews" offered them an alternative focus for their Judeocentric aspirations: the native tribes of North America. With growing "evidence" for the
Indians' origins either as descendants of the Lost Tribes of Israel or as
people who had retained a measure of cultural influence from their ancient
interactions with the Lost Tribes in the New World, this Jewish/Indian theory developed into a focal point for Puritan interest in Jewish affairs, and
it also led to new contacts between Puritans and *European* Jews. The settlement of so many Puritans in the New England colonies, where they had
frequent contact and interaction with Indians, fueled interest in the theory
on both sides of the Atlantic. If America could be shown to be the frontier,
literally, of gospel-propagation, and the penultimate resting place for the
last of the Lost Tribes before their restoration to Israel, the Puritan mission there would be invested with justifiable purpose even in the midst of
England's civil war crisis.[25] The mere assertion, however, that Indians were
Jews could hardly accomplish that. Just wishing that the Indians might in

fact be Jews could not in itself constitute sufficient grounds, and even fastidious attention to scriptural clues on the matter was not conclusive. A body of "Jewish" evidence was called for to corroborate the theory.

Thanks to the expanded mobility of the Sephardim throughout northwestern Europe and the Atlantic world, it was possible for English Puritans like Thomas Thorowgood to know that "The Jewes of the Netherlands . . . informe that, after much inquiry, they found some of the Ten Tribes to be in America."[26] Likewise, the philo-Semite John Dury recorded and published in Thorowgood's *Jewes in America* the stories he had heard in and among Holland's Jews. In the Hague, for instance, a Jewish jeweler had "with them of his Nation . . . received from Constantinople letters bringing . . . glad tidings of two special matters fallen out there"—the first, consisting of an abatement of taxes upon the Jews of the Ottoman Empire and the second, which proved to be the centerpiece for the entire Jewish Indian theory, that a messenger had come to the Jews from a distant land where the inhabitants had made "a resolution to live by themselves and observe the commandments of God." A journey of a year and a half's duration had brought this Jewish messenger into direct contact with a reconstituted Jewish nation, somewhere, presumably, in the wilds of the New World. Though the abatement of taxes for the Eastern Jews would appear to have had a minimal bearing on the concerns of anyone outside the Jewish world, the fact that Dury even mentioned it suggests that the affairs of actual Jews were becoming increasingly relevant outside the Jewish world, at least among Protestant reformers. In order to corroborate the various rumors and anecdotes pertaining to the Ten Tribes having resurfaced in America, Puritan theorists had to consult actual practicing Jews. In this endeavor, the Judeocentrists' primary Jewish interlocutor was Menasseh Ben Israel, the Amsterdam rabbi of Portuguese origin who had helped to instigate Cromwell's Whitehall Conference on Jewish readmission and had assisted the pioneering London Jews in situating themselves in that city.

For all of his messianic fervor, not to mention his willingness to serve as a steady interlocutor to several Puritans who would have liked nothing better than to have affected his conversion, Rabbi Menasseh Ben Israel appears never to have been a mere foil for Puritan proselytizers. The "success" he found in the Christian world seems to have derived from his diplomatic skill, his ability to parlay his expertise among Christian millenarians without relinquishing all of his credibility as Jew. As Richard Popkin suggests, Ben Israel was savvy enough not "to argue against conversion"; he chose, rather, "to ignore it."[27] He was, however, the Sephardim's closest approximation to a Jewish ambassador to the Christian world, and he seems not to have hesitated to engage inquisitive Christians on the finer points of Judaic precedent when they sought his advice. As the Puritan missionary to the Indians John Eliot had it, Menasseh Ben Israel was an indispensable authority and intermediary, whose corroboration could only enhance his own missionary efforts among Native Americans. The hope of the "eastern Nations" conversion, according to Eliot, was always increasing, but it would be greatly expanded "especially if Rabbi Ben Israel can make it appear that some of the Israelites were brought to America."[28] The grounds of Eliot's hope lay in Ben Israel's inclusion of one compelling anecdote in his book *The Hope of Israel* (1650), whose reception among the Dutch Jews and English Puritans had brought about a powerful if temporary stir. The story had originated with one Antoine de Montezinos, a Portuguese *converso* whose adventures in a remote area of the Andes had brought him into contact with a band of curiously bearded and robed "Jewish" remnants who proved their religious lineage to him by reciting the *shema* to him at a meeting place along the edge of a river which they would not permit him to cross for fear of any corrupting influences from outsiders, however Jewish they might claim to be.

Not surprisingly, Jewish/Indian theorists found themselves having to qualify their obvious admiration for the Jewish rabbi upon whose knowledge and worldliness they so heavily relied in proffering their argument for the Indians' Jewish origin. "When that treatise [Thorowgood was referring to Ben Israel's *The Hope of Israel*] came forth," the author of *Jewes in America* wrote,

> I found some sprinklings of his National errors, so I cannot commend divers passages; and lest any conceive me also to Judaize, and to be in love even with the wanderings of that unhappy people, I will here professe, I am not yet perfectly reconciled to them, in respect to those horrid injuries they did to our most dear savior . . . but we shall be friends, when they with Repentence . . . [will] be reconciled to Christ; in the meantime, I have not

onely affection for them, as well; but I do honour them, chiefly, for that to them were committed the oracles of God . . . and they have with faithfulnesse and care transmitted them unto us Gentiles.[29]

The eventuality of a Jewish reconciliation to Christ made possible such an effusive acknowledgement of Ben Israel's and his correligionists' worthiness. So too did the Jews' undisputed status as the bearers of God's commandments. Thorowgood's expression here was hardly out of keeping with anything that his Puritan contemporaries might have said. After all, in the Judeocentrists' view, unlike Catholics and Muslims, the Jews were destined to "be on the winning side in the battle of Armageddon."[30] Thorowgood's acknowledgment that "Judaizing" in any form might be forgivable, however, and that zealotry in defense of Christianity's Jewish legacy might make it possible even "to be in love with" the history of the Jews, was startling. A good Protestant, as Glenn Moots puts it, "was to draw on the Old Testament, [but] he was not to become a 'Judaizer.'"[31] Not only was "this Israelite worthy of commendation . . . for maintaining the total sanctification of the Sabbath," wrote Thorowgood, but he was "abundantly learned, and morally good, and hath also given fair respect in the dedication of his book to the Parliament of England."[32]

Despite their small numbers, not only in England itself but especially in the Puritan colonies of North America, Jews, Jewish history, and Jewish practice would soon become subjects of considerable attention. More often than not, particularly in the seventeenth century, Jewish stories were transparently Puritan stories, and Englishmen learned to think of themselves as "the historically errant Israelites . . . in search of an unfulfilled divine promise of deliverance."[33] In 1669, Increase Mather published his case for such an imminent conversion in the form of The Mystery of Israel's Salvation. Remarkably, given its release merely two decades after the emergence of the Jewish Indian theory, Mather's book made no mention of the Indians, but concentrated its entire efforts instead on the "Eastern" Jews of Europe and Asia who, the author expected, would soon see the light of Christ. Though Mather's conversion tract took shape in response to the growing millennial excitement within Puritan circles and as a direct result of his hopes for the Jews' salvation, it was motivated by his misgivings and ambivalence about New England's faltering present and uncertain future.

The Mystery was one of many Puritan pamphlets in the jeremiad tradition, in which New Englanders expressed the idea of "chosenness and a deep anxiety about the prospects of continued blessings."[34] Mather believed, as William Scheick puts it, that "all the biblical prophecies that literally appl[ied] to the Jews likewise allegorically appl[ied] to the latter day New Israelite elect throughout the world," most especially in New England.[35] A central theme in The Mystery was the guilt that followed from the ancient Jews—as well as their modern counterparts—having believed wrongly in the improvement of this world as an endpoint. His preoccupation with what he alleged to be the Jews' tendency to seek meaning and fulfillment in the world was related to his concern about New England's latter-day Puritan Israelites' efforts to reinvent a heavenly kingdom on earth. Whether Mather and future New Englanders were aware or not of the strong parallels that their Judeocentric efforts would establish between unconverted Jews and faltering Christians, their attention to the severe transgressions and moral failings committed by the Jews through history would soon develop into a consistent reference point in their pursuit of solutions to a crisis in identity that was bound to intensify in the coming years.

CHAPTER ONE

"JEWS, TURKS . . . AND ANTI-CHRISTIANS"
Alien Encounters with Puritan Hebraism

NEW ENGLAND PURITANS COULD never make up their minds about whether or how actual Jews were important. Right up until the end of the seventeenth century the arrival and temporary settlement of at least a dozen Jews in, respectively, Massachusetts, Connecticut, and Rhode Island eluded the focused attention of the same New Englanders who, whether they fancied themselves latter-day Israelites or sought figural guidance from the Hebrew Bible on their New World exile, consistently invoked the history of the Jews. Jews constituted one of several minority groups whose presence, though hardly welcomed or legally tolerated by Puritans, was an inevitable if lamentable result of New England's transatlantic exposure. Although some few of their immediate descendants would develop a keener interest in the Jews who entered their territory during the eighteenth century, the earliest generations of New England Puritans were too preoccupied by the presence of other more threatening and numerous aliens, not to mention their own theological and societal dilemmas, to notice Jews, let alone apply a standard treatment toward them. The Puritans' interest in Jewish history, on the other hand, allowed them to express their often contradictory attitudes toward all types of outsiders. In large part because the scriptural Jews who were the subject of so much self-reflective Puritan discourse could be understood according to context to be either God's Chosen People or perpetually exiled and despised strangers, actual Jews—and a host of other religious, cultural, and racial outsiders—would encounter a range of treatments at the hands of their Puritan "hosts."

The Jews as a separately constituted people with a distinct tribal past who were also the scriptural recipients of God's love and wrath figured prominently in Puritan discourse. Their collective history, not only through biblical times but during the long centuries of the Diaspora that had followed from the destruction of the Second Temple in 70 C.E., fascinated the Puritans, many of whom not only were seeking to establish a society on the model of ancient Israel's adherence to religious principles but also saw themselves as exiles in their own right venturing on what Perry Miller famously referred to as an "errand into the wilderness." If New England was not itself the Promised Land, the journey to it and away from a newly "desacralized England," as one historian points out, resembled the journey taken by the Children of Israel as they made their exodus from Egypt.[1] Over the last five decades, a succession of scholarly formulations has proposed, challenged, overturned, and revised the idea, most forcefully asserted by Sacvan Bercovitch, that the Puritans sought "the worldly protection, power, and privilege [God] had once granted the Hebrews."[2] Whether they were drawing comparisons between themselves and the ancient Jews or dismissing the relevance of such comparisons, New Englanders wrote or spoke about the Jews in their sermons, diaries, and legal discourse with significant frequency, in myriad ways, and for a broad range of purposes. Their writing about Jews offers insight into how Puritans attempted to cope with life on the transatlantic frontier while adhering to biblical precept. Puritan Hebraism, in New England especially, offered its practitioners a range of metaphors which they might employ in order to overcome the apparent discrepancies between "spiritual and temporal, faith and civic life."[3] While no such discrepancies existed in Judaism itself, since the Hebrew Bible itself did not allow for a sharp distinction between "practice and faith,"[4] the Calvinistic Hebraism of New England's first settlers offered no easy resolution to such dilemmas.

Despite their latter-day reputation as aspirant Old Testament prophets and crusaders for the restoration of early church purity, seventeenth-century practitioners of what came to be known as "the New England Way" often lacked the ability to articulate, let alone enforce, unequivocal laws of exclusion. The facts of life on the western fringe of the British Atlantic were not conducive to hermetic endeavors of any sort, and insofar as the Puritans themselves constituted a famously vociferous and factious assemblage of sectarians and spiritual misfits, their own religious doctrines and practices bred a social and cultural instability that opened the door, albeit inadvertently, to the arrival of aliens. The contradictions inherent in the Puritan theology, which, as one historian writes, insisted that "man had no power of his own," and yet at the same time compelled them to "forge new businesses, erect new colleges, and carve new cities out of the woods,"[5] sparked a series of spiritual crises that, in turn, resulted in the rise of all manner of economic and social dilemmas. The scriptural and historical precedent supplied by the Jews presented versatile, if inconsistent, guidance to New Englanders who wished to draw proper boundaries between themselves and those they wanted to ward off or exclude.

Puritans habitually sought and found typologies from the Hebrew Bible in order to predict, describe, and justify their actions in the New World. Although they often differed from and challenged one another when it came to reading the present-day implications of Jewish history, their investment in the subject was nearly universal. Their contrasting interpretations of the Hebrew Scriptures delineated one of the most profound splits that would ever develop in their ranks. One view, which came to be championed by such stalwarts as John Cotton, was that the biblical Hebrews could be looked to as exemplars of a proper covenantal relationship with God and that the strict laws that governed their firm treatment of outsiders offered a proper model for the Puritan saints' sharp policing of errant religious behavior. The language with which John Cotton expressed his views on such matters spoke frequently in terms of what Shira Wolosky calls "midsts"—of parishioners "being among, within, and outside of" the community which, in turn, was understood to be "closely knit together" on the model of the ancient Jews.[6] The Children of Israel, according to this formulation, had resisted idolatrous incursions by maintaining strong discipline and by not hesitating to prosecute violators. It was this view that predominated in Massachusetts Bay, Plymouth, and Connecticut and, for all of its paradoxical implications, ensured these colonies against any permanent incursion of actual Jews (not to mention Catholics and a host of other non-Reformist Protestants).

The opposing view did not dispense with the Hebrew Bible as a source of insight into how New Englanders might best cope with the presence of outsiders, whether they might be religious dissenters or foreigners. Most notably articulated by Roger Williams, this reading of the history of the

Jews placed particular emphasis on their many years of exile, as opposed
to their relatively brief experience of sovereignty in the land of Israel. As
exiles in foreign lands, the Jews had repeatedly benefited from the tolerant practices of their host monarchs. New Englanders, Williams argued,
would do well to display similar leniency and dispense with any notion that
they possessed the right to judge others' spiritual status, and thereby avoid
both the appearance and the reality of hypocrisy. "Rather than focusing
on the rule of God through national covenants in ancient Israel," writes
James Byrd, "Williams highlighted the passages [from the Hebrew Bible]
that describe God's people in bondage to foreign rulers"[7] As Williams was
able to implement his unconventional (by Puritan standards) views in the
founding of Rhode Island, his emphasis on the Jews' biblical experiences
of exile, particularly in Babylon, resulted in their modern-day descendants
receiving a considerably more indulgent treatment when a contingent of
them arrived in Newport in the latter decades of the seventeenth century
than they would have received in neighboring Massachusetts Bay.

Religious considerations, important as they were, did not constitute
the only basis upon which Puritan New Englanders shaped their policies
toward outsiders. When the Puritans crossed the Atlantic, religion and
economics were inseparable forces in their lives. While they were driven by
an Old World and Caribbean demand for such fish, fur, and timber as New
England might supply, they knew that their commerce "required control
by moral laws."[8] The tight congregational fellowships that the Puritans
sought either to replicate or to establish in Massachusetts, built as they
were around a paid preacher whom they had followed from England, were
simultaneously commercial and communitarian in their aspirations.[9]
Economics was not the sole driving force behind the Puritan emigration
from England, but it had supplied a significant enticement to a civil body
that faced stagnation at home. "Given the unusually strong appeal of non-
conformity to town dwellers and artisans," writes T. H. Breen, "there was
likely to be a marked congruence between disgruntled tradesmen and
disgruntled Puritans" coming to New England.[10] Religious reformers and
separatists, who happened as well to be seekers of economic stability,
would only be able to go so far in preventing their trading partners from
setting foot on the sacred soil of New England. Puritanism's susceptibility to internal dissent also bred economically individualistic behavior that,

in turn, created the proper conditions for occasional commercial engagement with non-Puritans. So it was that, as one historian of religious dissent in New England writes, "among the approximately twenty thousand colonists who settled in New England" between 1630 and 1660, "there were many individuals, ministers as well as laymen, whose Puritanism was not consonant with the official ideology of the Bay Colony."[11]

For all of their deliberate attempts to assert a self-consciously purified theological authority, the founders of New England had rather quickly found themselves not only unable to keep various religious dissenters at bay but, for that matter, subject to the fairly frequent incursions of the sorts of cultural outsiders who were necessary to the maintenance of trade. "In the seventeenth century," writes Richard Archer, "New Englanders sought profits and participated in a market economy. They bargained for higher prices of goods and labor if they were selling and for lower prices if they were buying."[12] This commercial spirit shaped the overall cultural atmosphere of Boston in which, by the mid-1600s, "sailors, artisans, merchants, colonywide officials, seekers of government favor, goodwives, farmers bringing produce to market, tavernkeepers, laborers, and prostitutes" jostled each other in an overall atmosphere which, inadvertent as it might have been, was quite cosmopolitan.[13] Although the most exclusionary Puritans never succeeded in eliminating the presence of outsiders, they did employ various rhetorical and legalistic means of attempting to do so. Their physical separation from the corrupting atmosphere of old England, however, neither guaranteed them against nor prepared them for the onslaught of alien exposures. If anything, their arrival on the wild western shore of the Atlantic placed them in close proximity not only to Indians, blacks, and other "internal" aliens but to their Dutch Calvinist neighbors in New Netherlands and, worst of all, to the French Catholics of Canada.

Both as they sought to govern themselves and as they tried to draw proper boundaries around their commonwealth, New Englanders frequently turned to the Hebrew Bible and to the example of the ancient Jews who, when they had inhabited their own kingdoms, had devised godly means of maintaining order. Although such resort hardly protected those who employed them from accusations of being legalistic and even "Judaical" in their lack of tolerance for other religious sects, including those who counted themselves Reformed Christians (i.e., Antinomians, Quakers, and Baptists), the Hebrew Bible provided a familiar body of law which bore the divine imprimatur. Though such usage generated its share of controversy among those increasing numbers of Puritans whose Calvinism emphasized a universally accessible free grace, its partisans could and did point confidently to its unique applicability to collective endeavors such as theirs, which sought to purify not only individuals but an entire "nation."[14] For the early settlers of Massachusetts Bay in particular, many of whom subscribed to what one recent historian refers to as a "Precisianist" brand of reform Protestantism that emphasized the steps that humans could and should take in order to examine their own lives and to "prepare" their souls for the salvation that only God could confer, the entire Bible might be looked to as "a kind of Torah," or book of the law that might assist them in such a difficult endeavor.[15] Those dissenters who found the strictures of this "Torah" used against them could not resist the temptation to proclaim their victimization in terms that equated the empowered orthodoxy of the Puritans with Judaism itself. In the 1670s, Quaker Peter Folger published a poem entitled "A Looking Glass":

> *New England* they are like the *Jews*,
> As like as like can be;
> they make large Promises to God,
> at home and at the Sea;
> They did proclaim free Liberty,
> they cut the calf in twain.[16]

Several historians have written about the earliest New England Puritans' efforts to adapt and occasionally adopt verbatim portions of the legal codes found in the Hebrew Bible. In its extreme form, this trend might translate into one early seventeenth-century English pastor's "methodical procedure" for honoring the Decalogue by meditations, in turn, on each commandment, a practice which could not but have struck at least some witnesses as achieving "a near-approximation of the Catholic confession."[17] This preference for Mosaic Law in a decidedly modern age was a salient contribution of Puritanism. Few would argue that any of the Puritans were deeply philo-Semitic; at best, as a mid-twentieth-century historian of New England religion put it, "the Puritans regarded the post-Biblical Jews as a misguided splinter group."[18] Particularly at the inception of their transatlantic errand, however, many Puritans were quite self-consciously interested in replicating ancient Israel's holy commonwealth and God's "calling forth of a chosen people."[19] Puritans sought and found moral and, more important, societal guidance in the only source they fully trusted— Scripture. They also argued the need "for each Christian to read the Bible himself."[20] Salvation itself was to be the result of a covenantal relationship between the individual (or the collective) and God (one sixteenth-century English theologian had referred to it as a "bargayn"[21]), and adherence to Scriptural precept, particularly from the Hebrew texts, was a necessary aid to men and women who wished to honor their side of that relationship. In order to ensure their fullest understanding of such "bargayns," New Englanders demonstrated a long-standing regard for the Hebrew language itself, on both sides of the Atlantic.

Rather than creating Judaizers, this massive-scale Puritan Hebraism was meant to deepen the Christian experience and, more particularly, to move Christianity as far as possible from the merely ceremonial and paganistic elements that Puritans were so eager to reject. Like the view of the Hebrew Bible itself as a foundation for the New Testament, this Puritan preference for the Bible's Hebraic elements was posited as a means for humbling the soul, as Larzer Ziff describes it, and "preparing him to will his salvation."[22] In keeping with all Christian doctrine, the Hebrew Bible could be relied upon as having predicted Christ's arrival.[23] What separated Puritans from the mass of Christians, however, was their attempt on a practical level to bring about an experience of daily life that might be led in keeping with biblical injunction. The more Mosaically inclined or "Precisianist" among them, as Theodore Bozeman describes it, were "pledged to a Hebraic and Deuteronomic scheme of laws, duties, rewards, and punishments."[24] Their Biblicism could be no mere injunction to revive a "Judaical" legalism, however. For ministers of John Cotton's ilk, Hebraism was a bridging device by which "the terms of the New Testament and old, interiority and exteriority, spirituality and legalism" might be made commensurate with each other.[25]

Ministers bolstered their practices as well through fastidious attention to the Hebrew language itself, which constituted significant curricular fare in their institutions of higher learning. None other than William Bradford doodled Hebrew grammar exercises on the inside cover of his work "Of Plimouth Plantation."[26] Roger Williams, another sometime Hebrew scholar, was tutored in that subject by John Milton, who, in turn, received Williams's instruction in Dutch.[27] Indeed, given how hard Bradford, Williams, and other stalwarts who followed in their footsteps had to work to get their Hebrew lessons, one might think that the language study itself, like the Hebrew Bible, constituted a sufficiently humbling ordeal to help a Christian soul in his or her preparation for salvation. Between 1642 and 1646, Harvard undergraduates were required to study Hebrew twice a day. Graduates were expected to translate random passages from the Hebrew Bible into Latin. During the seventeenth century, eighteen A.B. theses were written on Hebrew subjects, with more than half of those being produced in the ten years between 1640 and 1649.[28] In 1678 Cotton Mather produced a Harvard thesis arguing that the vowel markers, or "points" found in the Hebrew Bible were of divine origin.

Where the founding generation of Puritans came closest to reifying its devotion to the legacy of the ancient Jews, however, was in its attempts, beginning in the late 1630s, to bring about at least a partial adaptation of Mosaic Law. Several chroniclers of early New England have enumerated the founders' remarkable and quite widespread attempts to create, as well as to evoke through rhetorical means and typologies, a New Israel. Albert Ehrenfried cites Plymouth, New Haven, and Connecticut as all having "followed the ancient Hebrew pattern" in their law-making."[29] The attempt to do so could be quite deliberate, as the founders of New Haven made clear as early as 1644, when their preliminary effort to inscribe a set of laws indicated that "The judicial laws of God as they were delivered to Moses . . . shall be accounted of moral equity and generally bind all offenders and be a rule to the courts in this jurisdiction."[30] In 1652, a Connecticut court added a law stipulating equal punishment for violators of both the Hebrew Bible and the New Testament.[31] The New Haven code in particular, which was adopted in 1655, included a startlingly disproportionate number of statutes that derived from the Hebrew Bible, relative to the small number taken from the New Testament. New Haven's founders, as John Murrin writes, were eager to apply "retributive justice," and prosecuted crimes based on ancient Israel's "two witness rule," even for cases in which one of the two "witnesses" might be someone who had heard the defendant's confession. In one instance, an unregenerate man was convicted of bestiality based on the combination of his own coerced testimony and on the physical "witness" supplied by a deformed piglet whose resemblance to himself was seen as incontrovertible proof of his guilt.[32] The Puritans' "special regard for the Hebrew books" and adoption of the Jews' Bible as an "equal partner" with the New Testament, as Theodore Dwight Bozeman writes, was an aspect of their vehement rejection of Augustine and other "Catholic fathers" whose theology, in their judgment, was all too worldly.[33] If nothing else, the legalism of the Hebrew Bible would appear to offer a practical model for law-making. Its adoption was believed by some, most prominently the missionary John Eliot, to be "one of three civil components of the millennium" (the other two were the deposition of the civil monarchy and its replacement with congregational rule).[34] Indeed, for those Puritans who were eagerly awaiting the End of Days, the institution of Mosaic law would prove instrumental, according to Eliot, in enticing European Jews to convert to Christianity since it would undoubtedly coincide with "the elimination of Catholic images" from England's churches.[35]

On a less millenarian note, Mosaic law would also provide New Englanders with a means of properly legislating the boundaries that would mark their commonwealth. Since the Hebrews themselves had had considerable experience in maintaining a covenantal relationship with one another based on their collective identity as the people of God, New Englanders who wished to manage proper interaction with strangers favored a treatment of the Hebrew Bible that stressed the sovereignty of ancient Israel as God's kingdom on earth and as a precursor to Christ's eternal reign. In the 1630s and 1640s, as Puritans set about designing their laws, serious consideration was given not only to the Hebrew scriptures but to the Pentateuch in particular as an appropriate basis for a legal code which would include, among other strictures, rules governing the enforcement and maintenance of church membership. Progress toward such an outcome was by no means guaranteed, in large part owing to the fact that, for all of their regard for Jewish history, Puritans of all persuasions were also Calvinists who believed strongly in a predestinarianism that drew sharp lines of distinction between the covenant of grace and the covenant of works. Since the coming of Christ, salvation could only be attained through faith. No amount of proper, legally defined behavior could substitute, according to the strictest predestinarian formulation, for a divine sanctification that saw only a faithful Christian soul and cared nothing for outwardly virtuous action, including how many sermons a parishioner attended or how many hours she or he spent in prayer.

As legal historian Edgar McManus points out, Massachusetts Bay's drafting and eventual adoption of a permanent body of legal statutes was balanced in its application of Hebraic precedent. The Puritans, writes McManus, used "the light of Scripture" to fashion a "dynamic and progressive body of American law" which, in turn, was based upon and commensurate with English law.[36] When that process began, in the mid-1630s, at least a few of its initiators favored a relatively uncritical and even verbatim adoption of Jewish precedent. The formal process began in May 1635, when a committee was convened in Newtown (Cambridge), for the drafting of laws intended "for the well ordering of this Plantation."[37] John Winthrop apparently took the original position that "in the infancy of plantation, justice should be administered with more leniency than in a settled place."[38] Whether or not he himself was eager to achieve such an equalizing effect, the committee itself was influenced not only by biblical precedent but by English history as well; they wished to bring about some "resemblance to a Magna Charta."[39] Initially, however, the committee—whose members included Henry Vane, John Cotton, Thomas Hooker, and John Wilson, as well as Winthrop himself—expressed broad disagreement with Winthrop's preference for leniency. On the contrary, these latter-day Hebrews argued that strict discipline, both in criminal offenses and in martial affairs, "was more needful in plantations than in a settled state."[40]

Accordingly, Cotton set about devising two reports which he called "A Model of Moses his Judicials" and, later, "How Far Moses Judicialls Bind Mass[achusetts]" to set before the committee for their approval, on the assumption that, given the primitivist impulse that had guided its initial settlement, Mosaic law could be said to have been "designed for the ages, and for New England itself."[41] Though a set of proposed laws bearing that exact title has not been recovered, a version of it, dating from 1641, was found among Cotton's papers upon his death. In "An Abstract of the Laws of New England, as They Are Now Established," the imprint of the Hebrew Bible, and especially the Pentateuch, was unmistakable and, as William

Manuscript pages from John Cotton's 1641 draft of the *Abstract of the Laws of New England as They Are Now Established*, hand-copied by William Gray in 1767. The featured pages are from the section on "Crimes." Note the right-hand margin notes on page 13, each of which refers to precedents set by specific passages from the Hebrew Bible, including the Pentateuch. For instance, "To put in practice the betraying of ye *Countrey*" to any Spanish, French, or Dutch interest is likened to precepts laid out in Numbers 12, 13, 14 and is punishable by death. Courtesy of the Massachusetts Historical Society.

Aspinwall wrote in his preface to a 1655 edition of it, Cotton "would undoubtedly have made a more thorough search of all the rules and laws of judgment and justice scattered here and there in the Books of Moses" had he had the time.[42] "Not to have made God's law part of the colony," writes Edgar McManus, "would have defeated the purpose that brought Puritans to New England."[43] Though certain sections of the "Abstract" did not make explicit reference to the Hebrew Bible, several sections did, including the criminal code and long list of capital offenses, as well as the section devoted to the election and service of public officials. The margins of the manuscript copy were carefully labeled with specific citations from throughout the Hebrew Bible. Indeed, in among a few dozen references to books ranging from Genesis through those of the prophets, only one of the margin notes referred to any part of the New Testament—the section of the capital offense code that speaks of "reviling religion." Among the many parts of Cotton's proposed code that did refer directly to the Hebrew Bible was language befitting Moses himself: "To worship God in a molten or graven image, to be punished with death." As Theodore Dwight

Bozeman notes, "even a certainly indifferent provision for an agricultural storehouse in each town was grounded upon Deuteronomic rule."[44]

Cotton's adherence to the precedent of ancient Israel was unremitting and, as Perry Miller wrote, "as close to literal Biblicism as one can come."[45] Another committee, whose work was completed with the somewhat more compromised adoption, in 1641, of Nathaniel Ward's *Body of Liberties*, rejected some of Cotton's proposals (included among them were execution for heresy and the profanation of the sabbath).[46] In 1648 the *Laws and Liberties of Massachusetts* was brought into fuller conformity with both Cotton's proposals and English law and formally adopted by Massachusetts Bay.[47] In one of the meetings held to discuss the potential adoption of the Mosaic Code, the less Hebraically inclined participants asked why Christians ought to be bound "to establish the lawes and Penalties set down in script as they were given to the Jewes & none other than they."[48] Excessive adherence to the strictures of the Hebrew Bible could endanger the entire Puritan experiment, making it susceptible, as one Anglican author's pronouncement proved, to accusations of Judaizing. "To search into the *Veiles* and *Shadowes* of the *Old Testament*," wrote John Prideaux, in connection with the Puritans' attempts to regulate the keeping of the Sabbath, "is to fall into the Toyles of Judaism."[49] Given the obvious apostasy of post-biblical Jewish practice, the committee asked whether "If the Jewes be now still under the bond of them . . . then are we bound to observe them?"[50] "Moses Judicialls bind," the answer suggested, only in the absence of Christ's more recent command—"Love thy neighbor as thy selfe." Thus, a central question for the law-making committee seems to have been to what extent the Hebrew Bible was "antiquated" by the New Testament. Accordingly, in his account of her trial for antinomianism, Edward Johnson wrote that Anne Hutchinson had compared the magistrates who had so vociferously opposed her to "a company of legal Professors . . . going on the Law which Christ hath abolished."[51]

No historian questions the Puritans' wholehearted endorsement of Christianity, but the propensity of some stalwarts for elevating the injunctions of the Books of Moses stretched the utility of their Hebraic outlook. Only "those Judicialls" that were foretold or mentioned in the New Testament could possibly hold. Otherwise, in the words of one questioner, "the church of the Old Testament" would appear to have been "superior to the new."[52] Bozeman, who holds to a more pragmatic view of the debate over Mosaic law, argues that Cotton's version "failed of acceptance" only "because it fell short of meeting the demands of the popular party bent upon abridging the magistracy's discretionary privileges."[53] Cotton's preference for a Mosaic code precluded any mandated replacement of magistrates and, in the spirit of the ancient Hebrew precedent, conferred upon those magistrates an unfettered power to interpret and apply God's law. Ultimately, because "the Puritan self was foundationally constructed through its participation in community," Jewish precedent, controversial as it might be, could be made to fit the common interest.[54]

Massachusetts' adoption of the *Body of Liberties* in 1641 and the *Laws and Liberties of Massachusetts* in 1648 spoke both to the Puritans' scripturally based idealism and to the spirit of pragmatism that had made it possible for them to emigrate to the New World in the first place. It did not make them latter-day Israelites, or even remote aspirants to that title. Even the most committed Hebraists among the Puritans were leery of considering themselves God's chosen reincarnate. Fanciful references to Massachusetts as "the New Jerusalem" constituted a "literal castle in the air," as Reiner Smolinski puts it.[55] Puritans practiced a Judeocentrism that acknowledged the existence of actual Jews, even as it wished wholeheartedly for their eventual conversion, and the existence of those actual Jews meant that any New Jerusalem would have to be a metaphorical kingdom. When the millennium came, it would bring about the sovereignty of these actual (and, albeit converted) Jews: "If the Puritan prophets had laid claim to Elijah's mantle," Smolinski writes, "they knew only too well that they [had] attired themselves in borrowed robes."[56]

Puritans' practical, if determinedly "primitivist" reading of Mosaic law helped to guide their adoption of an exclusionary policy toward unwelcome outsiders which warned, in 1657, that "Strangers . . arriving in this colony must give an account of themselves."[57] So although it may bear the appearance of a supreme irony, the application of such policies toward the few actual Jews who entered Massachusetts would hardly have struck its enforcers as in any way hypocritical or inconsistent, let alone "intolerant." Latter-day Jews were, at best, decrepit shadows of Israel's former glories. Though the threat they posed to the Puritan colonies paled in comparison to that posed by Catholic (or "Jesuitical") agents, Indians, and other more obviously dangerous aliens, Jews were complete outsiders who merited no sort of preferential treatment. Not surprisingly, the entire Jewish presence in Massachusetts preceding the turn of the eighteenth century can be summed up by the handful of documents pertaining to three experiences of three individuals, only one of whom left any firsthand record of his time there. Although the stories of Solomon Franco, Gideon Rowland, and Solomon "the malatta Jew" contain no indication that these men were singled out on the basis of their Jewish identity, neither do the records pertaining to their time in the Bay suggest that the magistrates who would have heard their cases considered their Jewishness as a marker of anything other than an alien status. These Jews suffered considerably less at the hands of Puritans than did the Quakers who faced summary public whippings, exile and, upon their return to Massachusetts, execution but, then again, Quakers, who frequently proselytized, constituted a numerically significant and deliberate threat to Puritan hegemony.

New Englanders had brought their Mosaic predilections to bear upon the Quakers, whose unabashed denial of any authority other than that of their own Christian consciences, could be considered to make them practitioners of an unambiguous form of heresy and even idolatry. No evidence exists to suggest that the three Jews who entered the Bay before 1695 wished to settle permanently in Massachusetts, much less preach their faith publicly in the manner of the Quakers. Long-standing Judaical thinking on the part of the Puritans helped to ensure the exclusion of Jews, but Bay authorities probably did not find it necessary to proclaim their exclusionary principles or announce their Deuteronomic objections to latter-day Hebrew idolatry. Jews who sought to settle permanently in North America instead found their way to the Dutch settlement in New Amsterdam (soon to become the English settlement of New York), where a reluctant Peter Stuyvesant, though hardly an advocate of tolerance toward Jews, was bound by the governors of the Dutch West India Company to avoid alienating the Jewish traders and financiers of Amsterdam and had been explicitly advised not to ban Jews from his colony. The Jews who entered Boston could not but have known that their welcome there, such as it was, would be temporary and provisional.

Something of the generally inhospitable atmosphere of seventeenth-century Boston and its citizens' suspicion of any non-English sojourners is conveyed in the journal account of two Dutchmen—Jasper Danckaerts and Peter Sluyter—who traveled there from New York in 1680 in order to find a ship that might take them across the Atlantic to England. In their own words, they were "as great enemies of [Catholicism] as any persons could be," but their staunch Calvinism did little to earn them the trust of New Englanders who took automatic offense at their inability to speak English and their reliance upon French in its stead. Perhaps their own skepticism toward the religious practices of the Puritans, which they viewed as lacking in "respect" and "reverence" and weak in comparison to the religion of New York's Dutch Calvinists, had upset their hosts. Despite the polite reception they received at the home of Governor Simon Bradstreet, they despaired of finding lodging in the settlement among the English. Among the Puritans, only John Eliot, Roxbury's "Apostle to the Indians," received them warmly. When, a few days in advance of their transatlantic voyage, they went to purchase wine at the home of one John Taylor, the reason for the coldness of their reception in Massachusetts was finally made plain to them:

> He said we must be pleased to excuse him if he did not give us admission to his house, he durst not do it in consequence of there being a certain evil report in the city concerning us; they had been to warn him not to have too much communication with us, if he wished to avoid censure; they said we certainly were Jesuits, who had come there for not good, for we were quiet and modest, and an entirely different people from themselves; that we could speak several languages, were cunning and subtle of mind and judgment, had come there without carrying on any traffic or any other business, except only to see the place and country that this seemed fabulous as it was unusual in these parts.[58]

Taylor concluded his warning to Danckaerts and Sluyter by telling them about the recent arrival in Boston of a Canadian "Jesuit" who had gone among the New Englanders in disguise before being detected and summarily banished. No Jew could possibly have expected to receive a warmer reception than that which greeted these two Dutch Calvinists. Those few who did put Massachusetts to the test seem to have arrived there almost inadvertently.

The historical consensus is that Solomon Franco, who is known to have spent a period of three months in Boston in 1649, represented the earliest Jewish presence in the area. Franco arrived in Boston in his capacity as an accompanying supercargo for a freight shipment originating in the Netherlands that entered the harbor under the authority of Major General Edward Gibbons. As the goods were offloaded, Franco sought payment for the duties he had performed. For reasons that remain unclear, neither Gibbons nor the chief officer on the ship itself, Immanuel Perada, was willing to pay Franco his due, so the Jewish supercargo filed suit. Our one extant document explains only the result of Franco's suit. The authorities seem to have struck some sort of balance between an out-and-out rebuff of Franco and a humane acceptance of his human rights. In the language of the document, "The court did not find any clear ground whereupon" either Gibbons or Perada might pay him. Nor would the City on a Hill offer any kind of permanent refuge. But the court did "allow the said Solomon Franco sixe shillings per week out of the treasury for ten weeks for his subsistence till he can get his passage into Holland."[59] Though Franco was not officially "warned out" of Boston (that official practice didn't begin until 1656), his treatment, as outlined in the officials' decision, was in keeping with such a response. Well before any Englishmen came to New England, they had formed the habit, based on a principle called "inhabitancy," of disallowing the permanent residency in their rural villages of *any* alien who lacked a demonstrable means of support, including the ability to tithe.[60] Solomon Franco's stay was a short one, but Boston was a small outpost in 1649, in which few arrivals or temporary residents could go unnoticed. As Jacob Marcus puts it, "Solomon Franco, supercargo, walked the streets of Boston in a day when John Alden and Miles Standish were still alive."[61]

Absent any further documentary evidence from the Boston court, not to mention any firsthand testimony from Gibbons, Perada, or Franco, for that matter, we can only surmise so much from the Franco story. On the other hand, thoughtful attention to both the broader economic and social context in which the shipping took place, as well as to other Jewish narratives from this first period of a Jewish presence in New England, may lend insight. Certain questions beg attention. Why, for instance, was a ship with an Ibero-Catholic agent and a Sephardic Jewish supercargo docking in Boston in the first place? If his foreign presence, even temporarily, was forbidden in Massachusetts Bay, why was Franco left behind, even taking

into account the vicissitudes of his unresolved claim? Franco's story serves
as a reminder of how, even as relatively early in the Puritan errand as 1649,
Massachusetts Bay was fully engaged in an inter-colonial, transatlantic
trade that precluded any sort of hermetic existence. Franco himself, as
Ellen Smith writes, was "allied with the broad network of English, Dutch,
and Italian merchants who helped link Europe, the West Indies, Africa,
and the North American colonies through commerce, trade, and family
connections."[62] Notwithstanding their steadfast adherence to an adaptation of Mosaic strictures that forbade the permanent settlement of idolatrous, or at least non-Reformed Christian practitioners, the ruling magistrates of Massachusetts Bay had no interest in impeding a transatlantic
trade that was the key to the prosperity of their commonwealth.

By the mid-to-late seventeenth century, places like Boston were well
on their way to becoming "prosperous mercantile centers with relatively
large, concentrated, heterogeneous populations."[63] While the coming of
a Solomon Franco was hardly an everyday occurrence, neither was it an
especially noteworthy exception to the developing norm, in which some
four hundred ships would dock in Boston annually by 1680, and nearly two
hundred ships would be registered in that seaport by 1698,[64] bearing as
part of their crews a motley assemblage of not only Englishmen but sailors of many other European nationalities as well. As a Sephardic *converso*,
Solomon Franco would have been quite used to a marginalized existence.
Since the Inquisition had outlawed Judaism, first in Spain in 1492 and
shortly afterward in Portugal in 1497, either the Sephardim had sought
refuge in sheltering pockets of Italy, southern France, and, eventually, the
Netherlands, or they had undergone a conversion to Catholicism and were
living, outwardly, at least, as Christians. As David Graizbord puts it, *conversos* like Franco, whether they were practicing Catholicism or had reclaimed
their Judaism in the Sephardic diaspora, inhabited a "cultural threshold"
that was, at once "a boundary and a crossroads between the Jewish and
Christian worlds."[65] Collectively, the Sephardim manifested an unprecedented hybridity "of the European, American, Old, and New Worlds,"[66]
and their growing involvement in the transatlantic trade might serve as a
reminder to even the most xenophobic Puritans that "routes" could be as
important as "roots."[67] For his part, Franco appears to have known this
threshold existence his whole life. After he found his passage from Boston

to Holland he made his way from there to London's growing Sephardic community, where he undoubtedly gained considerable notoriety when, in 1668, he left his family in the care of the synagogue and published a pamphlet, "Truth Springing Out of the Earth," in which he stated his recent "devest[ment] of [his] former Mosaical Zeal" and embraced Christianity.[68]

Strictures against any permanent alien presence were not sufficient to keep Jews out of New England's most "Judaical" colony of Connecticut where, in 1659, "David the Jew" was fined ten shillings for trading, or attempting to trade, dry goods in a Hartford home in which the parents were absent and only a teenaged child was on hand. Some ten years later, Hartford records spoke of one John Allyn's bearing "ten shillings for the Jews."[69] Whether or not David was any longer a part of this group, a 1661 document referred to "the Jews living at John Marsh's" having been "granted permission to remain in the city [Hartford] for seven months" (Marsh, who later moved to Hadley, Massachusetts, had been among Hartford's founders).[70] Jacob the Jew appeared the winter of 1667–1668 as a horse trader doing business with neighboring New York. Though his trade was of an itinerant nature, David the Jew was listed in his final appearance in the records of Hartford (in 1670) as an "inhabitant."[71] In October of that same year court records from Connecticut also recorded the charges filed against another Jew, the New York merchant Jacob Lucena, for "lascivious dalliance and wanton Carriage and profers to several women."[72] Lucena's punishment was light, however; thanks to supporting witness from Asser Levy, who apparently traveled all the way to Connecticut from New York in order to assist his friend, the former's fine was decreased "as a token of respect," so the official records indicated, "to the said Mr. Assur Levy."

Authorities in Essex County, Massachusetts, did bring Hebraic principles to bear in the case of a "malatta Jew" named Solomon, a trader who made the mistake of choosing to travel "through Wenham on his way toward Piscataqua" (Portsmouth, New Hampshire) on a Sunday in 1668. Between 1635 and 1653, Massachusetts officials passed a series of increasingly severe penalties for violation of the Sabbath, including a law that expressly forbade travel on Sundays. If one historian's assessment of the results of the ban is any guide, one immediate outcome of such strictures was that residents of the Bay who sought to avoid both attending church services and being penalized for traveling on the Sabbath developed the habit of leaving their home villages on Saturday nights until authorities in Boston went to the extreme of banning travel on Saturday night as well.[73] Where the invocation and institution of Mosaic laws had once been an expression of first-generation "precisianist" idealism and spiritual rigor (Bozeman refers to Sabbath-keeping, because of its public function, as the "showpiece of preparationism"[74]), by the time that Solomon made his way along the roads of Essex County its application had evolved into a reactionary gesture on the part of churches whose membership rolls were dwindling in the face of antinomian challenges, defections to Rhode Island, and a growing social instability. By reputation, at least, those practitioners who held the promise of free grace as of a higher order than any legalistic strictures upon actual behavior were suspected of teaching that, in John Winthrop's paraphrase, "the Sabbath is but as other days."[75] Solomon was a Jew who merely happened to have run afoul of a policy that held all New Englanders accountable for maintaining a congregational order and discipline whose heyday was rapidly passing.

Still, the influence of Judaical principles, even if their strict enforcement could no longer be maintained, would continue to shape discursive efforts to draw proper boundaries around the Puritan experiment. In the 1670s, Boston saw the arrival and brief settlement of Rowland Gideon, a Sephardic merchant and the scion of a large and prosperous family of Judaized *marranos* who had left Lisbon for Amsterdam and later Hamburg.[76] Rowland Gideon's own voyage from the Old World to the New has not been documented, but Lee Friedman, who wrote an essay in the 1930s about the history of the London-based Gideon clan, was convinced that the merchant was joining an already existing family group in the West Indies when he came there. The documentation pertaining to Gideon's Boston experience is limited to a set of court papers from July 1675 outlining a suit filed by Benjamin Gibbs appealing Gideon's initial claim that he and his partner, Baruch Lousada, were owed money for a tobacco transaction. A year before the suit was filed "Rowland Gideon ye Jew" had appeared in Boston rolls as having been taxed at the relatively high rate of 216 pence,[77] a fact that would necessarily have given him a significant, if impermanent footing among the relatively small number of Boston merchants who, by 1670, were said to be worth "from ten to thirty thousand pounds."[78] Most of the details pertaining to the case, including the exact nature of Gideon's claim and the basis for Gibbs's defense, are lost. Upon the filing, however, of Gibbs's appeal (the court had initially ruled in favor of Gideon's claim), Rowland Gideon authored what looks to be the earliest example of first-person testimony, or first-person writing of any kind, by a Jew in New England.

After enumerating his and Lousada's concerns and a litany of Benjamin Gibbs's apparent failures to furnish clear bookkeeping and promised recompense, Gideon offered the following plea: "As God commands our fathers that the same law should be for the strangers and sojourners as for the Israelitt, I may expect equal justice. Thus, and committing my case to this Honnourable Court and Gentlemen of the Jure, praying for the prosperity of your Government and that you may be further fathers of this scattered nation . . ."[79] Seeking equal redress and an evenhanded dispensation of fairness, Gideon's claim rested on his references to a set of books, or ledgers, that Gibbs, for all his apparent opportunities to do so, had repeatedly failed to produce. Gibbs's "appeal," Gideon testified, "speaks without books"; if, at one time, a man's word (especially in a Christian commonwealth) were sufficient, written proof was required in the current milieu. The vaunted legalism of the Puritans, in other words, their self-styled attempts to mimic the laws of ancient Israel, provided the central legitimizing context for Gideon's claim. Gideon appeared in his petition to be hedging his bets, aligning himself as both insider and outsider. As Ellen Smith suggests, he seemed loath to commit to either status; the apparent obsequiousness of his petition also expressed his awareness that "no particular outcome could be guaranteed him."[80]

Gideon pinned a certain amount of hope on the idea that, because of the justice of his claim, he and Lousada would be treated fairly as "strangers and sojourners"—in a land governed, presumably, by a native, or at least dominant, population of "Israelitts." His use of the phrase "further fathers" emphasized his keen awareness of the Puritans' metaphorical identification as belated Israelites. Whether Gideon intended any sort of suggestion that, in accordance with their claims of such a status, the Puritan authorities represented a "Jewish" or "Israelitt" point of view is impossible to know. The petition's reference to "Israelitts" could in fact have been chosen almost arbitrarily, in keeping with the biblically informed rhetorical practices of the time or, as Jacob Marcus puts it, Gideon's effort to show that "he could cite scripture as deftly as a Puritan."[81] Such a reference, given the Bay's firm grounding in the Hebrew Bible, would have an obvious connotative effect within which the majority population would be obvious stand-ins for Israelites. That the sentence immediately following from the "Israelitt" reference projected an entirely denotative identification on the speaker's part with the "scattered people" of the Jewish diaspora, on the other hand, suggests that Gideon's earlier references to Israelites was not entirely offhand or unself-conscious. Moreover, leaving aside the legal code's unequivocal insistence that the only officially tolerated foreigners could be those who "profess the true Christian religion," Massachusetts' *Body of Liberties*, as drafted by Nathaniel Ward, also stipulated the general principle that "people of other nations . . . shall be entertained and succoured amongst us."[82] In the name of the typologically conceived biblical covenant upon which the Bay was founded, as well as the historical one within which Gideon had been raised as a self-identified Jew, in other words, the petitioner expressed his hope that the Bay's civil authorities would find in his favor.

Whether he was successful in his 1675 claim is unknown, but Gideon apparently found Boston to be either inhospitable or unrewarding from a financial point of view; he left the city and returned to the West Indies in 1679. He reappeared in Barbados in 1692 and then in London in 1694, where he entered the established Sephardic community there by marrying into the prosperous family of Esther de Porto and becoming involved in the affairs of the Bevis Marks synagogue until his death in 1722.[83] Lousada was formally endenized, or naturalized, in Barbados a year after he and Gideon pleaded their case in Boston and then went on to become a prominent member of the London congregation as well.[84]

Twenty years would pass before the next Jews would appear in Boston. During those intervening years, those few "port Jews" who had the means and motivation to settle or at least trade in New England would find considerably more hospitable conditions in Newport, Rhode Island. Roger Williams had gone out of his way to establish a colony where, as Edgar McManus puts it, "the Bible citations that punctuated the Puritan codes were noticeably absent"[85] and an investment in Mosaic law as a means of outlawing idolatry was, for most residents, a bitter memory.

That Massachusetts had even practiced a severely limited tolerance toward a temporary Jewish presence within its jurisdictions, however, suggests that, even there, biblical principles could be held in suspense, or even ignored, in the interest of commerce. The Bay colony's reputation for severity toward religious and cultural outsiders is warranted by historical records, and the fact that a few Jews evidently survived their brief sojourns there does not constitute evidence to the contrary, let alone any kind of proof that Puritans harbored solicitous feelings toward the genealogical progeny of Israel. The limits of New England legalism, and the occasional "indulgent" attitude toward outsiders both spoke to the practical limitations attendant on authorities' efforts to maintain the primitivist and "precisianist" principle that had motivated their settlement in the New World. Every now and then affairs of the world intruded upon their dedicated attempt to apply religious strictures. Moreover, the spirit of mercy might occasionally infuse Puritan lawmakers, as it did when, in 1700, they decided that shipwrecked "Jesuits" might be spared execution if and when they washed up on the shores of Massachusetts.[86]

One of the most dramatic illustrations of this phenomenon had occurred in connection with Massachusetts' effort, in 1650, to affect an advantageous defense against the Iroquois. In a colony whose very identity and origin derived from its settlers' deep antipathy toward Catholicism and rejection of all "Popish" influences, a French Jesuit priest was welcomed as an ambassador, and also enjoyed audiences with Governor Dudley in Roxbury and William Bradford in Plymouth. Father Gabriel Druillettes had served as a missionary to the Montagnais and Abenakis before he was sent by the French authorities in Quebec to attempt to convince the New England colonies to join France's effort to form a bulwark against the Iroquois. As one historian describes Druillettes's visit to Bradford, the priest was even served fish on Friday in deference to Catholic practice. Before leaving Massachusetts, Druillettes also visited John Eliot, who supplied the Bay Colony's closest approximation to Quebec's intrepid missionaries. According to the Frenchman, Eliot had even invited him to spend the winter with him.[87] Druillettes was unsuccessful in convincing his Puritan hosts to join an alliance with Quebec, but the indulgent treatment he received at their hands suggested that attitudes toward outsiders, including those whose identity practically equated them with the anti-Christ, could be adjusted in accordance with diplomatic interest. The Jews who entered the Puritan colonies during the seventeenth century had represented a considerably more innocuous presence.

Massachusetts' attempted adherence to Mosaic principles and to an idea of theocratic sovereignty that looked to the biblical kingdoms of the Jews for guidance precluded any official conferral of rights upon non-Reformed Christians. Notwithstanding the irony attendant on such a situation, the very orthodox Puritan legalism that privileged a biblically sanctioned communitarianism that was to be based on "Jewish" precedent was fundamentally incompatible with the sort of practical leniency that would have been necessary for Jews and members of non-Reformed sects to experience anything approaching tolerance in the Bay. Only the large-scale *rejection* of Hebraic legalism, as put into practice by such stalwart New Testament readers as Rhode Island's Roger Williams, would allow for the development of an actual Jewish community in colonial New England. Williams and others of his ilk who rejected the Judaical tendencies that they ascribed to the Bay authorities had nonetheless been *influenced* in their actions by their reading of the Hebrew Bible. Their vociferousness had not arisen in a vacuum, and their contrary interpretations of Jewish precedent derived from many of the exact same theological impulses that had guided their more legalistic opponents. Those same New Englanders who rejected the "precisianism" of the empowered orthodoxy were no less dedicated to the purifying mission that had peopled the shores of New England with men and women who wished to sunder their connections to a corrupt official church in England. As Dwight Bozeman describes it, both "sides" of the debate over the centrality of Hebraic precedent were profoundly affected by a "well-practiced pose of embattlement" which had arisen before any Puritans had even crossed the Atlantic, as they had learned "to frame their identity in antithesis."[88]

Puritanism invited dissent and, for that matter, diversity. As Philip Gura suggests, some form of separatism and challenge to institutional orthodoxy comprised the "premises of the very congregationalism on which" Puritanism was based.[89] "All errors take Sanctuary in Independency" was how Thomas Edwards put it in 1646, and "independency" was what New England was all about.[90] Where Janice Knight and others point to the strictly theological fractiousness that defined the Puritan experience and gave it its intellectual and social resilience, other historians have in recent years worked to overturn any idea of *cultural* homogeneity as inherent in the region's history.[91] Bernard Bailyn sums up this reading of the earliest phases of the English colonial experience in New England by referring to

Puritanism as "a range of beliefs, ideas, and attitudes."[92] "The dissenters," in this view, "were no less 'Puritan' than the elder Winthrop and his clerical establishment."[93] In his tellingly entitled work on the seventeenth century in the region, Richard Archer argues for a diversified polity even at the earliest stages of settlement. "Not everyone was a Puritan, and English, and male, and a minister or a magistrate," Archer asserts in *Fissures in the Rock*.[94] "The builders of the Bay Colony and all of New England were a diverse people" who numbered among themselves "skeptics, lukewarm believers, Baptists, Anglicans, Quakers, Jews, shamans, [and] practitioners of magic."[95]

When Williams was cast out of Massachusetts Bay, his banishment came about not because he was timid in his assertion of faith, but because in his very stridency he had argued forcefully for a severance of all ties to the Church of England. *The Bloudy Tenent of Persecution*, Williams's 1644 polemic, used the New Testament to refute any supremacy of or equivalency of the Hebrew Bible and argued against "State worship"—which "profaned the holy name of God and Christ by putting their names and ordinances upon unclean and unholy persons."[96] Thus Williams offered a rebuke to church hierarchy whose extremism far outdid the founding extremism that created the errand in the first place. It is ironic that in his privileging of a New Testament–based theology, in which freedom of worship was the only means by which the Puritan mission could be truly achieved, he made it possible for a Jewish influx to take place. His argument in *The Tenent* embodied a fervent separatism that could not be contained by anything other than an impartial civility which would have, by definition, to tolerate all beliefs as equal under the law. Less than two decades passed before word of this experiment in civic tolerance inspired by religious extremism reached the ears of an itinerant group of Sephardic merchants who had survived the Inquisition as *conversos* or as practicing Jews in Holland, sought freedom and fortune in South America or the West Indies and then, upon the Spanish and Portuguese defeat of the Dutch in the tropics and the reintroduction there of the Inquisition, found themselves seeking a haven in North America.

The Bloudy Tenent, which appeared during Williams's visit to London in 1644, constituted an extended manifesto on religious tolerance. The argument it presented, however, was not a pluralistic plea for the natural rights of religious dissenters, let alone non-Christians. As one of the

English influences on Williams, Henry Ainsworth, had demonstrated, the argument against applying the example of Israel in the modern world "was not an instrument of secularization," but an attempt to deepen religious faith in accordance with a pietistic view of God that deemphasized the importance of the law.[97] Williams, as another historian puts it, was as careful a reader of "Judaical" precedent as any other Puritan, and, on that basis, "could not abide the deep political divide that separated the Puritan emphasis on God's victorious nation of Israel in the Old Testament and the New Testament idea of God's people as political outcasts."[98] Rather, the *Tenent* argued in favor of tolerance as a means of bringing about a deeper purification for the separatist congregations, whose excessive reliance on coercive measures, in Williams's view, detracted from their parishioners' unimpeded ability to know and experience true grace.

Williams's argument turned on the example of the "National Church and State of the Jewes," whose ancient history demonstrated two central principles. First, he stated forcefully and repeatedly that any over-arching institution of Mosaic law, as sought by the likes of John Cotton and other stalwart opponents of tolerance, was intrinsically non-Christian. Though he never went to the length, as Anne Hutchinson apparently had during her trial for antinomianism, of actually accusing his prosecutors of *being* "Jewes" themselves, the implication was unmistakable: "They that follow *Moses Church Constitution*," he argued, "which the *New English* . . . implicitly doe, must cease to pretend to be *Lord Jesus Christ* and his institutions."[99] In other words, as was pointed out to Cotton in the course of the Bay's debate over the adoption of a Hebraic legal code, the wholesale adoption of laws derived from the Hebrew Bible would have either to be proven to be entirely commensurate with the universal moral precepts of the New Testament or dismissed as superannuated, superseded *Jewish* law. With the "appearing of the Body and Substance, the Sun of Righteousnesse" in the form of Christ, Williams asserted that this "figurative" Jewish state "vanished."[100] Second, Williams tried to show that even the "Jewish church," when it was passing judgments, knew and adhered to a proper distinction between "civil" and "spiritual" affairs. Williams's version of the Hebrew Bible, as James Byrd explains, "provided vivid examples of religious liberty and courageous opposition to malicious kings and governments."[101] Williams applied a versatile typology in order to discredit his rivals' efforts to build their commonwealth in too close an accordance with the Jewish legacy.[102]

Williams argued that within a modern, or, more properly, post–New Testament world, "The State of the Land of Israel . . . is proved figurative and ceremoniall, and no patterne or precedent for any kingdom or civill state in the world to follow."[103] In this way, Williams's argumentation, which was no less steeped in scripture than that of his orthodox opponents, prefigured an approach that became more common years later, as the Unitarian influence of the nineteenth century urged a "metaphorical" reading of the Bible. The Hebrew Bible recounted the story of "the Seed or offspring of one man, Abraham," but since the coming of Christ, that offspring, aside from the case of its Jewish remnants, whom Williams didn't even mention, had become a "spiritual" rather than familial offspring, and "no paradigm for a Christian commonwealth."[104] "They only that are Christ's," Williams wrote, "are only Abraham's Seed and Heires," according to the promise, but that promise had only spiritual validity and could not be employed as it had been in the Jewish civil state as a basis for legislative restriction over worldly affairs. The Jews of old had been "selected and separated to the Lord," and they enacted all manner of delineating practices to establish and maintain their distinct lineage, such as "circumcision, the Passover, and matters of Gods worship, but even to temporall and civill things."[105] Where, however, "hath the God of Heaven in the Gospel," as opposed to the Hebrew Bible, "separated whole nations or kingdoms (English, Scotch, Irish, French, Dutch, &c) as a peculiar people and Antitype of the people of Israel? Yea, where the least footing in all the Scripture for a Nationall church after Christ's coming?"[106] Since no group (aside, again, from the Jews, but they did not figure into Williams's reasoning) in the world can be said to be "Israel's parallel and Antitype,"[107] the laws of Israel could only have been relevant in a spiritual or metaphorical capacity "as a type of Christ's church, not the secular state."[108] In questioning the Hebrew Bible's legitimacy as a model for the creation of a post–New Testament state, in which ancestries were to be mixed, Williams laid the foundation for a religious tolerance that, ironically, would before long extend to the tiny minority of "Abraham's Seed" who continued to adhere to that code.

Having established the largely figurative relevance of Hebrew law and its limitations as an arbiter on civil matters in the modern English or New

English state, Williams was thus able to argue that spiritual matters ought not to be subject to civil disputation. His promotion of religious tolerance was predicated on his assertion that all people might potentially come to Christ. Just as a garden contained vegetation that its keepers might not wish to harvest, society could not possibly banish all "hereticks" and not hazard the potential loss of souls to Christ. "He that's a briar, that is, a Jew, a Turke, a Pagan, an anti-Christian today," wrote Williams, "may be . . . a member of Jesus Christ tomorrow cut out of the wilde olive, and planted into the true."[109] In a civil state within which the tribalism of the Hebrew Bible had since lost its relevance, the proper objective was civil peace. By definition, Williams argued, such a state, containing as it does the progeny of so many mixed ancestries, is not hermetic but "an Heterogeniall commixture of joining of things most different."[110] Within such a context "who knows but not that many seducing teachers, either of the Paganish, Jewish, Turkish, or Anti-Christian Religion may be free and clear from scandalous offenses in their life as also from disobedience to the Civill Lawes of a State."[111] Indeed, by the time of Christ, even the Jews, whose legal code Williams elsewhere rejected as a universally applicable model for modern civil legislation, seemed to have recognized the necessity, or inevitability, of religious pluralism. "Whence Israel was under the Romanes," he reminded his readers, "lived divers sects of Religiones, as Herodians, Thadducees and Samaritanes, beside the common religion of the Jewes, Christ and his Apostles."[112] Accordingly, James Byrd argues that Williams "embraced the political imputations of the Old Testament"[113] and particularly valued the passages within its latter sections "that concerned the people of God in bondage to pagan governments."[114]

As in England, the chaos and tumult of the Reformation led directly, in Rhode Island's case, to the admission of Jews. In the maelstrom of economic activity that took shape as an ever-growing number of Puritan dissidents entered the new colony, Jews would shortly become participants, albeit marginalized ones. Developments in England had a shaping influence on such events, as some of the most strident devotees of the Puritan revolution saw the use, from an economic standpoint, of admitting Jewish merchants into a land that had formerly banished all Jews from entering in 1290. Hugh Peter, who had served the congregation in Salem, Massachusetts, before returning to England to raise funds for the Bay in the late 1640s, took the position in his 1647 pamphlet, "A Word for the Armie; and Two Words for the Kingdome," that a properly reformed England, in order to keep its place in the world and to keep peace with other European powers, should loosen restrictions. Here was no Roger Williams, arguing for the entire separation of the church from civil society, but a hard-headed, albeit radical adherent of congregational discipline. Peter combined an economic argument with a religious one, invoking English commercial ambitions while simultaneously drawing attention to Puritans' millennial aspirations. The concluding section of his pamphlet suggested "that merchants have all manner of encouragement, the law of merchants set up, and strangers, even *Jewes*, [be] admitted to trade and live with us, that it may not be said we pray for their conversion, with whom we will not converse, but being all but strangers on the Earth."[115] Peter's pronouncement sought both to expand England's economic horizons and to encourage a deeper theological consistency, in which the risk of admitting non-Christians into the kingdom would be made worthwhile by the potential advancement of the Gospel. Peter, like Roger Williams, would prove to be an early spokesperson for what Patricia Bonomi refers to as a modernistic latitudinarianism, wherein Protestant Christianity engendered a *loosening* of sectarian discipline and exclusivity as a key to the growth of the faith and the advancement of God's will.[116]

Williams, though hardly enamored of Judaism itself, echoed Hugh Peter's endorsement of lifting the ban on Jews entering England. "I have desired to labor in Europe, in America, with the English, with Barbarians," he wrote, "yea, and also I have longed after some trading with Jews themselves, for whose hard measure, I fear, the nations and England have yet a score to pay."[117] Williams made clear mention of Jews in the context of a wider set of references to aliens in general and, more specifically, to the idea of an expanded trade for the new colony. As early as 1647, Providence's code contained the language that "all men may walk as their conscience persuades them."[118] As Holly Snyder and other skeptics point out, the primary motivating context for the adoption of such tolerant statutes was hardly philo-Semitism, or even necessarily an economically motivated eagerness to lure Sephardic merchants to the colony. Rather, "the true tenor of the argument," Snyder suggests, "was that if even Jews (or Muslims) might, theoretically, be encompassed in such a Christian commonwealth, certainly any Christian would be welcome there."[119] The royal charter that was eventually secured for Rhode Island in 1663 made no explicit mention of

Jews or of any other religious group, for that matter, but its language was unambiguous on the subject of liberty of conscience, granting "full libertie in religious concernement." In the name of "true pietye rightly grounded upon gospel principles," the charter asserted, the colony's subjects would be left to shape their own spiritual lives in accordance with their individual consciences.

The question of exactly when the first Jews arrived in Newport remains unresolved. Filiopietism appears to underlie the claims of a few of the early twentieth-century American Jewish historians who may have wished to bring Rhode Island's Jewish history into closer proximity with that of New York, where a group of Jews is known to have settled, if only temporarily, in 1654.[120] In Newport's case, the earliest known firsthand surviving document pointing to any Jewish settlement is a deed from 1677 establishing a burial ground purchased by Mordecai Campanal and Moses Pacheco for the "Jews and their Nation Society or Friends."[121] Most of the speculation regarding an earlier establishment of the community derives from the existence of a single transcribed document belonging to an early nineteenth-century (non-Jewish) resident of Newport, N. H. Gould. The note itself establishes 1658 as the year by which Jews had first settled in the town, and describes not only what would have been the first settled Jewish presence in New England, but the earliest appearance of the Masonic Rite in North America, by Jew or Gentile: "On ye 5th day of ye 9th month 1658, ye 2nd Tisri A.A. 5518 we assembled at ye house of Mordecai Campanall and gave a degree to Abraham Moses."[122]

The most convincing evidence for the 1658 arrival comes to us in the form of the burial plot deed of 1677—the same piece of evidence that has been used to establish a later initial settlement. The conclusion to the deed called significant attention to the period *preceding* 1677 during which the Jews, according to the wording of the document, had already *left* Newport. In keeping with Jewish tradition that stipulates that burial sites ought only to be located adjacent to existing Jewish communities, the deed called for the abandonment of this one if the Jews should happen to leave. It also made clear that the community had been deserted once already:

> This witnesseth that I Nathaniel Dickins of Newport in Rhode Island have sold for a Valuable consideration in hand Received unto Mordecay Campanell & Moses Pacheickoe Jews unto their Nation Society of Friends

a Piece of Land for a burial Place. . . . I have for my Self and my heirs and Assigns or Successors for them to Possess and Enjoy for the Use as above said forever from thenceforth but if it should so fall out that ye Jews should all depart the Island Again so as that these shall be left to keep up & Maintain this Fences as aforesaid then the said Land shall Return Again to the Said Nathaniel Dickins for heir Executors Administrators or Assigns for him to Possess and Enjoy Again As if no such Sale had been made.[123]

The establishment of the cemetery in 1677 supplies sufficient evidence of a pre-existing community in need of a burial site.[124] Pacheco had to have been a more recent arrival than Campanal had been, as he is known to have been living in Hamburg between 1654 and 1660 (where he served as president of the Sephardic synagogue) and later endenized (in 1662), as were several others among the Newport Jews, in Barbados. As for the cemetery itself, its entirety comprises a small proportion of the Newport Jewish burial ground as it was delineated in the late eighteenth century.

Even if the group of Jews did indeed first come to Newport in 1658, chroniclers of the experience all concur that *between* that date and 1677, they "only resided there sporadically, or perhaps seasonally, as their commercial affairs required,"[125] having returned, according to those who argue for the earlier date, to Barbados. A succession of Navigation Acts handed down from English authorities in 1651, 1660, and 1663 prohibited any non-endenized aliens from trading. Notwithstanding Williams's relatively liberal policies on freedom of religious observation, the authorities' efforts to establish a firm hold on who might actually conduct trade appears to have been enforced. By 1684, a point in time by which no historian disputes a Jewish presence in Newport, some eight families had settled there permanently and, to the degree that their trade was unhampered, were conducting business in and beyond the town. Somewhat in the same spirit as Rowland Gideon in Boston in 1674, Simon Mendes and David Brown, two Newport Jews whose trade had been interfered with owing to their status as "Enemy Aliens"[126] under the latest round of Navigation Laws petitioned the Rhode Island legislature that "they could expect as good protection [there] as any stranger, not being of our nation, residing amongst us in his Majesty's colony ought to have, being obedient to his Majesty's laws."[127] Not for the last time, Jews in New England would be resorting to an appeal over the heads of local authorities, to officials in London, where the royal council could easily afford to indulge the requests of commercially active Jewish traders. As William Pencak points out, Rhode Island's comparatively liberal charter regarding religious toleration of dissenters seems to have both resulted from and necessitated a much higher degree of cooperation with English authorities than could be found in Massachusetts.[128] Ironically, the man who sought to prosecute the two merchants, William Dyer, was the son of one of Massachusetts Bay's most famous Quaker martyrs, Mary Dyer, whose much-decried public execution for heresy had helped to turn the tide against that colony's severe treatment of errancy.[129]

The Rhode Island court returned a decision in favor of the Jews on the same day that Dyer had filed his charges. A year later, Dyer attempted prosecution of several more Newport Jews, including the same Mordecai Campanal whose name appears in association with the 1658 document and the cemetery deed. An initial confiscation of their property occurred. Dyer was once again rebuffed, the jury found in favor of the defendants, and their property was restored.[130] Abraham Campanal, who may have been Mordecai's son,[131] applied for and received a license to sell liquor;[132] he was also charged in court for fornication.[133] David Campanal is known to have commanded a Newport-based sloop in the 1690s.[134] Thus, several decades before their community reached its peak of power and influence, the Jews of Newport were, according to Morris Gutstein, "permitted to hold property, and become freemen,"[135] even if the Assembly's "protection" of them also highlighted their "public position . . . as outsiders."[136] The community moved toward solidifying its status in the 1690s, when ninety more Jews arrived from the Dutch West Indies island of Curaçao.[137] From its earliest beginnings to its eventual eclipse in the face of the British occupation of the 1770s and 1780s, the Jewish presence in Newport was a function of wide-ranging, transatlantic commerce which, alongside of all manner of dueling theologies, had shaped the settlement of New England and its place both in the context of North America's colonization and as an increasingly important center for trade.

The arrival of Jews there in the mid-seventeenth century coincided with the solidification of Rhode Island's status as a politically viable counterpart to Massachusetts' more tightly woven commonwealth. For a period of time in the late seventeenth and early eighteenth centuries, Newport's centrality as a seaport, as well as its growing status as a trading haven for

Sephardic Jewish merchants, outstripped New York's. The town offered direct evidence of New England's participation in a transnational, inter-colonial and cultural commerce. Its seventeenth-century economic history, particularly *because* of the Jews' presence, was an aspect of its rising fortunes, and illustrates Bernard Bailyn's claim that seventeenth-century North America "becomes more fully comprehensible when seen as the exotic far western periphery, a marchland of the metropolitan European cultural system."[138] As they had been when they lived on Europe's periphery, the Jews of Newport were overwhelmingly merchants, as opposed to crafts- or tradespeople; their very itinerancy spoke to New England's trans-atlantic reach. The Jews' existence at the apparent margins of society was a function not so much of their separateness as of their full-fledged engagement with an outside world. "Their horizons," writes Eli Faber, "encompassed not just their immediate surroundings but the entire Atlantic world."[139] Commercial connections among Jews often transcended established boundaries among colonies as well as the width of the Atlantic. In 1674, for instance, legal proceedings were enjoined upon Asser Levy of New York, who was accused by Dutch authorities in that city (control over which had briefly reverted to Dutch hands after the English takeover of 1664) of having "received a letter from New England." In his successful defense, Levy argued that he had not been home when the letter was delivered, that his wife had "unwittingly accepted it but did not read it."[140]

That these Jews had arrived in Newport in the course of a circuitous, decades-long journey that had taken them first from the Iberian peninsula to Holland, thence to either South America or the West Indies, and, finally, to one of New England's busiest seaports was a consequence not only of their marginalized status within the Christian world but of the ceaseless transformations, migrations, displacements, and reformations that were creating a "new Mediterranean" out of the Atlantic. The toleration that growing numbers of Sephardic Jews were finding in Holland, England, and various pockets in the New World was hardly enough to place them in the mainstream of any society, but their "threshold" existence, as David Graizbord describes it, their straddling of Jewish and Christian, Protestant and Catholic, New and Old World, and, for that matter, temperate and semi-tropical climates helped to confer a similar status on New England itself.[141] The relative mobility of the Newport Jews, even at this early stage of settlement, was an outgrowth of the strong kinship ties that bound so many of them as members of the "Nation," as Spanish and Portuguese *conversos* commonly referred to themselves. Their shared identity as Jews, their even clannish insularity, also ensured their movement and interaction back and forth across these many thresholds. The Jews' peripheral existence gave evidence of Puritanism's susceptibility to in-built centripetal forces that had given rise to it in the first place. Rhode Island itself, as Joseph Conforti points out, was a territorial manifestation of the same tendency, "a kind of refugee camp from Puritanism" that only Puritanism could have created and occasioned.[142]

The presence of a Jewish community in Newport confirmed Rhode Island's marginal status and its role as a "receptacle" for an essentially individualistic deviance that had been born of the Reformation's more radical tendencies. Despite the worst accusations and fears of the ever-beleaguered Massachusetts clergy who had launched Rhode Island by banishing such figures as Anne Hutchinson and Roger Williams to it, and despite Williams's and others' spirited rejection of the congregational and social discipline implied by the use of Mosaic law, the Rhode Island experiment would go a long way toward illustrating the ordering efficacy of church and state separation. Whether this tendency spoke more volubly to Puritanism's emphasis on a Mosaic or exilic reading of Hebraic precedent, its preference either for an unmediated experience of "conviction" or for the more ambitious pursuit, through "works," of an achievable salvation, its application reminds us, once again, of the movement's intriguing engagement with Judaical subjects, as well as of its orthodoxy's "impressive capacity to reinvent itself," as Michael Winship puts it, "while being in principle fixed."[143] Whether physically present as agents of their own and their gentile neighbors' future in New England or as merely implied through all manner of discursive deployments of their scriptural legacy, Jews were increasingly important participants in the life and consistently integral subjects of the theology of seventeenth-century New England. Their small numbers could hardly minimize the extent of the "rhetorical importance"[144] they bore, as Puritan writers sought justification and stability in the face of quickly multiplying theological dilemmas and social crises.

CHAPTER TWO

"NEW-ENGLAND IS SELDOM WHOLLY WITHOUT THEM"

Boston's Frazon Brothers and the Limits of Puritan Zeal

ON NOVEMBER 22, 1705, the *Boston News-Letter's* correspondent in Barbados received word that Samuel Frazon, a Boston merchant of Sephardic parentage who was initially "feared to be Lost in coming from on board a Man of War" while sailing to Antigua from Boston had in fact survived his ordeal. The story that appeared in the March 11, 1706 edition of the paper offered readers the full scope of Frazon's adventures. Caught by a storm in the Caribbean, he and his black slave survived six days without food or water and eventually washed ashore on the island of St. Vincent, "where the Indians stripped him naked as soon as he landed."[1] The merchant and his slave lived through their captivity, but the two sailors accompanying them perished. Eventually, although Frazon was evidently unable to ransom the slave, he was able to pay for his own freedom for the price of "17 or 18 Pistoles."[2] From the West Indies he made his way back to Boston by way of Martinique, "ready," according to Jacob Marcus, "to do business again" in partnership with his brothers Joseph and Moses. Frazon's story was remarkable as an adventure on the high seas, but it was no less fantastic for its dramatization of the extreme itinerancy of the Sephardic merchant class. The Frazon brothers' participation in the New England economy was a fleeting one, but it represented a cosmopolitan and integrally Jewish incursion nonetheless, and—as the *Boston News-Letter's* coverage suggested—it did not go unnoticed. The presence of unapologetic and self-identified Jews in the Massachusetts Bay colony also helped to inspire a renewed Puritan discourse on the legacy of Judaism, particularly as it related to the question of whether or not church members ought to take active steps toward achieving New England's salvation.

The man likely to have been the Boston merchants' grandfather, Samuel Frazoa, had himself been born in the New Christian community in Portugal, made his way to the large Jewish enclave in Dutch Brazil in the early1640s, and served that community as a teacher of Hebrew. At some point between the family's flight from Recife in 1654 and the settlement of the younger Samuel and his brother Joseph in Boston in the late 1690s (Moses was their consistent business partner but seems never to have come to New England), the Frazons (or Frazoas) became members first of the Jewish congregation in London and later were affiliated with the Jewish community of Barbados, where they were endenized in March 1693. Joseph is thought to have been buried in Newport, Rhode Island, in the Jewish cemetery that had been purchased in 1677 by Mordecai Campanal and Moses Pacheco. Samuel, whose official residence at the time of his prematurely announced death was noted as "Boston, New-England," actually died in Jamaica in 1706. Both Samuel and Joseph Frazon were residents of Boston for "at least a decade," according to Marcus's accounting, from about 1695 to 1705.[3]

For the Frazons, like many other Sephardim, itinerancy functioned as a mode of economic advancement. Their collective experience, which included ship-ownership, captaincy, slave-trading, and the proprietorship of a warehouse, was a testament to the trans-oceanic versatility of colonial-era Jews. The British Atlantic, with its many economic and cultural enticements, offered endless possibilities for reinvention. Free from the shadow of the Inquisition, whose oppressive influence nonetheless inspired an invigoration of extended kindred ties among the members of La Nacion, the Frazons and their ilk might easily have surged headlong into the commercial fray with minimal regard for their previous ties to Judaism. For better or worse, however, they seem not to have been overly eager on this account. Instead of severing their ties to the Old World, the Frazons did their best to make the most of their Jewish connections on both sides of the Atlantic, as well as between New England and the West Indies. How important Judaism itself was to them is difficult to ascertain on the basis of what scant evidence we have, but their identity as Jews was of more than incidental interest to at least three prominent New Englanders who wrote about them during their time in Boston. If economics was the primary inspiring force behind their itinerancy, religious and cultural identities appear to have shaped many of their commercial interactions. From the perspective of the three Boston notables who cared about such things— Samuel Sewall, Increase Mather, and Cotton Mather—the Frazons were objects of attention *because* they were unconverted Jews. After half a century of discoursing *about* Jews, publishing pamphlets calling for their conversion, identifying the surrounding native population as biblical offspring, and apparently barely even noticing when actual Jews like Solomon Franco or Rowland Gideon traded in their midst, prominent New Englanders noted the presence of actual Jews. Even if Boston's Frazon brothers were not part of a larger local community of Jews, a short distance to the southwest a numerically significant number of Jews was assembling in Newport, reinforced by the temporary establishment of ninety new members from Curaçao in 1694.[4] By 1712, the town that had been founded by Anne Hutchinson—the woman who had caused a great courtroom stir by referring contemptuously to her panel of judges in Boston as a committee of "Old Jewes,"—would have its own "Jew Street" and "Jews Alley."[5]

As delighted as he ought to have been at the prospect of a massive conversion of the Jews, Massachusetts Chief Justice Samuel Sewall was reserved in his attitude toward the idea. Born in 1652, Sewall spanned the second and third generations, having come to Massachusetts from England at age nine to join his grandfather, who had settled in the town of Newbury.[6] The diary he kept from 1675 until 1727 was a testament to his extreme sensitivity and candor. The diary also provides insight into his diplomatic aspect and his ability to maintain cordial friendships with Bostonians whose ecclesiastical views varied widely. Sewall was no less convinced than any of his fellow Puritans that the Jews were misguided in their apostasy, and his eschatology was posited on the idea of New England itself being at the geographic center of an imminent Second Coming. Though he was himself a fairly orthodox practitioner who sought as best as he could to uphold the first generation's high standards of Calvinistic rigor and never questioned the importance of the performance of spiritual confession as a prerequisite for church membership, Sewall was more speculative than activist in his writing on Jewish conversion.

Sewall's primary inheritance seems to have been the founders' pietism.

He avoided making the sorts of public pronouncements that other second- and third-generation Puritans produced. As Larzer Ziff explains, Sewall "inclin[ed] to a religion of sensibility" which actually "permitted a degree of self indulgence in religious devotion"[7] as opposed to aspirational prayer. In a world in which "daily reality [was] fragmenting beyond confident doctrinal explanation" it made more sense to work at relinquishing the illusion that prayer or any other human activity might be sufficiently powerful in and of itself to shape outcomes that were entirely in God's hands.[8] Sewall also appears to have been less pained than Mather was by the dissolution of congregational authority. His willingness to cede control where he was powerless to exercise it, notwithstanding his privately expressed misgivings over all manner of impious indulgences, from the use of pagan names for the days of the week to the wearing of periwigs,[9] rendered the conversion of the Jews, as well as many other public events, less urgent matters for Sewall than they were for many of his contemporaries. Like John Cotton, John Winthrop, and several other pragmatists of an earlier generation, he was committed to creating "'a city on a hill' more perfect than man had known, [but] . . . did not believe that even a chosen people would be free from error."[10]

Cotton Mather, who only outlived his father Increase by five years, faced a more difficult time parlaying the orthodoxy of the founders into the more manageable piety that enabled Sewall and other transitional figures to adjust to the new New England. The conversion of the Jews was a more vexing matter for Mather than it was for Sewall, owing perhaps to the former's more proprietary, not to mention fraught relationship to the founders and their legacy. As far as Mather was concerned, the presence of Jews and the prospect of their conversion bore powerful symbolic significance as New England itself, well into its third generation of continual English settlement, sought a new kind of vindication. In his private meditations and public pronouncements on the subject of Jewish conversion, Mather played the part both of the dutiful son honoring the legacy of Christianity's "fathers" and of the chastening father calling the errant "sons" of the commandment to task for failing to recognize the divinity of Christ. His dualistic demeanor toward Jewish conversion mirrored his evident ambivalence toward the imposing legacy of the founders, whose looming example both lent him legitimacy and threatened to render his ministry irrelevant.

In the face of both real and imagined states of "declension" among late seventeenth- and early eighteenth-century Puritans, apologists like Mather had found it necessary to redeploy the old parallels between ancient Israel and New England in new ways. The year 1689 had brought the Glorious Revolution to Massachusetts. In the aftermath of the deposition in England of the "Jesuitical" James II and Parliament's replacement of him with William and Mary, New Englanders conducted their own bloodless coup and removed Governor Edmund Andros from power, reviving the old charter that had been revoked by an imperious English colonial authority. For some New Englanders, as Mark Peterson writes, the events of 1689 restored not only a long dormant sense of their own autonomy but a feeling that, as in the heady days of the Cromwellian revolution, they "could finally link their aspirations to a powerful political and military force that they could plausibly imagine might turn dreams" of a "Protestant International into reality."[11] The peaceful restoration of Protestant hegemony in England, as glorious as it did indeed look from the point of view of New Englanders who had all but written off the importance of England with the ultimate failure of Cromwell's revolution in 1660, would also necessitate a new balancing act on the part of the American Puritans. New Englanders had not only adopted their own compromises in the form of the Halfway Covenant and its "opening" of the way to a less than spiritually qualified church membership but were now obliged to submit gracefully to a Protestant crown which had chosen to approve a policy of universal tolerance to all dissenting sects. Thus, as "re-Anglicization" became the norm even for testy New Englanders who included among them the grandsons of the Cottons, Winthrops, and Mathers, the previous parallel with Israel had to be adapted so as not to seem to impute an excess of exceptionalism to what was now just another English New World colony. The "strong association with ancient Israel" that "had originated in New England's sense of moral and cultural distance from the homeland"[12] now had to be reshaped as to avoid offense and, at the same time, in such a way as to reinvigorate a population that was growing increasingly restless with endless debates over ecclesiastical purity and distracted by burgeoning opportunities for commercial growth.

Jewish merchants, for their part, would only have been oblivious or at least indifferent to New England's struggle to manage its religious future

Samuel Sewall (1652–1730). Oil on canvas by Nathaniel Emmons, 1728. Courtesy of the Massachusetts Historical Society.

in accordance with or opposition to its earliest founding principles. Re-Anglicization certainly boded well for them, as the extension of crown authority over the New England trade meant that they would be less susceptible to the arbitrary and protectionist whims of such colonial authorities as Rhode Island's William Dyer, who had created such a nuisance for the Newport Sephardim in the 1680s. How and why the Frazons chose to base their trade in Boston, particularly as Newport was both nominally and practically speaking a more hospitable location for Sephardim, is difficult to know. Samuel Sewall, who made the brothers' acquaintance sometime shortly after their arrival in Boston in 1695, learned from them that both their father and grandfather had been among the "very numerous" Jewish residents "in the Dutch plantations in Brasil."[13] Whether or not the Frazons were the source of Sewall's broader knowledge of contemporary Jewish life as well, the Puritan judge had clearly been paying close attention to some Jewish source as he produced his *Phaenomena Quaedam Apocalyptica* in 1697. "Now it is manifest to all," he wrote, "that very considerable numbers of Jews are seated in the New World; where they merchandize, have their *Synagogues*, and places of burial. At *Spikes* in *Barbados*, there is a street called *Jews* Street . . . At *Jamaica* there are a great many, and *Port Royal* also hath its *Jews* Street."[14] Sewall mentioned the Jewish community in New York before passing on to his discussion of the Frazons. His somewhat exaggerated sense of a Jewish presence in North America, including its salutary Boston manifestation, emphasized one point—*actual* Jews had established permanent inroads in the Americas, and they had done so quite visibly or at least in such a way as to be "manifest" to all. "New-England," he said, "was never wholly without them." This remark, it seems, was the direct result of his interaction with "Joseph Frazon & Samuel his brother," Sewall wrote, "to whom I am beholden for a sight of the *Spanish Bible*."[15]

The Frazons' arrival in Boston followed immediately from their endenization, in Barbados, in March 1693. They are known to have owned a warehouse in Charlestown. In 1702, their part ownership of the "square stern'd vessel of burthen of about one hundred and fifty tons" *Joseph and Rachel* "built at Salem . . . anno 1700" was noted by two Boston lawyers.[16] As his later adventure on the high seas proved, Samuel Frazon was the more volatile of the two men. He was cited twice in Boston courts in connection with the physical abuse of other men's slaves.[17] Aside from their interactions with Sewall himself, as well as with Cotton Mather, their primary notoriety in Boston derived from Samuel's adventures as recounted in the *News-Letter*, but also, at least in one case, from the fact of their uniquely Jewish knowledge. On November 29, 1699, Joseph Frazon was called upon by Massachusetts governor Richard Coote (the Earl of Bellomont) to help in identifying a man whom court authorities believed to be James Gilliam, a former associate of William Kidd who was known to have been forcibly circumcised and converted to Islam while adventuring off the coast of

India. Wishing to affect a positive identification of the alleged pirate, the court authorities consulted Joseph Frazon on the matter of the outlaw's circumcision. In the language of the affidavit to which he was sworn after visiting the captive in jail, Frazon affirmed his authority on the subject by stating that he himself was "of the Jewish Nation by both his parents."[18] His Jewish background enabled him upon his examination of Gilliam, to "find that he ha[d] been circumcised but not after the manner practiced by the Jewes according to Leviticall Law the prepuce being taken of [sic] round and not sloping as the manner of the Jews is to cut."[19] Joseph Frazon and his brothers supplied New Englanders, who had always been fascinated by the legacy of the Jews, with firsthand knowledge of the actuality of Jewish existence and custom.

For his part, Sewall himself recorded several observations of Jewish life in his diary, going back to the 1680s. While on an extended sojourn in England, where he had been sent to assist in Increase Mather's attempt to regain the Massachusetts charter, the Massachusetts judge had taken notice of the arrival by the Harwich coach (which would have fetched passengers just arriving over the North Sea from Holland) of a new "Priest" for the Bevis Marks Jewish congregation of London. Perhaps Sewall's general curiosity had been piqued by the Jews' excitement over this event. Shortly afterwards, in any case, he made his way to the Bevis Marks burial ground itself, at Mile End. He recorded the following entry in his diary, striking for its candor, level of detail and, finally, for the charming story it related of the stalwart Puritan joining in a communion, of sorts, with an actual Jew. "Some bodies" in the cemetery, Sewall noted

> were laid East and West; but now all are ordered to be laid North and South. Many tombs. Engravings are Hebrew, Latin, Spanish, English, sometimes on the same stone. Part of the Ground is improv'd as a Garden, the dead are carried through th' keeper's house. First tomb is abt. The year 1659. Brick wall built abt part. ont's two sides 5444 Christi 1684, Tamuz 2, June, 23, as I remember—I told the keepr afterwards wisht might meet in Heaven. He answered, and drink a glass of Beer together, which we were then doing.[20]

Sewall had managed to breach more than just the brick wall surrounding the Jewish burial site. The idea of the heavenly meeting, suggesting as it did not only an occasion for a toast of fellowship but a fanciful breaking

Mile End Cemetery, London. The seventeenth- and eighteenth-century Sephardic cemetery, which Samuel Sewall visited on his trip to England in the 1680s, is the oldest Jewish burial ground in Great Britain. This contemporary view is provided through the courtesy of the photographer, Philip Walker of London, England.

Bevis Marks, London. Established by the Sephardic community in 1701, it is oldest synagogue in England. This view of the candle-lighting is provided through the courtesy of the photographer, Philip Walker of London, England.

down of the wall of belief separating the Christian and Jewish perspectives, invites us to view both Sewall and the Jewish groundskeeper as surprisingly indulgent of each other's convictions. Indeed, if either of the two religions can be said to have prevailed in the exchange, it would have to been that of the Jews, which generally placed less emphasis on the afterlife than Christianity did. As the groundskeeper elevated the seemingly mundane act of sharing of a glass of beer—an act that he and Sewall were at that very moment participating in—to the level of a heavenly exchange, the Puritan judge appears to have gone along cheerfully.

That London—that other center of the Puritan universe—had become host to a growing and increasingly visible Jewish community beginning in 1657 was a factor in the evolution of New England's developing awareness of an actual Jewry. Following from Cromwell's dedicated but not altogether successful efforts to bring about the readmission of Jews to England, a small number of Sephardic traders were able to settle and establish a congregation, first at Creechurch Lane and, eventually, at Bevis Marks. Most of the London Jews, at least before the eighteenth century, were of the same Sephardic stock that went on to populate the New World outposts to which Sewall referred in his diary. They came to London from Amsterdam, as well as various Dutch outposts in the New World, and brought with them a fairly advanced Judaic background, including a set liturgy, congregational structure, and mechanisms to ensure Hebrew training for young men. The congregation whose burial site Sewall had visited represented a committed and sometimes quite insular Judaism, notwithstanding the cosmopolitanism of its members. If these Sephardic merchants were merely seeking economic betterment, they would not have gone to such lengths to fortify their Jewish life.

The Sephardic diaspora took several routes—northward into Holland and eventually England; southward and eastward into, among other places, southern France, Italy, North Africa, the eastern Mediterranean, and the Middle East; and, finally, westward across the Atlantic. Since many Sephardim had been living in Holland for several decades following from the Inquisition, their movement into several of the Dutch colonies came naturally, especially with their myriad commercial enticements. An especially large number chose to settle in Brazil where, by 1645, half of the fifteen hundred European colonists were Jews. That colony was in Dutch hands for a barely a year, from 1624 to 1625, before it was conquered by Portugal. The Dutch returned in 1630 and remained in power until Portugal re-conquered it in 1654. The Dutch West India Company compact that governed the Dutch recovery of 1630 openly stipulated religious tolerance. "The liberty of Spaniard, Portuguese, and natives," it read, "whether they be Roman Catholics or Jews will be respected."[21] Though not all of the *marranos* present in Brazil during the Dutch occupation re-embraced their Judaism, a significant number did. Indeed, as one historian suggests, notwithstanding the language of the charter, the Jews fared better under the Dutch regime than did the Portuguese Catholics, who had been conquered, after all.[22] Within a relatively short space of time, in any case, the Jews had organized two formal congregations—Zur Israel in the larger settlement of Recife and Magen Abraham in Mauricia.[23]

The spiritual leader of Zur Israel was the renowned Amsterdam rabbi Ahoab de Fonseca (1605–1693), who distinguished himself in 1646 by writing the first Hebrew poem ever produced in the New World and may also have been among the first Jews to visit, if not settle, in Newport, Rhode Island. Ahoab had first come to Recife in 1642, and was paid a handsome salary of 1600 florins annually for his services.[24] The congregation took relatively little time to organize itself in accordance with the Amsterdam model, adopting a requisite forty-two regulations, or *Acuerdos*. One rule in particular, the one that governed the terms of congregational membership, would have given a host of Puritan ministers and magistrates pause to reflect on their own policies; its unambiguous lineage-based guidelines stood in stark contrast to the vexed and often theologically obtuse regulations that guided congregational membership among New England churches. As translated by Arnold Witnitzer, the twentieth-century historian who brought out an edition of the congregation's 1649–1654 minute books, the rule stipulated that "all Brazilian Jews who had been present at the plenary meeting . . . or who at that time resided in other parts of Brazil, as well as those Jews who in the future would migrate to that country would also be considered members of congregation Zur Israel and would be subject to its regulations and responsible for its debts and for general assessments imposed upon the Jewish community."[25] Membership was instituted (or imposed) upon a given Jew's signing of the congregation's minute book. Among the names recorded there in 1649 are those of Jacob, Joseph, and Samuel (or Semuel)

Frazoa. The last, who was most likely the grandfather of the Frazons who lived in turn-of-the-eighteenth-century Boston, held the official post of "ruby," which Witnitzer defines as "instructor in the lower classes of the Talmud Torah," or Hebrew school. Whatever the fortunes of the congregation as a whole may have been, the minute book shows that the elder Frazon's own salary shrank over the course of his five-year term—from a starting point of 600 florins in 1649 to 250 florins annually in 1653, the year preceding the congregation's dissolution.[26]

When the Portuguese recovered Brazil from the Dutch in 1654, the Jews were given three months to leave by order of the conquering but "reasonably lenient" General Barreto. According to one evacuee's diary, the general had "caused it to be proclaimed throughout his Army that every one of his soldiers should be careful not to wrong or persecute any of the Children of Israel."[27] Like the majority of fleeing Sephardim, the Frazons made their way back to Holland (fifteen of the sixteen ships that left Recife with Jews aboard them after the Portuguese conquest made the return trip to Amsterdam; the sixteenth vessel was the one whose shipwrecked passengers, after being rescued by the French vessel St. Catherine, sailed to New Amsterdam instead, and whose arrival there marked the first long-term Jewish sojourn in North America). How long the Frazons remained in Holland before joining the London congregation is unknown. When the time came for the younger Frazons to leave the Old World once again for the New—in this case, Barbados—they had experienced membership in three closely knit Jewish congregations. Regardless of the level of their own personal interest in religious matters, their exposure was sufficient to give them a firm sense of what it meant to be identifiably Jewish in a Christian world. Their marrano heritage belied what had to have been an impressive immersion in Judaic practice and rabbinical scholarship.

Among other efforts undertaken by the London Jews of the late seventeenth century to inculcate a form of orthodoxy was the congregation's purposed pursuit and installment of a succession of "learned rabbis," as their Puritan neighbors would have put it. One of these rabbis may very well have exerted an influence on at least one of the Frazon brothers. Sewall himself was the source of this information, as in his recounting of his interaction with the Frazons, he indicated that Joseph "was sometime scholar to the learned Yeoshuah da Sylva."[28] Da Silva was the

London group's second rabbi, after Jacob Sasportas. Like his predecessor and his successor, da Silva had been trained in Amsterdam, northwestern Europe's most well-established Jewish center and a long-standing haven for members of the Sephardic diaspora. Da Silva was the rabbi, or *haham*, of the London congregation from 1670 until his death in 1679, when he became the first rabbi to be buried in the same cemetery that Sewall was to visit ten years later. Since a congregational census that appears to have been completed in December 1680 makes mention of Jacob Frazoa, his wife, and two sons, and because Sewall's notation indicates that Joseph had studied with da Silva, we can safely assume that the Frazon brothers were members of the Bevis Marks congregation during some part of the 1670s at least.

How fully immersed they were in their Judaism can only be extrapolated on the basis of what we know about their earlier participation in other congregations, since no Jewish community as such existed in Boston. Given the interest that Sewall and, as we shall see, Cotton Mather himself had in the Frazon brothers and their Judaism, it would appear to have been the case that the London experience, if not those of Amsterdam, Brazil, and Barbados as well, had exerted a palpable influence upon them. As far as London was concerned, at any rate, congregational discipline appears to have been firm and—in a manner not so very dissimilar from the norm among the Puritans of New England—not uninvolved in the management not only of religious conduct but of day-to-day affairs as well. The records of the London Jewish congregation from its founding in 1657 and into the years that it was served by Joseph Frazon's teacher, da Silva, presented a succession of rules. These *acuerdos* governed liturgical affairs and the conduct of Jews on the street, in among the general population of English gentiles, whose government had not really sanctioned tolerance so much as it had decided to look the other way as a growing population of Jews assumed inhabitancy and conducted business. *Escarme* number 31 laid down that "No Jew may hold dispute or argument on matters of religion with Guim [Goyim] . . . because to do otherwise is to disturb the liberty which we enjoy and make us disliked." Another rule forbade the publication of any book in Hebrew, Ladino, or any other language without the full consent of the complete *Mahamad*, or membership.[29]

Congregational order was sought but not necessarily fully established

among the London Jews. Measures had to be taken regularly to counteract everything from the loudness of the worshippers to the protocols surrounding the movement of members in and out of the synagogue when
the Torah was being removed from the ark, the proper use of tfillin, and
even the appropriate composition of a minyan. Nor could order be found
within the talmud torah, or Hebrew school. In 1674, the membership saw
fit to hire a new parnas, or teacher "to be given a section in the synagogue
in a part where he shall be within view of the Talmudim [students], devot-
ing especial care to controlling them."[30] Whether or not one or all of the
Frazon brothers were among the members of this young rabble is a matter of speculation. If, as Sewall indicates on the basis of his conversations
with Joseph Frazon, the latter had indeed been one of da Silva's pupils, he
had to have been relatively advanced in his studies by the time he came to
Boston. When Isaac Davila was chosen to serve in the role of parnas in 1675,
at a salary of 30 pounds annually, the congregational record book went on
to explain that his job would be "to teach the Talmudim from Aleph Beth
as far as reading Parashea in Hebrew inasmuch as other lessons from that
point upwards devolved upon our St. Jehoshuah da Silva."[31] In meeting
Joseph Frazon, then, Samuel Sewall and Cotton Mather may not have been
discoursing with a "learned rabbi," but neither were they encountering an
uninformed merchant who had barely learned his "Aleph Beth." Frazon
had undergone relatively advanced training in Judaism.

Although da Silva may have gained less notoriety than either his predecessor or his successor, both of whom left more permanent records of
their time at the head of the London congregation, he earned significant
respect among the learned Sephardim for his "science and erudition," as
one of his memorialists among the Amsterdam Jews recounted. Shortly
after his death in 1679, da Silva's widow brought out a print edition, in
Portuguese, of his Thirteen Articles, a series of sermons he had delivered to
the Creechurch Lane congregation. The book was one of the first publications to be issued by the London Jews, and was intended to showcase
the rabbi's dedication to the Law and, as Isaac Aboab put it in his introductory note, "the benefit and utility" of the "Republic of Israel."[32] That
Joseph Frazon, and perhaps Samuel as well, had been even a "sometime"
pupil of so accomplished a scholar as da Silva could only have bolstered
his awareness of, if not his reverence for, Jewish teaching and tradition.

In one of several prefaces to the Thirteen Articles, Selamoh de Oliveyra indicated not only that da Silva had inspired general admiration on the part of his fellow Jews for his scholarly achievements but that his sermons on the sanctity and contemporary relevance of Mosaic Law displayed the sort of spiritual illumination that suggested superior sensitivity and wisdom on his part. Applying celestial similes to his description of the learned rabbi, De Oliveyra suggested that da Silva's teachings were like the "phases of the resplendent moon" to Moses' "clear and luminous sun." No man who had spent even a part of his boyhood and youth studying under the guidance of such a teacher, as Joseph Frazon had, could have avoided imbibing a sense of what it meant to be a Jew.

If Samuel Sewall ever sought to bring Joseph Frazon or his brothers into the Christian fold, he never did write about it, and his diary was about as candid a personal recounting as any produced by a colonial New Englander. Sewall's writing on the subject of Jewish conversion articulated a minimal level of personal investment. In the Phaenomena, where he spoke in the greatest detail both about the Frazons and about Jews in general, he offered the fairly bland comment, in connection with the Jews associated with the Dutch colonies of Surinam and Curaçao, that "Probably these Jews will be converted." His use of the passive voice conveyed a less than activist mentality, a sense that the conversion would be resolved "when the time . . . shall come."[33] His calculations concerning the Jews, which included a fairly detailed recounting of the history of the diaspora following from the Inquisition of 1492, led to a relatively balanced conclusion. Given the direction that world events had been taking, Jewish conversion (which might also have encompassed those native American Israelites who had found their way to the New World in the course of their wanderings) was going to be the inevitable result of God's efforts to bring about His own desired ends.

Sewall's own minister, Samuel Willard, had himself issued a sermon on the subject of "A National Conversion of the Jews" in 1694. The sermon, entitled "The Fountain Opened," was eventually published in the form of a pamphlet, including one edition in 1727 that was appended to a reissue of Sewall's own Phaenomena. Willard, who served also as the acting vice-president of Harvard until his death in 1707, had wished to weigh in on the question of whether and how "God's ancient people" would be restored to their former glory. As Increase Mather had in *The Mystery*, Willard had first to refute the idea that the Jewish conversion of biblical prophecy had occurred in ancient times when the early Christians were won over to the cause of Christ. Opinions had long been divided among Protestants on this matter, as the apparently cursed and forlorn condition of the world's Jews, in the view of some Christians, precluded any warrant or possibility of their eventual conversion. Many were convinced that all relevant Jewish conversions had occurred in Jesus' own time and its immediate aftermath, when born Jews like St. Paul had become Christians. Among other things, adherence to such a view licensed an unfettered anti-Jewish prejudice, since the conversion of actual Jews was rendered entirely irrelevant by it to Christian prophecies of the Second Coming. Like many other Puritans whose eschatology was posited on changes that had not yet occurred, however, Willard was interested in real, living Jews, as distinguished from the "Spiritual Israel" (who numbered among them the Puritans themselves), including those wandering Israelites who constituted at least a portion of the indigenous population of the Americas, but most especially the miserable, misguided Jews of Europe.

The Fountain was at least in part a charity pamphlet, as it called repeatedly for the relief and redress of a poor, suffering, benighted, and *geographically distant* population of benighted Jews. Willard's pronouncement addressed itself to real-world conditions and events, including that of the Sephardic Diaspora and the Jews of Salonica who, as he wrote, "have synagogues, especially those of Castile, Portugal, and Italy, besides two colleges that contain about 10,000 students who arrive there from all parts of the Ottoman Empire." Indeed, he wrote, "the City is for the most part inhabited by Jews."[34] Willard noted with some sympathy, and in keeping with a Puritan mindset that saw two major foes arrayed in opposition to the achievement of God's true purpose of establishing the worldwide sway of Protestantism, that the Sephardim had escaped the tortures of the Catholic Inquisition only to find themselves at the mercy of the Mohammedans. According to this calculus, the numerically miniscule Jews, who were to be commended for at least once having been God's chosen, emerged as especially deserving of Puritan sympathy. Recalling the days when Europeans themselves had been pagans, Willard wrote appreciatively of the Jews that "They once prayed for us; we therefore owe this duty to them."[35] Like

Sewall, however, Willard avoided exhorting his readers to agitate for the immediate conversion of the Jews. Rather, describing the plight of the Jews, Willard hoped to inspire a spiritual effort in their behalf. "The thing [the national conversion] is a matter of faith," he wrote, "and so it calls for Prayer." The Fountain resonated with the Puritans' tendency to place stress on the workings of grace, which might be meditated upon and even hoped for, but not necessarily sought after through active pursuit of works calculated to accelerate the progress of God's intention.

Whether or not he was directly influenced by Willard's thinking on such matters, Sewall's oddly tolerant and bemused attitude toward Jews and their eventual conversion appears to have resulted, at least in part, from his pursuit of a more adaptive form of Puritanism's most Calvinistic, or at least pietistic tendencies. As at least two recent biographies of the judge (by Richard Francis and Eve LaPlante) have shown, Sewall was an exception to the Puritan norm in his impressive capacity for introspection and, ultimately, his unique willingness not only to challenge disagreeable policies but to admit to his own moral failings. One of four Massachusetts leaders who are depicted in a series of murals that grace the walls of the State House in Boston (the other three are John Winthrop, John Hancock, and John Adams), Sewall has been commemorated in the popular memory for having apologized publicly for his role as a condemning judge in the Salem Witch Trials. On January 14, 1697, the congregants of Boston's Third Church heard as Samuel Willard read before them Sewall's confession, his acceptance of "the blame and shame" resulting from his participation in the trials.[36] Sewall himself stood as his confession was read. It was in the aftermath of that apology that, among other things, he produced the Phaenomena. The immediate trigger for the apology, as Eve LaPlante suggests, had been the recent death of one of Sewall's children, but a larger contextual element in so profound a change of heart was an evolving attitude regarding Satan himself, who, as Sewall apparently realized, was "less physical and more psychological or spiritual" than the witch-hunters had conceived.[37] This "more proximate Satan" could only be opposed as "Puritans took more responsibility for their own sins and their souls."[38] Sewall's transformation over the issue of the Salem Witch Trials, which may have been a factor as well in his beliefs regarding Jewish conversion, suggests a recovery and modification of the same inner-directed piety that

Cotton Mather (1663–1728). Mezzotint engraving on laid paper by Peter Pelham, 1728. Courtesy of the Massachusetts Historical Society.

had motivated those Puritans of the preceding generations who had themselves hoped to establish "a commonwealth more perfect than man had known," and in so doing, to avoid any attempt to foment a grace and justice that was God's, not theirs, to confer.

The world of 1697, in other words, was drastically different from that of 1650, or 1662, or even 1689. The Puritan movement was still defined by many of the same internal struggles that had shaped its first generations, but congregational dictates were losing their influence over external circumstances of life in the Commonwealth. Ironically, efforts on the part of an embattled New England orthodoxy to re-instill a strict adherence to the disciplined practices of the founders, or at least to involve the *example* of the founders as an instrument of moral guidance, grew. Although men like Cotton Mather were fighting a losing battle against forces of social and cultural change that originated both in England and in Massachusetts, they made the attempt anyway. Cotton Mather's writing in particular bore singular witness to the "cultural pressures and dilemmas" that resulted from the Puritan orthodoxy's early eighteenth-century attempt to restore the old order.[39] Owing to his prolific output of sermons, books, and tracts, the younger Mather himself, with his eclectic interests not only in theological matters but in the occult, natural phenomena, and human history, embodied New England's multifaceted transition from Puritanism to Dissent—a transition which, in a few short decades and thanks in part to its adaptation of Newtonian physics (of which Mather himself was an adherent), would further mature into the Enlightenment itself.[40] Mather was a far more complex figure than his historical detractors, dating back as far as Washington Irving, gave him credit for being, and his very complexity and versatility were outgrowths of the ferment that characterized late-period Puritanism.

For the likes of Cotton Mather, the conversion of the Jews, like the effort to expand church membership and to promote moral behavior, was something to be acted upon, as opposed merely to be longed for or predicted. Where Sewall might have invoked the spirit of the first generation by reviving their humility and wonder at the magnificence and grace of God's power and mercy, Cotton Mather manifested a more "activist" attitude that sought to plant the seeds of millennial change by more direct means. He was no John Cotton or John Winthrop, however, and he knew that no amount of legalistic discourse could enforce rapidly loosening strictures concerning church membership. By 1710, as Francis Bremer writes, Mather "began to dispense with theological disputation and to work toward achieving an ecumenical pietistic consensus" among the various constituencies within New England.[41] Mather's ecumenical efforts were the product of his times and, as such, bore little resemblance to Roger Williams's mid-seventeenth-century attempts to argue for religious tolerance. Where Williams had been motivated by a radically separatist agenda that wished to counteract the more "Judaicall" tendencies of the established non-separatist clergy, Mather—himself the product of two generations of empowered religious orthodoxy and the single most visible, not to mention prolific advocate of the New England Way—was spurred on by a desire to maximize congregationalism's waning influence in New England. His hopes for a "national" conversion of the Jews were part and parcel of the more ambitious attitude that he bore toward the propagation of a proper religious life. If Williams's tolerance had been intended as a weapon of principle and as a means of depriving the orthodoxy of central authority, Mather's was intended as a tool for the restoration of that authority to its former arbiters. All the same, Mather demonstrated a surprising willingness to sanction most variants of Protestant deviance in the quest to maintain order. "He had," writes Perry Miller, "come face-to-face with a dilemma from which he and other orthodox leaders were never to escape; they detested heresy," but under the terms of the Glorious Revolution "could no longer prosecute it."[42] Instead, he and his fellow orthodox ministers had to "learn to regard themselves as no more than a majority of Dissenters within the most loyal of British provinces."[43] The key to assembling this "ecumenical pietistic consensus" was the encouragement of good works and proper social behavior, as Arminian as that might have seemed to the sensibilities of the earlier generations, Mather's own grandfathers included. Accordingly, by the early eighteenth century, "the land was filled," as one historian puts it, "with pious, upright, moral, but unregenerate people."[44]

For all of his fervent belief in the covenant of *grace*, in other words, Mather had adjusted himself to life in a bustling, increasingly religiously diverse working New England, where an emphasis on "doing" would, as Dana Nelson suggests, "highlight the economic dynamic that was newly operative."[45] Though his Puritanism would appear to have separated him from the famously Deistic Benjamin Franklin, Mather shared with Franklin, whom he had known when the latter was a boy, a seeming indefatigability and tendency to elevate production and achievement over mere reflection. In 1710, more than twenty years ahead of the first *Poor Richard* publications, Mather published his book *Bonifacius, Essays to Do Good;* indeed, Franklin himself readily acknowledged Mather's influence upon him, not least in naming his first fictional character, created when he was sixteen years old, for his brother James's newspaper, *The New England Courant,* Silence Dogood. Mather's latter-day image as the last scion of New England orthodoxy misses the mark for several reasons, not the least of which proves to have been his lifelong tendency to promote good *behavior* on the part of New England's growing population of imperfect souls, as opposed to mere preparation for sanctification or some other appropriately cautious Calvinistic approach. In 1706, for instance, Mather produced an essay arguing that it was "every Christian slave-holder's duty," as Dana Nelson puts it, "to Christianize his slave."[46] Similarly, Mather sought to be an *active* proselytizer of Jews. Conversion of the Jews, as we have seen, was an active subject of Puritan discourse, even in the evident absence of any visible Jewish presence. "One suspects that these books, essays, and discourses were on the whole academic," writes Jacob Marcus about the Puritan conversion tracts in general, "semantic exercises within which preachers titillated the intellectual and emotional palates of their patient listeners."[47] Cotton Mather, at least, had located a couple of Jews upon whom he was able or at least determined to test his powers of persuasion. Evidently, the arrival of the Frazon brothers in Boston coincided with, or maybe inspired, a flurry of hope on his part. His diary of July 18, 1699, in characteristically dramatic fashion, recorded his ambition. "This day, from the dust, where I lay prostrate, before the Lord," he wrote, "I lifted up my cries: For the conversion of the Jewish nation, and for my own having the happiness . . . to baptize a Jew, that should by my ministry be brought home to the Lord."[48]

To a greater degree than any of his seventeenth-century predecessors, Mather was a lifelong devotee of Jewish knowledge and ephemera. According to historian Arthur Hertzberg, the famed minister "donned a skullcap" in 1696 and also "took to calling himself rabbi."[49] He was an accomplished Hebraist as well, fond of displaying his Judaic knowledge in an offhand manner, as when he referred to Harvard as "New England's Beit Midrash."[50] The Mathers' family library, which Mark Peterson describes as nothing less than "a conglomerate artifact of Atlantic culture from the fifteenth through the eighteenth centuries," contained eleven books in Hebrew, including not only the requisite Bibles and grammars that had been prepared by Christian Hebraists such as Johann Buxtorf, but volumes by Menasseh ben Israel and Mordecai Nathan, a Jewish physician of fifteenth-century Avignon.[51] Regardless of his personal practices, in his authorship of dozens of published and unpublished writings, including the six-folio *Biblia Americana*, Cotton Mather gave frequent attention to Judaic scholarship and practice, as well as to various episodes of Common Era Jewish history. The Judaic interests of the younger Mather surpassed those of his father because Cotton Mather, beginning in his time at Harvard, possessed an inexhaustible interest in the Hebrew language itself. While studying at the college, he produced a Masters thesis that "argued for the divine origin of the Hebrew vowel points."[52] Mather developed his Hebrew studies, which included a pursuit of the *kabbalah*, in order to be brought closer to the "divine revelation" that he and other Christian Hebraists believed to be contained in the original language of the Bible.[53] He also used Hebrew and a sustained study of Jewish history in order to facilitate his "adaptation of Hebraic concepts," one of which, as John Erwin explains, was that of the "Nishmath Chajim," or "breath of life," which allowed him to write more effectively about the soul's progress toward the divine presence.

Still, as Louis Feldman suggests, Mather held "ambiguous" views about Jews.[54] He was generally unguarded in his outright condemnations of Jewish wickedness and intransigence. Toward the end of his life, the revisionist eschatology he presented in his pamphlet *Tripardisus* would dismiss the Jews as helpless apostates whose conversion was no longer worth waiting for and, apparently, irrelevant to the Second Coming.[55] Nonetheless, few other non-Jews of his time developed as deep an interest in Jewish affairs, and still fewer could be so outspoken on the subject of the Jews' persecution at the hands of Christians. Where his father took a somewhat distant and abstract view of Jewish conversion as "one of the primary signs indicating the last days prior to the dawn of the millennium,"[56] Cotton Mather expressed significant private hope for such an eventuality, not just on the world stage but on a human scale and in his own lifetime. Like the diary entry from 1699, several more of his diary entries articulate passionate hopes that he himself might someday be an instrument in the conversion of at least one Jew.

His modest but passionate hopes in this latter matter developed in keeping with his characteristic filiopiety. Mather and his cohort had been born too late to witness, much less have a hand in creating the New Jerusalem. For them it no longer made sense to live and write as if New England were poised at the very edge of the millennium, and the "national conversion" of the Jews was to have been part and parcel of events occurring on this massive scale. "The age of the fathers," writes Andrew Delbanco, "was becoming the touchstone of all value,"[57] and only that age and the men who had led New England's earliest congregations could possibly have overseen such grand undertakings. Mather distinguished himself from other Puritan conversion enthusiasts by investing in scriptural conjecture and tracking the progress of actual conversion efforts worldwide. He manifested a spiritual impatience similar to the one that had defined the theology and practice of a host of previous "preparationist" Puritan ministers for whom the mere unfolding of God's grace could never constitute a sufficient object of desire. While the most pietistic Puritans of a previous generation (for whom even English Protestant converts to the true church had long been required to prove their spiritual worth not through the ritual recitation of a creed, much less through ceremonial baptism, but through a rigorous questioning; see Chapter 3 for an extended consideration of one such case) would have been skeptical about any mass conversion of Jews, Mather was eager to see such an event to its fruition.

Mather's enthusiasm emerged from the pages of his most focused effort at instigating a conversion of the Jews, *The Faith of the Fathers*, which was published in Boston in 1699 as a "catechism of the Christian religion."[58] Although his motivations certainly extended beyond the particularities of his own immediate time and place, the production of the pamphlet seems to have been inspired by the Frazons' presence in Boston, as his diary made clear: "Whereas, I have for divers years, employ'd much prayer for and some discourse with an infidel Jew in this town; thro' a Desire to glorify my Lord Jesus Christ in the conversion of that infidel if Hee please to accept mee . . . I this day renewed my Request unto Heaven for it. And

writing a short letter to the Jew, wherein I enclosed my *Faith of the Fathers*
. . . sent it to him."[59] In character with the common Puritan practice of
advancing theological arguments dialectically, the pamphlet posed questions based on the author's anticipation of Jewish objections to Christian
doctrine and then answered them with cited portions of the Hebrew Bible.
For instance, to Jews who might doubt Jesus' divinity on the basis of
his having been unconvincing in his presentation of his messiah-hood,
Mather asked, "When the Messiah first Appears to the Jewish Nation, is
He to be Despised and Rejected of that Nation?" Isaiah had stipulated that,
indeed, the messiah shall be "Despised and Rejected of men."[60] Mather's
approach offered no noticeable departure from the centuries' worth of
conversion tracts that appeared before and after 1699. If it made its own
mark, it was in the breathtakingly confrontational rhetorical stance with
which, at its inception, it took the Jews to task for their steadfast denial of
Christ's divinity.

Assuming that Frazon had received the delivery, it is difficult to image
him or any other Jew having progressed beyond the opening sentences in
his reading:

> One thing that satisfies us Christians, in the truth of Christianity, is your
> obstinate Aversion to that Holy Religion of our Blessed JESUS. The Author
> of our Faith, foretold your continuance under the circumstances now come
> upon you, until the Times of the Gentiles . . . are Expired. And your own
> Inspired Prophets, who are now more ours than yours, foretold your being
> poenally given to the Deafness, Blindness, and Hardness now upon you.[61]

Although Mather almost always strikes current-day readers as so broadly
hyperbolic as to be out of touch with audience sensibilities on any given
topic (he had a similar effect on his contemporaries as well), *Faith of the
Fathers* presented such a high degree of antagonism toward its purported
audience that it begs an alternative reading, in which an altogether different readership may have figured as the intended target. Notwithstanding
Jacob Marcus's dismissive assessment of published Puritan conversion
efforts as amounting to little more than a large-scale performance of mere
semantic exercises calculated to impress other ministers, Mather's *Faith of
the Fathers* can also be read as one more in a long line of latter-day Puritan
jeremiads whose purpose it was to chasten the author's fellow congre-

gants and New Englanders in general for their having fallen short, as the pamphlet's title suggests, of their fathers' mission.

While the Jews of Salonica or London or Newport would never set eyes on Mather's tract, the Christian "Jews" of the New English Israel—those chosen of God whose grandfathers had crossed the Atlantic to found a city on a hill—would certainly listen, or so Mather might have hoped. Thus, near the conclusion of *Faith*, Mather posed the following question "When the *Jews* are by God, given up to *Blindness* of Mind, and *Hardness* of Heart, must the Gentiles be brought into the knowledge of God, and His *Messiah*?"[62] The scripturally pertinent answer was, of course, "Yes," as indicated in Isaiah, but the historically operative answer was meant to suggest another sort of "Yes." In the aftermath of the Glorious Revolution, when Mather produced *Faith of the Fathers*, many ministers were taking New England's moral decline for granted. Three generations of Puritans had been describing themselves as Israelites, but these Israelites were behaving badly now, had lost their way, and relied too heavily upon the tribal, or "Judaical" basis for their church membership. The members of the third generation amounted to so many blind, intransigent, and self-satisfied Jews bent on maximizing their commercial prospects and social mobility at the expense of their *fathers'* faith. The way had therefore to be opened to whichever "Gentiles" might be up to the task of filling their shoes. Such people, presumably, would have included all manner of "Gentiles" who might previously have been labeled as incorrigible and, worse yet, religiously tepid Anglican dissenters but whose membership could no longer be spurned by New England Congregationalists. That Mather's stylized self-denunciation, as Miller refers to the jeremiad tradition, assumed the form of an indictment of the Jews for failing to see the light of Christ was a testament to the rhetorical power that the Puritans-as-Jews metaphor had accrued by 1699. "One must think," writes religious historian Thomas Kidd, "about the cultural work such a pamphlet might do for New Englanders' identity."[63] Like the Jews, New Englanders like Mather knew God's love could and did assume many forms, that "He will afflict us," as Bercovitch puts it, "because He would save us."[64] Indeed, *Faith of the Fathers* ended on as uplifting a note as might be hoped, as the "Jews" whose conversion Mather so fervently desired were welcomed into the heavenly fold upon their acceptance of the messiah, "while *Others* are Damned into eternal confusion."[65] Legalistic and Judaical Congregationalists needed to heed this "Jewish" lesson carefully, lest they spurn their best opportunity to experience true grace.

Mather was sufficiently interested in worldly events as to devote considerable reading attention to modern Jewish history, at least as it might have been related to millennial prospects. His immense *Biblia Americana*, which absorbed his intermittent attention from 1693 well into the first decade and a half of the eighteenth century, was a perpetual work in progress. Louis Feldman refers to it as an "extended exegesis of the complete Bible," and its structure, at least, reflected such an intention on the author's part.[66] The complete manuscript has the appearance of a pastiche effort, and although its overall shape was determined by the content of each book of the Bible in the order of its appearance, Mather inserted various appendices throughout, in accordance with his discrete interests. From a Jewish perspective, the appendix that followed from Mather's treatment of the Book of Acts contained the *Biblia*'s most compelling material. In his 1706 advertisement for the book, for which he never did receive sufficient publication subscriptions, he described this "Jewish" appendix as "A sort of Twenty-Ninth chapter of the Acts; or an Elaborate and Entertaining History of what has befallen the Israelitish Nation."[67] For all of his rhetorical extravagance, verbosity, and pedantic imperiousness, Mather was certainly an ambitious reader of eclectic materials. The appendix that followed from his discussion of Acts was replete not only with scripturally based interpretations of Jewish liturgy and belief, but with an impressive assemblage of factual data on the Jewish historical experience.

As Feldman suggests, Mather seems to have been less interested in abstract points of theological interest than he was in the "facts of history, geography, and the natural sciences."[68] The Acts appendix, thanks in large part to Mather's reading of and more or less verbatim borrowings from European Christian historians of Judaism such as Jacques Basnage (1653–1723), presented a detailed and quite sympathetic history of the Jews' sufferings from the Middle Ages right through into Mather's own era. Mather recounted several pogroms, each time leaving little doubt as to where his sympathies lay. Surely, he suggested, any Christian hopes of bringing about a massive conversion would never be advanced by senseless violence against the Jews. Accordingly, Mather illustrated this principle with his recitation of the horrific events that had been visited upon the Jews through many historical eras. For all of the intolerance that he previously displayed in Faith of the Fathers and would go on to articulate in the Tripardisus, his unequivocal defense of Jewish rights in the Biblia was striking. Mather made his greatest impression on the collective memory of New England's history by acquiescing to the use of spectral evidence in the Salem Witch Trials, but in his writings on Jewish history, he was eager to debunk all manner of superstitious anti-Jewish prejudices. "An old woman at Bavaria, A.D. 1286 confessed her delivering a child [to?] ye Jews," Mather wrote, "who drained all his Blood with Needles, to make a sacrifice." This reference to the blood libel occasioned his narrating the subsequent massacre of the area's Jews: "The people of Munich rose, and without staying for the sentence of ye Judge, knock'd on ye head, all ye Jews they could meet with. The officers in vain opposing this fury, advised ye [men?] of that Nation, to take Sanctuary in a Synagogue which was of stone. This made their misery but the more general; the people pursued them thither, sett fire to ye Place and burn't 'em alive . . ."[69] Mather's attention to the mob's irrational and cruel fervor, not to mention their evident disdain for the rule of law, struck a familiar chord, coming as it did on the heels of the witch scare in Salem, about which he may have had some misgivings by the early years of the eighteenth century. More important, it was pertinent to the general state of affairs in New England where people displayed an increasingly common disregard if not for rule of law then at least for the opinions of magistrates and ministers.

The anecdote about the Bavarian pogrom was followed by several more. Gradually, the stories presented not only Mather's contempt for the various folk prejudices against Jews but his admiration for the Jews' characteristically steadfast retention of their religious principles. Faced by a later pogrom in another section of Germany, one group of Jews, as Mather put it, "chose to Burn themselves with their Furniture, Wives, and Children, than to be thrown into the fire by the Christians."[70] In 1400, Jews throughout Germany, Italy, and Provence were "Accused of poisoning Wells," Mather wrote. "Tho ye misery was so great, that this like was never seen since ye Destruction of Jerusalem, yet nobody forsook his Religion."[71] In anecdotes such as these, Mather displayed a singular sympathy for the same "Nation" that, in Faith of the Fathers, he singled out for unrelenting rhetorical censure. Once again, the operative subtext suggested a broader interest on Mather's part than unqualified philo-Semitism.

In effect, the same Jewish stubbornness he had posited in *Faith of the Fathers* as an analogy for his own congregants' growing degree of legalistic self-satisfaction he was now depicting as an antidote for a new excess of liberality. The *Biblia*'s engagement of Jewish history revised Mather's earlier depiction of Jewish intransigence into an admiring view of Jewish faith and stiff-neckedness in order to counter the growing influence of the Brattle Street Church in Cambridge and of Solomon Stoddard in western Massachusetts. Brattle Street was the collective endeavor of several enterprising Boston merchants who were quickly losing patience with the Mathers and other proponents of the founders' more rigorous and doctrinaire Calvinistic congregational practices. Beginning in 1690, Stoddard, the autocratic but broad-minded minister of the Northampton Congregational Church, loosened restrictions on who might receive communion and published sermons and pamphlets counseling New Englanders against an excessive regard for the exclusivist membership practices that had so long been in place in the eastern churches. In the face of this dual pressure to part company with the fathers' practices, Cotton Mather may well have gained a new appreciative insight into the Jews' stiff-necked resistance to all temptations to relent on matters of religious principle. As Joseph Conforti writes, Mather had great concern about what he called the "Criolian [i.e., hybridizing] degeneracy that would inevitably result from irreligious declension."[72] If nothing else, the Jews could always be looked to for an example of resistance to outside pressures to change.

No pogrom before the Holocaust had a more devastating effect on world-wide Judaism than the Inquisition, whose effects were still widely felt by the Jews with whom New England Puritans were most likely to come into contact—the Sephardim. Mather's descriptions of the Inquisition, like his anecdotes concerning earlier anti-Jewish violence in Europe, were striking for their tone of sympathy. New England Puritans and Sephardic Jews shared a common enemy, and Mather's sympathy derived in large part from his antipathy toward Roman Catholicism. His comments on the Inquisition were quite in character with the Protestant millenarianism of his day, which read the cruelties of the Jewish persecution as yet another sign of the Catholic Church's demonic sway. Mather included in his depiction the story of the original marranos, who, as he must have known, were the immediate ancestors of the Frazons and of the Newport Jews. Even if his description was primarily informed by his disdain for the Catholic church that fomented the Inquisition, it still struck a sympathetic chord on behalf of the Jewish victims:

> The Inquisition is watchful of these New Christians; as they are called tho' two hundred years have rolled since ye conversion of their ancestors. The cruel ministers of the Tribunal often & on the least occasion enrich themselves with the spoils of this forsaken people. [It is in] these Acts of Faits [auto da fes], in which they [the Jews] are burnt in ye most horrible way this is ever seen upon the face of the Earth.[73]

A similar passage in the Biblia mentioned an auto da fe in which, "in the year 1605 a Dominican with a crucifix in his hand, put himself at the head of a mob who plundered and ravaged, and killed four or five hundred of these New Christians."[74] The evident parallels between Jewish victims of the Inquisition and the burning of Shadrach, Meshach, and Abednego in the Book of Daniel could not have been lost on Mather, who admired the Jews for their steadfast faith. But lest he confer excessive admiration upon the same errant people who, after all, in his father's Mystery of Israel's Salvation, were judged "guilty of the most horrid blasphemy against the Son of God,"[75] Mather also advanced a certain amount of contempt for the suffering Jews who took their persecution as a sign of sanctification.

"The Jewish historians," he wrote, "make bitter complaines of these violences. Thus they comfort themselves with ye character of martyrs put upon ye sufferers; & with pretty stories of Miracles now and then wrought upon their Martyrdoms."[76] Mather's dismissal of Jewish martyrdom under the Inquisition may remind us that, not many years before his time, all manner of dissenters had met a similar fate in the Commonwealth and, undoubtedly, had also been thought of as delusional in their religious beliefs. In any case, it would have been difficult for him, or any other spokesman for the New England orthodoxy, to acknowledge the contradictions inherent in his pronouncements. Mather could seem inexplicably oblivious in his rendition of Jewish martyrdom to the tradition within Christianity itself, and among the Puritans especially, of associating affliction with sanctification. Indeed, he seems not even to have been able to see the afflicted conditions of his own age, so fixated was he, as Andrew Delbanco has it, on the persecuted "militant spirit of his immigrant fathers."[77] But Mather's writing about Jews betrayed more than mere blindness on his part. His contempt toward the Jews for their willful ignorance of the true religion was tempered, or at least complicated, by the frequency with which his writing about Jews presented a thinly veiled commentary on the state of Christianity, particularly in a New England context.

In keeping with the age's obsession with the legacy of the first generation, much of the "Jewish" material in the Biblia spoke to his simultaneous reverence for and, at least on a sublimated level, rebellion against the founders. The Jews, after all, were the fathers of Christianity, the original guardians, as Thomas Thorowgood had explained in 1650, of God's Law. At the same time, the Jews were errant children, criminally misguided in their "superstitious" adherence to an obsolete and, therefore, wicked religious practice. On a metaphorical level, since there were so few of these Jewish fathers/sons on hand to worry about, Cotton Mather's obsession with the Jews was suggestive of his own ambivalence toward the legacy of his grandfathers, whose rigorous example may have inspired him to vilify the declining present but also left him with little recourse to building a similar glory out of his own age. Mather was merely among the earliest of "American sons who have," as Delbanco puts it, "periodically coped with feelings of smallness beside their pioneer fathers by exalting the fathers extremely."[78] His obsession with Jews and Jewish history was an outlet for the anxiety engendered by all that filiopietism.

The father/son metaphor, as a commentary not only on the Jews' relationship to Christianity but on the author's troubled relationship to the faith of his own fathers, offers a useful lens through which not only to view Mather's own interest in Jews, but to understand why he chose certain materials for inclusion in the Biblia. The Biblia was as much a showcase for its author's wide reading as it was an outlet for his theological judgments and misgivings regarding the legacy of the founders. In a way that surpassed even the most Hebraically engaged efforts of his predecessors, including his own father, who was certainly a devotee of Jewish conversion efforts, Mather amassed a contemporary knowledge of Jewish life that would serve to reinforce his authority. He wrote about the Jews of England and the efforts that Cromwell had made on behalf of their readmission. He wrote about the indulgence of the Dutch toward the Jews of Amsterdam, those prosperous Sephardim who spawned congregations in London, the West Indies, and North America. He also wrote about an English Christian whose millennial hopes, one presumes, were sufficient to inspire him to collect funds on behalf of the Jews of Palestine when similar efforts on the part of the Amsterdam Jews were coming up short. Mather's attention to such details and, particularly, to the story of the English philo-Semites having rescued the Jews of Palestine from a desperate fate spoke to his paternalistic outlook and was also an aspect of the "doing good" tendency that, a few years earlier, had motivated his tract on the virtues of Christianizing blacks.

The more obviously filial side of Mather's Jewish interest emerged from the Biblia's final appendix, "Synagoga, On the Origin of Synagogues." Like the rest of the Biblia, "Synagoga" was incomplete. It consisted primarily of notes on evolving liturgy within Jewish practice through the ages. This section was yet another showcase for Mather's knowledge of Hebrew. Like the work of his predecessors, this writing also betrayed a particularly inquisitive spirit on his part, in which knowledge of what many of his peers might have dismissed as Jewish arcana figured quite prominently. In a congregational atmosphere in which church hierarchy was quickly losing its sway, thanks in part to the growth of commercial interests, as well as to the liberalizing membership policies of Brattle Street and Solomon Stoddard's Northampton church, Mather's attention to the "sacerdotal order" of Jewish synagogues may have served a larger chastening purpose. Whether the cause of such slippage in New England ministerial power was the universal moral declension for which Perry Miller, echoing the eighteenth-century jeremiads, argued or the economic and social changes that instigated the struggle among the varying levels of clerical and governmental authority, as later historians like T. H. Breen have contended, attention on Mather's part to the work of the synagogues' official clergy offered insight into how the Puritan fathers had sought to ensure order in their congregations.[79]

Mather's extended passage on Jewish liturgy carried a tone of filiopietistic reverence and admiration at least for the ancient Jews, who seemed in his formulation not to have been plagued by the sort of internal dissent that was playing havoc among New Englanders.

That order might be performed, there were in every *Synagogue* some *Fixed Ministers* to look after ye Religious duties to be performed . . . and they were solemnly ordained thereunto. There were *elders* of the Synagogue who governed all the affairs of it. . . . One of them . . . was *the Minister of the Synagogue* who . . . was, as the *Messenger* delegated from ye people to Speak in Prayer to God for them . . . called *Sholiach Zibbor*, that is, the Angel of the Church. Yet others were sometimes extraordinarily called forth for the discharge of [duty], provided they were by Skill, Age, and piety qualified for it. Next to the sholiach zabor, were the Deacons . . . in Hebrew called Chazzanim. . . .[80]

Abstracted from any particular time or place, the liturgy described here was ordered and inherently hierarchical. Indeed, as Mather went on to describe the reading of the Torah, he outlined still more fixed practices—the blessings first of the priestly class, or *Cohenim*, followed by that of the Levites, as well as the calendrically ordered reading of the weekly *parsha*. Though it didn't by any means suggest that Jewish ritual practice was superior to the Protestant liturgy, "Synagoga's" deliberate and sustained recounting of the traditional Jewish liturgy's *predictability* would necessarily have stood in stark contrast to the less than stable state of affairs that conservatively inclined New England Congregationalists were, by the early 1700s, encountering in their churches. Mather's attention to Jewish history and practice in the *Biblia* served a multiple purpose in this context. His knowledge of Judaism and, hence, of the origins of Christian belief, enabled him to honor the founding tenets of 1630 and, by extension, the example of his grandfathers. At the same time, as he heaped criticism and contempt upon the misguided Jews, he gave voice—albeit in sublimated and indirect fashion—to his anxiety about having been forced by the circumstances of his birth to inhabit and preside quite falteringly over a compromised New England. Reverence for the fathers could only take him so far. His attention to the intrinsic fallibility of the Jews provided a means by which he could delineate the limitations of his own filiopiety and justifiably hold the example of one set of long dead fathers in contempt.

The conversion of Jews itself provided an opportunity in which proselytizing Puritans could play the roles of dutiful sons, conferring upon the chosen people the mantle of sanctification that generations of foregoing Jews had so blindly rejected. At the same time, and particularly if they chose to ape Mather's finger-wagging style, Christian proselytizers played a paternal role as well, warning their fatally misguided audiences—to the extent that such audiences could be said to exist—of the dangers that were attendant upon their persistent apostasy. Pamphlets like *Faith of the Fathers*, as well as a life's work like the *Biblia*, even if they failed to reach a Jewish audience, may still have offered Mather opportunities to reach a Puritan audience whose spiritual growth was stunted by the paralyzing shadow of the first generation. In his attempt to convert an actual Jew, however, Mather appears to have transcended the limits of mere rhetoric and performance.

Unfortunately, we lack the one piece of direct evidence that would shed the greatest light on Mather's conversion attempt, its aftermath, and implications: testimony from the actual Jew in question. Samuel Sewall, whose relationship with Mather was long-standing and cordial, if not always approving, recorded the outlines of Mather's effort in 1706, and in so doing, provided some limited insight. The chronological circumstances of the case suggest that Samuel Frazon was Mather's intended target (Joseph Frazon, also according to Sewall's diary, had died in 1704), and that one or both of the brothers had been the object of Mather's prayers for some time. Referring to a previous instance of what he called Mather's "youthful vanity," Sewall noted that he found "Him in spirituals as failable as Politicks, or he would not have attempted a *Pretended Vision*, to have converted *Mr. Frazier, a Jew*, who had before conceiv'd some good Notions of Christianity: The Consequence was, that the Forgery was so plainly detected that Mr. C.M. confest it; after which, *Mr. Frazier* would never be persuaded to hear any more of Christianity."[81] What the written forgery actually consisted of remains a mystery, but the fact that Sewall's adumbration of the event indicated that it had a dramatic element as well as a written one, and that Mather was playacting as well as conjuring false scriptural evidence provides an intriguing perspective on the inherently performative nature of the minister's attempt, not to mention the dilemma that resulted from his having been born the hapless grandson of two of New England's most prominent founding fathers.

Mather seems not to have been able to decide whether he ought to have played father or son. An overwrought filial reverence on his part for Frazon's Judaism would likely have been seen as ingratiating, if not transparently manipulative. By the same token, no amount of paternalistic sanctimony would have won the day either. If our knowledge of the Frazons' background can serve as a guide, the several generations during which they had retained their Judaism on both sides of the Atlantic would have prepared them for efforts like Mather's. Moreover, knowledge of their own tradition, which had surely been imparted in the talmudim of Amsterdam, Recife, London, and Barbados, would have made all of the ordinary Christian arguments, like the ones that Mather had proffered in Faith of the Fathers, quite familiar to them. Mather's reversion to the seemingly primitive tactic of conjuring up a vision and fabricating a text may strike us as odd, and it only seems to have repulsed Samuel Frazon. This was the man, after all, who had survived a shipwreck and near starvation in the West Indies, and who, upon his return to New England, was "hauled into a Boston court," as Jacob Marcus has it, "for beating another man's Negro servant."[82]

Mere scriptural evidence, however, could hardly be expected to have won the day with Frazon either. One of Mather's better known works had been The Wonders of the Invisible World (1693), which he wrote in the immediate aftermath of the Salem Witch Trials, and which offered readers a carefully rationalized but nonetheless exhaustive catalogue of strange providences. His interest in "prodigies," while it may look to us today like an enthusiasm for the supernatural, or even like mere superstition, had been a bridge between religious belief and science, and offered evidence of his own and his age's struggle to adjust to epistemological changes that were difficult for even the most learned of scholars to fathom, let alone assimilate.[83] It is no wonder that when all the ordinary means of persuasion were so obviously proving to be ineffective, Mather found himself changing his tactics. For all of his erudition and theological sophistication, Cotton Mather had sought recourse to extraordinary measures because neither filiopiety nor paternalism was effective in the face of the two major obstacles he faced. First, Frazon evidently possessed a sufficient familiarity with the Hebrew bible as a bar mitzvah, or son of the Torah, to "spot a forgery," not to mention what was obviously a manufactured reverence for his Judaic bona fides. Second, like his brother before him, he had achieved a level of economic self-sufficiency that made it altogether possible for him to get by in Boston as a Jew; he did not need to be ministered to by any kind of elder.

Modern historians agree, by and large, that the men and women of

Salem who made accusations of witchcraft were, among other things, manifesting Puritanism's limitations as a politically and socially effective instrument of order. Cotton Mather was a veteran of that experience, and for all of his subsequent ambivalence about his role in its prosecution, he had been famously suggestible as to the uses of spectral evidence. His having resorted to the *purveying* of such evidence in his attempt to win Samuel Frazon over to Christianity offers additional insight into yet another insoluble Puritan dilemma—the inability of the third generation to transcend or even anticipate its own impending obsolescence and to decide whether to persevere in revering the fathers or to acquiesce, finally, to their overthrow. Visions, whether manufactured or genuine, were dangerously unreliable indices of eventualities, even if they might be useful outlets for unresolved cultural tensions. An anonymously written letter from 1707 recounted how a woman once had been brought before Increase and Cotton Mather and insisted on telling them their future. She made three predictions, including one that "a Jew [presumably Samuel Frazon] who Mather the Elder has taken great pains with to convert to the Xtian faith shall be converted."[84] The author of the note recounted, with some evident cynical triumph, that despite the woman's prediction, "the Jew went over to Jamaica and dyed a hardened wret[c]h."[85] What is more important is that, three years earlier, that Jew's brother Joseph had also died unconverted at the home of a Christian friend in Boston, from where, as Sewall's diary shortly afterwards recounted, he was "carried in Simon's coach to Bristow [Bristol, Rhode Island], from thence by water to Newport, where there is a Jews-burying place."[86] If Joseph Frazon could die and be properly buried as a Jew in New England, it was only a matter of time before significant numbers of other Jews would begin to *live* there permanently.

CHAPTER THREE

"A JEW RARELY COMES OVER TO US BUT HE BRINGS TREASURES WITH HIM"

The Conversion and Harvard Career of Judah Monis

COTTON MATHER'S FAILURE TO bring about a miracle with Samuel Frazon may have dampened his enthusiasm at the prospect of being an instrument of God's merciful redemption of the Jews, but conversion-minded New Englanders needed only to wait a few years before their prayers and efforts would achieve an even more fortuitous result. The recruitment, conversion, and appointment of a Hebrew instructor of Jewish birth by a committee of Harvard's most eminent clergy in the 1720s constituted the most visible and fraught achievement of nearly a century's worth of Hebraism in colonial Massachusetts. In the first decades of the eighteenth century, as congregational integrity slackened and social changes accelerated, the millennial hopes that had buoyed Calvinism's last holdouts had begun to fade, and ministers might well have worried that if New England's divine redemption came, the event would escape notice in the face of so many worldly distractions. The year 1720 brought a monetary crisis that had been sown in 1715, as public credits given in that year were suddenly due.[1] A smallpox epidemic that hit in 1721 killed one thousand of Boston's twelve thousand residents.[2] The same year also witnessed Governor Samuel Shute's halting attempt to finesse a middle path between assuaging British concern and mollifying the populism of Elisha Cook, Jr., on the subject of a renewal for the New England Charters.[3] The combination of these events and others could not help but "convince many Bostonians that clergymen did not necessarily have the right answers to many human problems."[4] Monis's public conversion ceremony, which took place at Cambridge's First Church in March 1722, represented a supreme, if problematic, effort to restore spiritual rigor and confidence in the church's mission in the face of such developments.

Although the "national" conversion of the Jews paled in comparison with the retention of Christians as a congregational priority, the conversion of one Jew engendered considerable excitement. Judah Monis's arrival at Harvard did not inspire the same predictions of an imminent Second Coming of Christ that it might have a few decades earlier, but it gave a temporary lift to local spirits because it promised to renew Puritanism's waning connection to its Hebraic roots. In 1718, in Cotton Mather's second attempt at a conversion tract that ostensibly targeted Jews, the man who had once prayed so fervently for the conversion of an entire nation suggested much more modestly that "If but one soul of that *Beloved People* should be found, and reach'd, and touch'd" by his proselytizing, his efforts would have been worthwhile.[5] Even the ministers who hovered over Monis's 1722 installment as a Hebrew instructor at Harvard harbored few illusions of his ushering in a mass conversion of other Jews, let alone a millennial age. If he might whip some lazy Harvard undergraduates into shape with his rigorous Hebrew exercises, he would be doing his part to contribute to the well-being of the Commonwealth. By the third decade of the eighteenth century, the legacy of the fathers lay so far in the past that undergoing difficult drills in Hebrew grammar constituted the fairest possibility of reliving the rigors that their spiritual life had once stipulated. Benjamin Franklin, whose "Silence Dogood" columns were increasing the readership of and interest in his brother's *New England Courant* during this period, had opined that Harvard was rejecting poor students who deserved admission and graduating successive classes of undeserving and intellectually inferior rich ones.[6] At a point in time when monetary interests were gaining an increasing influence over both clerical and secular affairs, the arrival of Judah Monis enabled New Englanders to purchase a small piece of their redemption at a low cost.

Within the newly commercial atmosphere, as religious life was losing its centrality, Monis's story dramatized the defining crises of early eighteenth-century New England theology. His conversion to Christianity made many Puritans uneasy. How could anyone know for sure if he "meant it"? Superficially, such doubts manifested a natural, if predictably prejudicial view that Monis had guilefully gained employment at Harvard and the economic stability that went along with it in apparent "exchange" for his change of heart. On a more profound level, however, the elusiveness of Monis's "true" intentions went right to the heart of Puritanism's as yet unresolved spiritual impasses. On the one hand, Monis's conversion and baptism hearkened back to New England's investment in a "federal" covenant; his declaration of loyalty to the Christian faith bore the trappings, at least, of a tribal ceremony of Abrahamic origin. It was a public gesture of official allegiance and, as such, mirrored Puritanism's now nearly full-fledged embrace of congregational expediency, by which any willing parishioner might sign his or her name to a church register in order to gain membership. At the same time, it bore as well the earmarks of an inspired, pietistic event, in which a deliberate, self-possessed adult confessed to a new faith in Christ and, in so doing, renewed Puritanism's earliest origins as a large-scale *eschewal* of ritual and hierarchy in favor of purely spiritual behavior. At the deepest level, and as a powerful example of cultural liminality, Monis was neither a Jew nor a Christian, neither a father nor a son, neither a teacher nor a student. His conversion and subsequent career presented New Englanders with what Shalom Goldman refers to as "unsettling questions" that exacerbated preexisting misgivings regarding church membership and parishioners' spiritual identities. If, as Goldman argues, "Jewish texts" could be experienced either as a "source of truth or a source of lies," what implications would the arrival of a purported expert on those texts and their translation bear?[7]

Although the myth of New England's spiritual decline into sudden degeneracy has long ago been lain to rest, few historians dispute the idea that, by the early eighteenth century, clerical authority in Massachusetts had been diffused. A potent combination of shifts in church membership policies, the distractions of frontier warfare with the French and their Native American allies, substantial changes in English imperial policy, and the rise and fall of colonial economic fortunes all contributed to a shift away from the tight communal structures that had once ensured congregational unity among New Englanders. Nothing could have made the declining influence of New England Congregationalism more palpable than the growth, in the midst of the same colonies whose original founding had occurred in *flight* from such things, of the Anglican church. In a few cases, Anglican influence had even occurred as a result of "defec-tions" from Congregationalism on the part of Puritan ministers. The greatest shock came in 1722, barely two decades beyond the founding of the new college in New Haven, when seven members of the Yale fac-ulty announced at commencement that they were going to convert to the Church of England and be ordained by a London bishop.[8] In the wake of such changes, Congregationalism sought every circumstantial advantage it could gain. Very little was left to compel church membership, and what requirements and strictures as might still be deployed were far weaker than those that had once ensured the packed meetinghouses of an earlier day. Even the most vocal defenders of the New England Way knew that they could only woo people back to orthodoxy gently, that scare tactics would no longer work. If resurgent "Anglicans had simplified doctrine and stressed morality for the sake of ensuring political unity,"[9] a man like Cotton Mather could only respond in kind, despite the fact that doing so would necessarily run contrary to the central Puritan teachings against the equation of works with grace. Mather was keenly aware of how much fur-ther arguments for "*Morality* and *Moral Honesty*" would take him than the older predestinarian fare ever could, and he was also anxious "to pre-serve his standing within elite culture,"[10] within which Anglicanism and other forms of socially pragmatic behavior were on the rise. By the 1720s Mather himself was a more or less willing participant in the transforma-tion of "Puritan theocracy" into a "merchant-dominated civic polity."[11] If his efforts to repopularize Congregationalism necessitated the relinquish-ment of central Puritan ideals, at least he might continue to exert an influ-ence over the enterprise.

The waning orthodox influence figured more prominently in the story of Judah Monis than did the eschatological zeal that had fueled earlier Puritan rhetorical efforts to convert Jews. As the remnants of ministerial authority sought retrenchment and renewal, they relinquished whatever larger aspi-rations they had once had to march at the vanguard of millennial change. Monis's arrival was timely insofar as it coincided with a broadly based appeal on the part of Harvard authorities to revive the spirit of the fathers by reasserting the power of the individual conversion experience as a com-munal spectacle. An ordinary renewal of faith could hardly be novel as it applied to men and women of the third generation, but if the Puritan spirit were to be reignited, who could possibly be better qualified to function as a catalyst for a revival of that spirit than an alien Jew? Notwithstanding intermittent efforts by John Eliot and a handful of other proselytizers to Christianize Indians, Puritanism generally embodied less missionary zeal—and gained less missionary success—than its nineteenth-century Protestant outgrowths. It was an intrinsically *internal* experience which could not be easily or advantageously explained to, much less imposed upon, outsiders. At best, as Yasuhide Kawashima writes, "the majority of praying Indians remained Christian in name only," and could hardly take well to Puritan civilizing missions, much less to the predestinarian credo and notion of original sin upon which the Puritan faith rested.[12] The revival of Congregationalism in early eighteenth-century, pre–Great Awakening New England would, by definition, involve a certain amount of "preaching to the converted," as opposed to a broader proselytizing, an appeal to the "gnawing guilt" of the spiritually errant offspring of a once devoted church membership.

The Jews constituted an appropriate locus for the orthodoxy's ambivalent views regarding the foregoing generations of Puritan progenitors. In February 1722, a writer calling himself "Johannes Clericus" published exactly such a view of the state of New England religion in the *New England Courant*. "If it were the Design of Men to Make our Religion a Dishonour and Reproach to the Jews, Mahometans and Heathens, could they do it by more effectual means?" the writer asked. For their part, the Jews' "Obstinacy . . . in Defense and Practice of their Religion," as the writer put it, could only "condemn our Coldness and Indifferency in ours."[13] As the people of God, who had once been more precious to Him than the people of any other nationality, the Jews occupied a similar place to that of the founders of New England. Like the errant Jews and as the progenitors of an increasingly idolatrous polity, the earliest New Englanders had once been a covenanted people. At the same time, the apostasy of the Jews had resembled that of New England's sons and grandsons who, in their clamorous eagerness to depart from the old ways, like ungrateful sons, were all too carelessly impervious to fatherly counsel.

When Judah Monis assumed his place on the Harvard faculty, he bore all of the weight of these inarticulate and inadvertent projections. Though his earlier life at Harvard suggests that some had initial hopes that he might prove to be an agent for a larger Jewish conversion, the context in which his own conversion took place suggests that most of the meaning underlying his experience derived less from his individual status as a Jewish convert to Christianity than it did from the fact that he had arrived at a time when the Congregational church was attempting its own renewal. Here at once was a "son" of the commandment come to fulfill his charge, much as the nominally Christian sons of New England, one hoped, would return to the fold. Moreover, Monis and his conversion represented a resounding affirmation of the oldest kind of covenantal faith, not to mention scriptural foundation. His having "come home" to the most pristine remaining haven of Protestant Christianity was a fitting reminder that the old religion still had life in it. Not long before Monis's arrival, Cotton Mather himself made an explicit connection between Jewish conversion and the renewal of Christian faith. His pamphlet Faith Encouraged recounted the story of three young Jewish girls in Berlin who had left their parents' home, gone to the local Lutheran pastor, and then declared their desire to convert to Christianity. At the end of his narrative account, which described the three girls' begging never to be separated from their "dearest Jesus," Mather asked his Christian readers, "How many Pious PARENTS are there who are Travailing for the Souls of their children to see a CHRIST formed in them?"[14] If three little Jewish girls who never had the advantage of attending church a single time in their lives could be so ready to leave not only their Judaism but their own parents for Jesus, ought not the ostensibly Christian families of New England to follow suit and fly to the arms of a church they had all but abandoned?

Historians have followed and attempted to piece together the parts of Monis's story since as far back as 1812, when Hannah Adams produced her two-volume History of the Jews. More scholarly attention came at the turn of the twentieth century, when Jewish American "investigators diligent to gather all that [could] be known about the early history of their people on this continent" published several articles on his career and legacy.[15] These historians' articles provide significant documentary value, as they review the extant primary sources and suggest the broader outlines of Monis's origins, arrival in America, time at Harvard, and eventual absorption into his wife's family and extended church community. The investigations of these early twentieth-century historians are limited, however, by their collective insistence on addressing themselves to a limited set of questions. As late as 1980, one historian was still hoping to resolve one central "mystery": "was [Monis's] conversion to Christianity . . . an act of faith or an act of opportunism?"[16] The question of whether Monis was a Jew or Christian at heart, however, besides being an impossible one to answer, represents an epistemological dead end. What matters is why and how Monis's conversion, regardless of what his innermost spiritual leanings may have been, was important to third-generation Puritans. Jews, it is safe to say, are unlikely to have taken any notice of it; if they did, we have no record of what they thought. New England's orthodoxy not only noticed but orchestrated it. Monis's story is important, therefore, because of what it tells us about latter-day Puritanism, and because it offers insight into what could happen when a theoretical Hebraism coincided with the presence of a person who, by birth at least, was closely associated with Judaism.

Based on the dates indicated on his gravestone in Northborough, Massachusetts, Monis is believed to have been born in 1683, but no consensus has been reached as to his birthplace, which is likely to have been "Italy or the Barbary States."[17] When George Alexander Kohut sought to investigate his genealogy, he hypothesized that, regardless of where Monis was born, he was of Portuguese *marrano* extraction. "Monis" bears a close enough resemblance to the common Portuguese name "Moniz" to suggest a *marrano* origin.[18] The evidence for the grammarian's Italian or, more specifically, Venetian background derives from Kohut's having found two gravestones with similar names engraved on them in a Jewish burial ground in Venice. An Italian origin was also likely, along with ties to the large Sephardic community in Amsterdam, owing to Monis's references throughout his scholarly career to specific rabbis who were well known among Italian Jews, as well as to the pronunciation key that he provided in his Hebrew grammar.[19] No historian, on the other hand, can offer any insight into why, in 1715, a thirty-two-year-old Monis crossed the Atlantic and settled in New York, where he appeared as one of five Jews on a list of "persons of foreign birth made natural born subjects." He was admitted as a freeman, or legally sanctioned merchant and local voter, in September 1715.[20]

While he was in New York, Monis operated a store, but he was also a tutor in Hebrew to both Jews and Christians. The announcement of his conversion that was made in the *New England Courant* in April 1722 indicated that he had been "the sometime Rabbi of the synagogue in Jamaica, and afterwards in New-York," and that he had studied "in the Jewish Academies of *Leghorn* and *Amsterdam*."[21] Throughout his career, Monis appears by necessity to have kept one foot in the world of religious study and the other in the world of merchandising. Neither New York nor Cambridge, in other words, could support him as a fulltime Hebrew scholar, whether Jewish or Christian. In New England, however, Monis represented enough of a novelty to generate interest and attention. The language of the *Courant* article suggested that, initially at least, Monis brought excitement on the basis of his linguistic expertise. The article's reference to him as "learned and ingenious," as well as its inclusion of his Judaic resume, speaks to an apparent admiration for a set of Jewish qualifications. Monis's Judaism was an enthralling and defining element of his appeal. It conferred extraordinary qualifications upon him on the basis of achievements that no New England pastor, no matter the extent of his Hebraic training, could attain. Despite his relatively young age, not to mention what would, in a rabbinical context, have been viewed as limited skill on his part, Monis merited respect among New England Puritans that might be accorded an elder.

When exactly Monis came to Massachusetts is unknown, although he first appeared in Cambridge records in September 1720, when he took a mortgage on the Corn Market Street house of Thomas and Sarah Boylston.[22] This same record indicates that the mortgage was cancelled four years later, within a few months of his appointment at Harvard and his marriage to Abigail Marrett of Cambridge on January 18, 1724. His letter to the Harvard corporation of June 29, 1720, in which he offered his services as a teacher of Hebrew, as well as an early copy of his Hebrew grammar, tells us that he was both diplomatic and ambitious. "Having made an Essay to facilitate the instruction of Youth in the Hebrew," Monis declared, "I make bold to present it."[23] The letter mentioned his lack of fluency in English, but it did so in such a way as to convey the author's misgivings on this account, so that he might come across as a willing and aware pupil even as he purported to preside over the instruction of other pupils. His efforts at producing a Hebrew grammar begged the "Judicious perusal" of his eminent readers. The letter referred as well, in attempting to round out the grammar's qualifications as a worthy text, to the "Learned

Gentlemen and Desenters of Different Churches." Monis knew his audience, to say the least. Regardless of the level of his learning in Hebrew—and his having shipped from western Europe's most advanced Jewish center in Amsterdam to New York at a time when the latter city, though it had a significant Jewish population, was hardly a center of Jewish learning or culture suggests that he may not have been the most promising of rabbinical students—Monis knew enough about New England Protestantism to know that Hebraic interest was likely to be highest among members of the "Desenting" sects. He was parlaying what was probably a rather middling ability in Hebrew to an audience who knew enough to value his expertise but perhaps not enough to get past his rhetorical appeal and their own reverential view of Jewish learning. In this respect, Monis was a transitional figure in more ways than one. Owing in part to the continual negotiations with which he sought to improve the fairly marginal status that he held over the course of a thirty-eight-year career at Harvard, he left a discursive record that spoke volubly to both his own and Harvard's sense of the potential economic value of his services.

The letter of 1720 suggested that Monis knew enough about Harvard's curricular interest in Hebrew to see that he might pique interest with his book. Leaving aside the long list of distinguished Hebraists with some connection to the school going back to the time of William Bradford himself, the college's first two presidents, Henry Dunster and Charles Chauncey, had been accomplished Hebraists.[24] In the seventeenth century, undergraduates had had to study the original language of the scriptures twice a day and be prepared to translate any portion of the Hebrew Bible into Latin.[25] In the 1640s, each Thursday was devoted in its entirety "to the study of Semitic languages."[26] Monis read Harvard's long-standing interest in Hebrew as an opportunity for advancement. Although his eventual conversion and his entire career at Harvard inspired some considerable skepticism on the part of both Christians and Jews who over the years have dismissed his appointment to the College, as well as his fairly long career there, as means by which he merely sought to improve his economic standing, such a hypothesis suggests not only an intrinsic prejudice but a troubling historical short-sightedness. Whatever his level of competence may have been, Monis was motivated by genuine scholarly interest. That he saw greater opportunities for a rewarding career in Puritan Cambridge than in New York's fledgling Jewish community seems no less likely a testament to his devotion to the study of Hebrew than to any small hope he may have had of striking it rich or, as Eisig Silberschlag puts it, "win[ning] an academic post with a secure though meager salary."[27] As Kings (later Columbia) College would not be founded until 1754, early eighteenth-century New York contained no possible outlet for Monis's scholarly ambitions. Whether or not Monis was entirely "sincere" in his crossing over to Christianity, neither his sense of common purpose with New England Puritanism nor his scholarly appreciation for Harvard's Hebraism have earned more than perfunctory recognition on the part of historians to date who have followed the arc of his career, even though such factors constitute the most telling and culturally significant reasons behind his move from New York to Massachusetts.

However deliberate or circumstantial the move may have been, Monis's appreciation for Puritan Hebraism and the high regard in which he was held at least initially by the Cambridge ministers explain the mutual affinity. Between the receipt of Monis's 1720 letter and the spring of 1722, in any case, the "sometime Rabbi" was matriculated into Harvard itself, where he went on record as the first and only Jewish recipient of a degree from that institution before the nineteenth century. The completion of his Hebrew grammar in manuscript form constituted his major undertaking for the degree; whether it was accompanied or followed by indoctrination in the Christian faith is unknown, but his official conversion occurred in advance of his appointment as an instructor.[28] Early on, in any case, he must have grown accustomed to receiving at least ostensible respect for his Hebrew achievements and abilities. Only a strongly capable scholar of Hebrew could possibly have passed Cotton Mather's muster. That that respect was nearly always mixed with condescension speaks more to the complexity of Monis's unwitting status as an experiment of Puritan Hebraism than it does to any "insincerity" on the part of his Cambridge patrons. If nothing else, Monis may have inadvertently influenced the rhetorical climate surrounding his relationship with the committee, or at least its patronizing aspect, with remarks of his own. As the committee members sought to adjust the terms of his financial relationship with Harvard, asking of him "what would he have for his trouble in coming over [to the College]?," Monis replied, with what may have been taken as a kind of haughtiness, that it "t'was the part of children not of men to drive a bargain about such a matter."[29] For better or worse, much of the extant documentation on Monis's long career at Harvard, as well as his life in Cambridge, was taken up with just such bargaining on his part. As the intrinsic value of clerical and scholarly achievement diminished in the face of New England's cultural transformation, Monis's worth would have to be spelled out, for better or worse, in monetary terms.

Monis's initial meeting with a group of Harvard officials resulted, in any case, in his being offered the opportunity to shore up his knowledge of Hebrew for the greater benefit of the college itself. He seems to have known what he was after, as the diary of Henry Flynt, one of the Harvard men to meet with him, made clear. Monis, Flynt wrote, "present[ed] a plan by which [Hebrew] would be taken out of the hands of the tutors and given to him with the proviso that the members of the upper classes should be compelled to take the subject and that only those students whose parents could convince the President that they did not need it should be exempt."[30] The proposal was hardly a modest one in the sense that it stipulated an unprecedented curricular change on Harvard's part. Well beyond the 1720s, all subjects were taught by tutors at Harvard; a professorship, as such, which was what Monis was proposing for himself, was nonexistent. Whether he bore delusions of grandeur or whether he was merely offering Harvard what it ought on the basis of its vaunted devotion to the study of Hebrew as a fundamental part of its curriculum to have desired anyway, Monis was bold. He prevailed, in any case, in securing a place for himself at the college, including what amounted to a remission of tuition, a small stipend and a "chamber in the house."[31] As Monis had never had the opportunity to earn a degree, Harvard saw fit to confer the M.A. as a means of giving him the necessary credentials for a post as an instructor there.

Every historian who has written about Monis has assumed that his conversion to Christianity, which took place upon his receipt of the M.A. and antecedent to his official appointment as an instructor of Hebrew to undergraduates, was a clearly defined stipulation of his gaining employment at Harvard. While circumstantial evidence does suggest such a connection, no written record of such a contract or anything resembling such an agreement exists. In the notes on his initial contact with the Harvard committee that oversaw his establishment there, we see only a record of his having agreed with the group to meet "every day at 3 a clock afternoon at Colledg to discourse about the Hebrew tongue."[32] The assumption that the 1722 transaction was some sort of officially contracted bargain is posited not only on the idea that a formal agreement existed to compromise the sincerity, and therefore the legitimacy of the conversion but also, and perhaps more important, on the still more problematic notion that New England Puritans might believe that Monis could be a Jew one day and become a Christian the next. Perhaps incredulity on this latter notion accounts for Clifford Shipton having suggested that the Harvard overseers actually *opposed* Monis's conversion. "They did not agree with him that he could be saved . . . by embracing Protestant Christianity," the Harvard historian noted, believing in apparent accord with a Calvinist view that "such a vain assumption of infallibility" was patently false.[33] In any case, the bulk of scholarship suggests, as Arthur Hertzberg does, that Monis's conversion was a "genuine" confirmation of the former rabbi's appreciation for Christianity.[34] Monis's biographers agree as well, to use Eisig Silberschlag's phrase, that Monis's "enigmatic personality" is surrounded by "an aura of mystery" that precludes any kind of final judgment on how Monis truly felt.[35] Most recently, David Gradwohl has succinctly concluded that everything about Monis, including the gravestone that commemorated him, "reflect[s] a unique person of complex and, indeed, conflicting identities" and a man "whose life still challenges our understanding today."[36] The religious and cultural tumult of early eighteenth-century New England was intrinsic to and only multiplied the circumstances and reverberations of that complexity.

Taken at his word, Monis looks to have "meant" every bit of his conversion. Indeed, on the traditional (if patently teleological) assumption that what one says on one's deathbed constitutes a be-all pronouncement on one's entire life, his having pointedly told his attendants in his final moments that he was eager to join Christ as opposed to "Abraham's bosom" would appear to dispel any obvious "mystery" regarding his spiritual leanings.[37] If posthumous messages constitute firm evidence of one's public intentions, so too does Monis's gravestone remove much of the ambiguity surrounding his apostasy, as Gradwohl and others have shown.[38] Based on such strong evidence then, Frederick Greenspahn's assertion that "Monis commitment to Judaism can be questioned" is a clear understatement.[39] A lurking hope owing perhaps not to Christian mistrust of a

Jew's reliability but to an eagerness on the part of American Jews to find in colonial New England some version of a "real" Jew confirming Weberian theories of an unambiguous Puritan philo-Semitism clings all the same to opposite interpretations of Monis's career. "Like Heine, Boerne, and others," wrote the early twentieth-century Reform Rabbi George Alexander Kohut, "he changed his faith in name only in order to reach the object of his ambitions."[40] Kohut went on to assert on what looks to be a combination of flimsy evidence and wishful thinking that, "though converted, [Monis] was a Jew at heart, and a Christian in public life."[41]

Historians' oscillations on the matter of whether or not Monis was "really" a Jew or "really" a Christian proceed from and result in a problematic narrowing of focus. Given the perseverance of an at least vestigial Calvinist theology in the early decades of the eighteenth century, a more salient question is whether and how Monis might have been thought to be of the *elect*. Despite his lifelong *professions* of Christianity or, for that matter, even in the face of whatever reluctance he may privately have maintained to relinquish Judaism or at least Judaic practice, the question of his outward or *covenantal* allegiance would have been moot. Accordingly, it is impossible to know from a Puritan point of view not only whether or not Monis "meant" his Christianity but how, on some assumption that he did, in fact, "mean" it, any pronouncement on his part could ever have been thought to be equivalent to his actual sanctification. For Puritans, who had so long lived in the absence of any assurances of their own election, however, Monis's profession was of primary importance as it related to just such a line of inquiry, insoluble as it was.

By 1722, and in the complete absence of any firsthand memory of what their Calvinism had looked like at the founding, they could not help but have been vexed and discomfited by a case that so thoroughly tested and displayed the limits of their own self-contradictory theological premises. For whatever reasons, existing scholarship on Monis abstracts his story from its historical context and projects a decidedly post-Puritan interpretive perspective upon his career. Since few, if any, other "events" in colonial New England's Jewish history were as thoroughly documented as Judah Monis's conversion was, no better opportunity presents itself for exploring these implications. The conversion was commemorated from multiple perspectives—both "objectively," in the form of a newspaper article, as well as from the point of view of Monis's Harvard sponsors, the most prominent of whom offered their own prefaces to his discourse. In addition, besides the testimony of Benjamin Colman, his primary sponsor, one of Colman's overseas correspondents provided epistolary commentary on the conversion. Finally, Monis's own tripartite discourse—*The Truth, The Whole Truth, and Nothing But the Truth*—offered the convert's own purported point of view. The compound effect of these records suggests that latter-day Puritan ambivalence regarding the relationship between covenantal and pietistic modes of spiritual affinity constituted the central subtext for the event. Those who wished to believe, presumably, that Monis had not duped them into hiring him on as a Hebrew instructor were sure indeed that his words amounted to the "truth, the whole truth, and nothing but the truth." His detractors, including some quite predictably prejudicial skeptics, felt that Monis's was no different from other apparently insincere conversions which were themselves "suspect as devices for promoting the material interests of a people looked upon as characteristically untrustworthy."[42] Notwithstanding such rather simplistic dichotomies between notions of a sincere versus a conniving Judah Monis, the documentary record of his conversion suggests a moment fraught with considerably more large-scale cultural meaning and import than the question of whether or not one man was being true or false to his inner convictions. Particularly as New Englanders struggled to shore up their once unbreakable congregational affinities in the face of growing economic and social pressures to pursue individual as opposed to communitarian interests, Monis's conversion was a salient reminder of what it meant to become a member of the spiritual community.

Each document referred to Monis's covenantal ties, first to his Judaic origins, or "his brethren of the flesh" and, in addition, to the new faith to which he was declaring his allegiance. The excitement which surrounded his conversion proceeded not merely from the fact that Monis was a Jew by birth, but that he had been so thoroughgoing a Jew by custom. The *New England Courant* article whose author had filed it the day after Monis had undergone the ceremony referred to Monis as a "Rabbi of the Synagogue in Jamaica, and afterwards in New-York," and as someone who had studied "in the Jewish Academies of *Leghorn* and *Amsterdam*."[43] The First Cambridge Church minutes for March 27, 1722, the day of the conversion, referred to Monis as "a Jew by birth and Education."[44] By the same token, both documents spoke to the covenantal finality of the gesture by which Monis forswore his old allegiance. To the extent that such things could matter within what would still have been at least a nominally predestinarian context, Monis's "Publick Profession of the Christian Religion" and his "Solemn Profession of his Faith in the Messiah already come" suggested the instantaneous substitution of one kind of tribal or at least doctrinaire belonging for another. The church minutes left a similar inference even more explicit, referring as they did to Monis's "being converted to the Christian Faith" and thereby having "owned the covenant."[45] Given that several generations of quite deliberate Christian-born predecessors had in many cases devoted their entire lives to bringing about a similar covenantal renewal for themselves, and that neither the clergy nor the laity equated even the most vociferous professions of faith with instant sanctification, the straightforward manner in which Monis's crossing from Judaism to Christianity was reported is odd.

In his lengthy discourse, "Moses a Witness unto our Lord Jesus Christ," which accompanied Monis's own discourses, Benjamin Colman addressed the subjects of baptism and circumcision directly and, in particular, their relevance as outward signs of a covenantal relationship between God and His people. Hardly hesitating to raise the specter of New England's own ongoing debates over the centrality of a covenantal congregationalism, and at the same time directly addressing the conversion of a man who had at birth been marked, in keeping with the practice of his forefathers, by their own badge of belonging, Colman pointed out that "circumcision indeed look'd to a church seed, a believing seed."[46] In his effort to justify baptism as a divinely sanctioned Christian adaptation of circumcision, he continued: "It [circumcision] was (as Baptism now is) a sacrament of Initiation into the covenant of Grace: a sign to represent, and a seal to ratify—and confirm, the Bonds and Blessings of it. It held forth the sufferings of CHRIST, whose blood began to be shed in His Circumcision."[47] In this way, Colman and, presumably, the other approving sponsors and witnesses to Monis's conversion sought not only to convince onlookers of the sacred validity of the moment and the sincerity of the man, but to revisit the vexing subject of a covenantal ritual practice in the context of a predestinarian theology.

Colman's endorsement of baptism hearkened back to the founders' own tireless but frequently frustrated efforts to convince a polity whose belief in election had caused them to be quite skeptical about excessive faith in ritualistic practices that might somehow forestall or displace the chillingly unpredictable workings of a God whose mind was already made up. His discourse, like the ceremony it accompanied and explained, held forth the possibility that human intention could actually amount to something in God's eyes, and it invoked the covenantal practices of two sets of forefathers—Jewish and Puritan—in order to substantiate its claim. As if to remind himself, Monis, and the gathered audience of its startling import, Colman made sure near the end of his discourse to state the facts plainly. "Believe me, sir," he indicated to the former "rabbin," "our Christian Baptism is a great solemnity in our Holy Religion. It is *a very* reverend and holy *ordinance* and supposes you in a State of *Grace*."[48] Such a supposition would certainly have stretched the bounds of credibility in the founders' day. Ironically, the idea that Monis could be both ratified and sealed in his newfound Christian beliefs, and thereby "earn" grace, would not have been thought possible two generations earlier, when much stricter expectation, at least among the non-dissenting congregants of Massachusetts Bay, had held sway. So complete a transformation had come about, however, that not only was such a thing possible at Harvard in 1722, but the fathers who might very well have prevented such a thing from taking place were now invoked at least indirectly through Colman's mention of the idea of "church seed" as the very guarantors of the practice.

The words spoken in College Hall that day, which were shortly afterwards printed, published, and distributed not only through New England but in England as well, confirmed the same fixation with covenantal ties and gestures that the baptism had symbolized. As the *Courant* article and First Church minutes demonstrated, Puritans took great pride in the fact of Monis's origins. Had he been any kind of previously Gentile convert, or a Christian by birth merely returning to the fold, Monis would not have engendered much enthusiasm. He was, however, and as Colman put it in his preface to the conversion discourses, "a Very Valuable Proselyte; (as a Learned Person has said to me of him) and he would be so esteemed by the learned & pious in one Profession or other of Christianity. He is truly read and learned in the Jewish *Kabbala* and *Rabbins*, a master and critic in the

Hebrew; He reads, speaks, writes and interprets it with great readiness and accuracy, and is truly . . . apt to teach."[49] Monis's Judaic background was the central factor behind his having been so warmly, or at least excitedly, received. Both Colman and Increase Mather, who, although his ill health had prevented him from having attended and presided over the ceremony himself, had contributed his own brief preface to the published version of Monis's three discourses, emphasized the convert's credentials as a scholar not only of the Hebrew language but of Jewish law.

Monis's conversion, however, for all of the momentary uplift it may have brought to Harvard, offered stark confirmation of the waning influence of an increasingly untenable founding belief in Calvinism. Conversion, not so much of Jews as of ordinary Christians, had long been the central focus for New England congregations. The intrinsic lack of assurance that had once defined the Puritan journey toward confirmation in Christ could not be maintained without some gesture in the direction of a more covenantal religious practice that would help parishioners to sustain at least a distant hope of their ability to *do* something toward affecting their status with Christ. As far back as the founding of Massachusetts Bay, therefore, Hebraism had supplied a means of furnishing this covenantal assurance. Monis represented an apotheosis of Puritan Hebraism, but just as covenantal strictures and guidelines had provoked what Theodore Dwight Bozeman calls "a distinctive redraft of the Christian redemption"[50] in the form of antinomianism whenever the early church fathers of the seventeenth century had deployed them in the interest of enforcing congregational discipline, Monis's eighteenth-century embodiment of a covenantal and Judaic Christianity would inevitably strain belief and tenability. Monis's conversion bore great potential as the ultimate achievement of the Hebraic and covenantal aspect of Puritanism, but it stood instead as a reminder of how, by 1722 at least, Hebraism had run its course as a viable instrument for legitimizing the orthodoxy's increasingly tenuous hold on congregational practice.

If Hebraism fell short as an effective rhetorical tool for enforcing a covenantal religiosity, Monis's Jewish background could be and was still invoked as a pretext for chastising not only Jews but lax and errant Christians whose devotion to the gospel left something to be desired. Increase Mather understood and appreciated the spiritual import of

Monis's conversion and referred to it on that basis as "an Effect of Divine Grace."[51] Particularly in the later portions of the work, Colman balanced Monis's status as a scion of the covenant with his evocation of a metaphorical climate that was more filial than paternalistic and, as a result, more pietistic than legalistic. Having begun his discourse with a sequence of references to Moses, the spiritual father of the Jews, and to Abraham, from whom the Jews derived their literal lineage, Colman concluded on a more Christ-centered note. He undertook a typological exploration of figures in the Hebrew Bible who prefigured the savior Himself. Hence, "the History of Abraham," in "offering up his . . . only son, Isaac, whom he loved,"[52] achieved a powerful attention to Jewish sons, of whom Monis, by figurative extension, offered a latter-day example. Even the means of Isaac's intended sacrifice bore typological significance: "The wood for the fire was laid for Isaac to bear as a figure of Christ's bearing His Cross. Isaac was the Lamb for the Burnt Offering; Christ is the Lamb of God without blemish and without spot. God freely gave His Son to die for us, the son of God freely laid down his own life, he made it his own Altar."[53] Colman's thematic emphasis on sons continued to include the story of Jacob's son Judah who, upon receiving his father's blessing, was named "He whom thy Brethren shall praise"— another foreshadowing manifestation of Christ's eventual arrival as the son who would rule over His people.[54]

Colman's remarks came to a head as he took note of the risks inherent in allowing too much to be made of Monis's past and, by extension, of Judaism's status as the parent religion. The shift in his talk away from the focus on Moses to the focus on Jesus also bore a broader significance as a means not only of reminding Monis of how far he had yet to go in renewing his soul but of reminding parishioners that no covenant, no legal system, could substitute for the internal conversion that had to take place before one achieved the possibility of receiving grace. It was here that baptism, signaling as it was meant to a rebirth in Christ, took on an additional meaning. If, on the one hand, it was meant to signify the mark of lineage, paternity, and covenantal belonging, it was significant as well, and in an opposite way, as a sign of a proselyte's figurative infancy. Much of the assurance that was accompanied by the covenantal promise of baptism was vacated in Colman's conclusion, where Monis and all of his Christian witnesses were duly warned about the tenuousness of his and anyone else's hold on grace. "It is *easy* for you to receive a place in the *Visible Church* and Kingdom of the *Messiah*," Colman pointed out, "but within it there is an *Invisible State of Grace and Salvation; Are you in that?*," the minister asked.[55]

The weight of Colman's remarks would assuredly have been lying heavily on Monis, the Jew who, on some level, had to have known that not only God but the people of New England were watching him to see how earnest he really was in his conversion to Christianity. Lest the witnesses of his monumental shift in allegiance be too lax with themselves, however, and take for granted their security in the *invisible* as opposed to the *visible* church, Colman's comments could very easily have served a dual purpose. If Monis was being asked to look into his own motivations, the bystanders present at his conversion ought to have been no less relentless with themselves. Though Colman's discourse would come to a fittingly uplifting conclusion, the penultimate passages served to remind listeners of the older rhetoric of the founders, whose charge had always been to demand a courageous introspection on the part of their parishioners. Whether or not Monis's joining the church was genuine, the terms to which he was being held and the tone with which he was addressed imputed a subordinated, appropriately filial status to him and to all others present in College Hall that day who might not have been fully committed to Christ's invisible, noncovenantal church. "Be sure that you have no *By-ends*, no sinister and corrupt *Views*, no *worldly* Advantages in what you do this day," Colman warned. "We can't be content with your good *Profession*; we seek your saving *Conversion* to Eternal Salvation. Is there a change in your *Heart* as well as in your *Principles*? You renounce your *Jewish infidelity*; do you renounce also *all sin*, every evil way? Is your *desire* true and fervent after *inward* Grace and Holiness?"[56] Content as they may have been to watch as Colman placed such strong demands upon the Jewish convert, the audience present at the ceremony, as well as the one implied in the print version of Colman's remarks, ought not to have been immune to its force. His concern lest Monis seek "*worldly* advantages" as a result of his conversion was addressed not only to the convert himself but to the larger body of parishioners who were growing increasingly liable to forge their congregational allegiances in connection with their mounting mercantile interests.

Even the guarded doubt that emerged from Increase Mather's measured acceptance of the conversion, as well as the more strident skepticism that found its way into the letters of an English correspondent of Colman's a few months after Monis's conversion, spoke volubly to church members' unstated misgivings regarding the intrusion of worldly motivations in a religious sphere. Mather's brief preface began with a salutary acknowledgment of all that Monis had "Exhibited," "Asserted," and "Proved" in the comments accompanying his conversion. It cited examples of "successful" Jewish conversions and placed them in the context of the "General Conversion of the Jewish Nation."[57] Near the close of his remarks, however, Mather cited the examples of two European Jews, "a Rabbinical Professor at *Vienna*" and a man named Conred Otton, both of whom "Returned to Judaism" after making particularly "zealous" and even "violent" professions against their former faith. Both men, at least in the apparent vociferousness of their initial rejection of Judaism, had evidently protested too much and, in doing so, bore an outward resemblance to Christian apologists for conversion whose rhetorical claims outran their own spiritual capacities. Mather's reference to the case of the Viennese professor was both prescient and pointed, insofar as that man was known, in the throes of his either feigned or fleeting apostasy, to have "Translated *Paul's Greek* Epistle to the Hebrew Tongue"; Monis's Hebrew grammar would eventually have appended to it both the Lord's Prayer and the Apostles' Creed rendered in Hebrew. In keeping with Mather's unstated but clearly hinted-at suspicion of Jewish converts' excess of zealotry, Harvard's overseers were apparently similarly discomfited by Monis's overstated zeal at his conversion, saying about him that, like so many other converts, "he went too far."[58]

Notwithstanding such misgivings, Mather wrote, "There is no cause to fear that *Mr. Monis* will Renounce his Christianity,"[59] and perhaps indeed suspicion of Monis as an individual was unwarranted. However, whether or not, as Colman had suggested in a pointed citation from the New Testament, Monis was "an Israelite indeed in whom there is no guile," the surrounding world contained many examples perhaps not of guileful Jews and Gentiles but of tempted ones, in any case, who employed outward demonstrations of faith in the interest of securing worldly status. Cotton Mather's 1718 pamphlet on the sudden conversion of the three young Jewish girls in Berlin had offered a particularly exaggerated example of Christian hypervigilance against a "Jewish" predilection for worldly temptation. When the three girls reported their intentions of converting to the Lutheran pastor in their district, he had gone out of his way to "feign to turn them off," first, by reminding them "how easily and comfortably they might live among the Jews, and that their father made fine Cloaths for them."[60] The girls' purported reply, which Mather rendered in italics in order to lend a catechistic tenor to the narrative, was that "*They did not value that at all; the cloaths must remain in the world; they would be children of Salvation.*"[61] The Lutheran priest undertook another effort, once again, on the operating assumption that Jews, even or especially when they are little girls, would care more for objects than they would for Jesus, saying, "They did very ill to forsake their Parents, who had such a tender Love for them, who would make them many fine Presents, and had brought some along with them: That on the contrary, they were to expect among *Christians* nothing but crosses and Afflictions, they would hardly get enough to satisfy their Hunger, but in a word, would be very Miserable."[62] Upon hearing this, the girls were all the more eager to cling to Jesus. How many New England congregations, in this age of burgeoning commercialism, could have been said to contain members whose devotion to Christ was as pure as that of these young Jewish girls?

As a primary sponsor of Monis's conversion and appointment at Harvard, Increase Mather restricted whatever suspicions he might have had regarding the new convert's worldly motivations to his remarks about the two European rabbis whose conversion had been "Perverted" in their motivation and results. On the other hand, Robert Wodrow, a Presbyterian minister in England who had read the copy of Monis's discourse that Colman had sent him, lost little time in expressing deeper reservations. In one of his letters to Colman, Wodrow made clear that his skepticism regarding the conversion at Harvard was at least in part motivated by a general sort of paranoid and racialist prejudice (he evidently feared that "opulent Jews," newly admitted to England under that nation's policy of religious tolerance, would "become able to purchase the City, whole country and be the lords of the Courts and the Patrons of our Churches").[63] Wodrow expressed a broader doubt as well, however, "of the sincerity of converts," and not only Jewish ones, "who act upon temporal motives towards a Temporal Messiah."[64] He quite expected Monis to revert to Judaism, comparing the

Hebrew instructor's case to that of Marcus Moses, a London Jew who had also published a discourse explaining his reasons for conversion but who, according to Wodrow, owed "his profession not to . . . the Gospel, but to an Act of Parliament which [gave] him a separate maintenance."[65] Monis himself, perhaps on Colman's prompting, later wrote to Wodrow, attesting (in Hebrew) to the lack of an ulterior motive for his conversion and his delight in Christ. As Milton Klein writes, no matter to what lengths Jewish converts might go to prove a lack of worldly interest behind their various professions of Christian faith, such gestures on their part "were generally suspect as devices for promoting the material interests of a people looked upon as characteristically untrustworthy."[66] Centuries of anti-Jewish prejudice could hardly be transcended by the solitary acts of individual converts. Moreover, within an overall cultural climate of declining church membership and waning ministerial influence, even the most earnest professions of religious conviction were automatically suspect. Falsely converted Jews were not the only suspicious parties in this milieu, as the growing influence of spiritual laxity within New England congregations led to the expansion of such institutions as the Brattle Street Church, whose very architecture spoke to its parishioners' burgeoning appreciation for material wealth and even "opulence" as appropriate accompaniments for Christian worship. Given the social, political, and economic advantages occasioned by *any* parishioner's membership in a Massachusetts church, established congregants could not help but be on the lookout for false confessions of faith from aspirant members.

Monis's conversion pamphlet was more performative than functional, as was evidenced by his having directed its first words to the Jews, or, as he put it, "My Brethren, According to the Flesh."[67] While it may very well have been the case that the author imagined a Jewish audience (his pamphlet was circulated in London, as well as in Boston, so from a purely practical standpoint, it could possibly have reached members of at least one organized Jewish community), his prefatory remarks, although ostensibly directed to other Jews, were calculated to achieve an effect among Christians. Indeed, if Monis's tripartite discourse ever did achieve anything like a dramatic result, an unevenness in texture, or the sort of "spontaneous" tenor for which people who sought evidence of a change of heart as opposed to a change of mind were seeking, it was in the preface, which betrayed a strikingly inconclusive ambivalence on his part toward the religion of his birth. Whether or not his conversion was "sincere," and regardless of whether his intended audience consisted of Jews or non-Jews, the preface wrought an emotionally wrenching leave-taking. Monis veered in his remarks from articulating an impatient anger toward Jews, to a solicitous consideration of their best spiritual interests, to an unguarded expression of his deepest desire that they might not lose their "brotherly affection and love" for him, despite his apostasy.

Ironically, Monis displayed his most spontaneous spiritual self as he addressed his fellow Jews. At one point in the pamphlet's final portion, he indicated that as he contemplated the state of the Jews' "spiritual darkness," he felt that his "heart [was] fit to burst."[68] Although skeptical Christians would have been the party most desirous of glimpsing an emotionally affected and spiritually vulnerable convert, Monis's deepest evocation of pathos came as he spoke directly to his fellow Jews. In the central portions of his discourse, on the other hand, which were more transparently intended to appeal to a Christian audience seeking proof of Monis's proper indoctrination, the speaker was deliberate, reasoned, abstract, and disproportionately argumentative. That his imagined Jewish audience apparently merited Monis's deepest expression of passion was inconsistent with Christian ascriptions of a logocentric and legalistic Judaic obsession with public covenants as opposed to private pieties. Likewise, in the extended exegetical performances featured in The Truth, The Whole Truth, and Nothing But the Truth, Monis gave his Christian readers the exact sort of abstract and calculatedly unsentimental treatment that his Jewish audience, based upon their own imputed history of dispassionate religiosity, would have deserved. In Nothing But the Truth Monis must have raised at least a few Christian eyebrows as his programmatic refutation of Arianism (a doctrine within Protestantism that, in the Puritan view, was tainted by Popish sentiments and practices) rose to such an accusatory pitch that Thomas Hollis, the London churchman who would eventually supply the Hebrew type needed for the publication of Monis's Hebrew grammar in 1735, advised the convert "not to judge too hastily of his neighbor and exclude from salvation everyone that differ[ed] from him in the exposition and belief of the article of the Trinity."[69]

The conversion pamphlet conjured the same dialectical relationship between covenantal and pietistic elements that characterized the Colman preface. His case for conversion manifested a similar tension and an analogous relevance to a broader set of third-generation Puritan concerns than an incidental or even vestigial millenarian interest in Jewish conversion would have occasioned. Once he got past his painful leave-taking, Monis seemed content to impute all manner of predictably legalistic and spiritually blind teachings to his fellow Jews. His resorting to such stereotypes showed that he was no less susceptible to the typical anti-Jewish prejudices and theological assumptions of his day than any Christian would have been. Knowing, however, that New England itself contained at most a few dozen Jews (nearly all of whom dwelled in Newport in 1722), it is altogether probable that, like the ministers who sponsored his conversion, and like their predecessors among the Puritan advocates of Jewish conversion, Monis considered that his writing might have borne some significant potential as a corrective instrument for *Christians* whose spiritual inner life and congregational alignment were problematically out of keeping with orthodox precedent. His many references in all three portions of his discourse to Judaic belief and practice argued a consistent association of the Jewish religion with, among other deficiencies of spiritual character, "Rottenness," "Superstition," "Stubbornness," and "Stiffneckedness." At the same time, and also in keeping with the patterns of Puritan Hebraism, Monis associated Jews with learnedness, steadfast adherence to monotheism, and piety.

Previous treatments of Monis's pamphlet suggest that some of its most outspoken arguments were not only overwrought but, on that exact basis, heavily influenced if not actually written by, among others, Increase Mather.[70] Whether or not Monis had such help (and the somewhat halting character of his letters to the authorities at Harvard suggests that his command of English would not have been up to the task of composing the discourses himself; nor would he have possessed the wherewithal to supply such detailed "and extensive knowledge of Protestant theology and controversy"[71]), his conversion pamphlet did directly engage problems originating in a Puritan milieu. Its author seemed unable to decide whether the Jews, and more specifically Jewish "rabbins," were elderly repositories of valuable religious knowledge or modernizing impostors. Monis varied between referring to the Jews' "own Rabbins of old" and, as one sequence in *The Truth* has it, their "new upstart *rabbins*" (elsewhere in *The Truth* he suggested that the Jews were susceptible to the teachings of so many faddish scholars whose "Modern Rabbins have newly Invented" all manner of unwarranted biblical interpretations).[72]

Specific references to specific rabbis, not surprisingly, elicited the least guarded and most reverent descriptions, as was the case with the author's tribute to Jacob Sasportas, the man would have been his rabbi during the time Monis was a pupil at the "Jewish Academy at *Amsterdam*." Sasportas, who remained a stalwart Jew his entire life, warranted blushingly effusive praise in *The Truth* as "The perfect wise Man, the Pious or Godly, the Theologe, Glory of the Wise Men, the Holy, One Teacher, My Teacher."[73] If merely personal considerations and loyalties occasioned such favorable treatment for one rabbi and such contempt for others, Monis's apparent inconsistency might be easily explained. A more profound and inadvertent sort of ambivalence was operative here, however, as Monis referred to the entire Jewish tradition at times as fossilized and decrepit and at other times as newfangled and modernistic. Consideration of the framing Puritan context, however, lends greater sense to Monis's apparently contradictory attitudes toward his "Brethren of the Flesh." The assistance he received from the New England authorities who sponsored his apostasy would supply at least a partial explanation for his apparent familiarity with a host of Puritan concerns. As the Puritans themselves had never been able to make up their minds about Jews, how might Monis ever have arrived at anything besides a profound inconsistency in his own discursive treatment of them?

The convert himself was unable to be univocal on many fronts. Were the Jews to be referred to in the first, second, or third person? (Monis relied for the most part on the third, but not without exception.) Were the Jews to be described as the author's "brethren," or were they to be thought of, as the passage on Sasportas suggested, as fathers? One section in *The Truth* offered an extended sequence of descriptors, each and none of which seemed entirely satisfactory to a speaker whose relationship to his birth religion was so fraught. In the Hebrew Bible, Monis indicated, God Himself was unable to settle on an appropriate term by which to address His People, varying between, "*My children, My first born, My Beloved;* [and] my peculiar People."[74] If God had so much difficulty making up His mind as to the nature of His relationship to the Jews, how might His fallible creation possibly negotiate such a mystery? Moreover, how might the proponents of the newer religion consider the legatees of its predecessor? The problems stemming from Monis's own inability to mark out his proper place in relationship to Judaism were inherent as well in the entire history of Puritanism, which had attempted to fashion a religion of grace on a foundation of covenantal precedent. Monis's divided loyalties were mirrored as well in New England's own complex and contradictory history as a laboratory for a unique form of religious primitivism that, despite its simplifying and traditionalist aspirations, lay astride a landscape and set of historical circumstances that mandated a transatlantic engagement of modernizing concerns.

Given the initial excitement created by the promise he seemed to embody as a man of Abraham's seed come to renew New England, Monis's actual career achievements at Harvard could only have disappointed both him and the larger spiritual community he had come to serve. Whether it was his own reputedly ineffective instructional methods or an intolerant view of him that underlay his treatment, Monis evidently sought but failed to gain authority in his classroom. Perhaps he had counted upon his erudition as a sufficient force in and of itself to compensate for his evident unpopularity. If the Cambridge ministers who had hired him had harbored an intrinsic respect for him, they apparently failed to convey their enthusiasm to the students. For his part, Monis himself may have been emboldened by the sentiments conveyed by Cotton Mather, who had once written in his diary that "a Jew rarely comes over to us but he brings treasures with him."[75] When Hebrew typeface was finally made available and Monis published his *Grammar of the Hebrew Tongue* in 1735 the advertisement that announced its appearance, in keeping with the idea that its creator's Hebraism conferred a certain paternal authority upon him, made all appropriate claims for the time-tested value of its subject-matter. The book would serve "all those that are desirous to obtain a clear Idea of the primitive Language, in order to aid their more distinct Acquaintance with the sacred Elements of the *Old Testament*, according to the original."[76]

As every historian who has undertaken a retelling of Monis's story has noted, his career as a grammarian was neither remunerative nor intellectually rewarding. Indeed, despite his stated interest in helping to unlock

Hand-copied pages from Judah Monis's *Hebrew Grammar*. From a manuscript copy made by John Cotton (1712–1789) when he was a student of Monis's at Harvard. Before Monis's text was published in 1734, students were required to prepare their own copies of it. Courtesy of the Massachusetts Historical Society.

various Hebrew obscurities and thereby advancing his students' Christianity, his grammar text and his teaching methods were far too "Judaical" for Harvard's tastes. Despite more than adequate precedent for such a thing on the part of language instructors of the day, his habit of requiring students to copy the text word for word appears to have alienated the unwitting scribes. In one of the handful of extant copies of these notebooks, John Cotton, with what looks to have been a measure of annoyance, indicated on his flyleaf that he had "Begun to recite in it Nov. 17, 1727" and "finished I don't know when 1728."[77] Cotton had apparently done his best to entertain himself in the process of copying out the book, as about midway through he began to experiment with several calligraphic variations on the right-hand headers, including "Monis's Hebrew Grammar," "Rabbi Judah Monis," and at one point, Monis's name in Hebrew letters. In one particularly cruel defacement of Monis's text, another student had changed the words "Composed and corrected by Judah Monis, M.A." to "confuted and accurately corrupted by Judah Monis, M(aker) of A(sses)."[78] Whether because of his reputedly awkward pronunciation scheme, the tedium of his methods, or latent hostility directed at a Jew of alien birth, students evidently turned the tables on their instructor, heaping upon him signs of disrespect.

Based on the complaints they were hearing, in May 1724, the Harvard corporation voted "to make enquiry of the method taken by" Monis to teach Hebrew and enforce discipline. One month later, the same body confirmed the previous vote and committed itself to see if the instructor's methods were "such as may answer to ye ends of" the "office and station" to which he had been appointed.[79] In 1758, some students "threw Bricks, Sticks, [and] Ashes at the door of the Hebrew School" while the then seventy-five-year-old instructor was teaching his classes. Though the five perpetrators were punished, this particularly barbarous episode was one of many such humiliations. The harassment of Monis was a frequent and popular activity which even merited its own specialized lingo—"Bulraging [bullyragging] Monis"—and often involved students breaking into the cellar of his home.[80] Harvard itself, as enthusiastically as it had first greeted him, relieved him of all undergraduate teaching responsibilities two years after his arrival. Doubts about his ability to discipline students were sufficient to have disqualified him from personally enforcing any of the College's strict rules pertaining to the study of Hebrew, so that when offenses occurred he was instructed to submit "a list of such as are absent or tardy" to "the President, or [the individual students'] respective tutors."[81]

While George Moore assumed that Monis's having been kept from disciplining his students proceeded from the Harvard overseers not having trusted him, a more contemporary reading by Thomas Siegel suggests that as an instructor, Monis simply did not merit the sorts of powers usually vested in tutors and that a larger debate occurring among the administrators of the college regarding the respective powers of the various officers resulted in the appearance of Monis having been personally slighted when such, in fact, was not the case. Whether or not Monis had been singled out as somehow less deserving of the college's high regard, a preponderance of evidence does show that he was, indeed, unable to gain the respect of the students he had been appointed to teach. Stephen Sewall, his successor in the Hebrew post at Harvard, wrote that during his time as a student of Monis's, despite having "attending his instructions and studied his grammar . . . [he] never could discover any form of comeliness in the language" as Monis taught it.[82] For all of his vaunted authority as a former pupil of Europe's great "rabbins," in other words, Monis had failed at the task of imparting such fatherly "treasures" as Jews were believed, or at least hoped, to bear. Another contemporary informant, Thaddeus Mason Harris, went on record as saying that despite Monis's "fondness for rabbinical lore, his criticism was so abstruse, and his conversation and manners so uncourteous, that he did not conciliate the respect of his pupils."[83] Monis was retained at Harvard until his voluntary retirement in 1760, but neither the record of his salary nor that of his correspondence with the college authorities and tax-levying officials of Cambridge, the latter of whom had an ostensible obligation to abate his fees as an employee of Harvard, suggests that his colleagues and neighbors thought any more highly of him than his students did.

Monis's charge, as he saw it, was "to Teach and Promote the Knowledge of the Hebrew Tongue at HARVARD COLLEGE, in New England, especially for the advantage of those that will Dedicate themselves to the service of the sanctuary."[84] The preface laid out the author's confident promise, based upon his previous learning, that his method allowed for "the Best, Clearest, and Most Necessary" means "to understand the WORD of GOD according to the Original."[85] At the same time, even the bold statements contained in Monis's advertisement were tempered by the instructor's attention to his own indebtedness to such rabbis as had provided him with his learning. Moreover, Monis's attention to his own and his grammar's distinction as imparting an old knowledge was tempered in the statements he made regarding the novelties contained in his book. Just as rabbinical Judaism could only go so far toward establishing Monis's good name among Puritan authorities, his grammar would have as well to offer some novelty along with its erudition. While its most prominent feature for doing so was its inclusion, in an appendix, of both the Lord's Prayer and the Apostles' Creed rendered in Hebrew, its pronunciation apparatus appears to have constituted Monis's boldest, if not entirely successful attempt to establish credibility as a spokesperson for something other than an antiquated Judaism. Despite the pronunciation system's having been "burdened," as Shalom Goldman puts it, "with a system of transliteration for English-speaking students" that severely compromised the book's utility, Monis's scheme did set his work apart from that of the many existing Hebrew grammars of his day that had been produced by Christian Hebraists.[86] "I am very sensible," Monis wrote, "that the way of my pronouncing it [Hebrew] will be somewhat new."[87] Here he claimed for himself and on the basis of his unique qualifications as a Jew by birth, that such novelty could be commensurate with Judaic precedent. "I am prone to think," he continued, "it is the Right and Genuine way, for besides that all the *Jewish Nation* in all their Dispersions do pronounce it as I do, which to me is of no Small Weight, I found in all my Travels, all the Learned in this Tongue that I conversed with among the Europeans (English excepted) do pronounce it the same way also."[88] At several points in the grammar, Monis referred to the use of the language in the present tense, among Jews of his own age, when he pointed out that the "*Hebrews* count by letters," "use the Feminine," or "comprehend" in a particular way. Elsewhere in the grammar, he was sufficiently bold as to name his primary references—"Rabbi David Kinkly, Rabbi Sam[uel] Archibolty, and Rabbi Solomon Temple"—as "the best Grammarians of ye Primitive Tongue hitherto."[89]

Having found initial favor among the promoters of an old-line and retrospective orthodoxy, Monis was an unwieldy vehicle for a Hebraism that had long since lost its privileged place in Puritan discourse. In 1724, Cotton Mather, one of the primary spokesmen for that displaced orthodoxy, referred in his diary to Monis as a "Christianized Jew at Cambridge, who is a Master of the Hebrew Language."[90] Mather thought he might "putt him [Monis] upon collecting and preserving the notable observations, which he makes in reading the Hebrew Bible," but such observations as Monis might have been wont to venture were of little interest to those who were looking for another sort of biblical revelation. Monis's "erudition," to use Mather's word, was not so much rigorous as it was, as several of his students were to write, "tedious," not to mention erratic. If it proceeded from his newfound wonder in Christ's divinity, it was not needed by students who had inherited such faith and taken it for granted their whole lives. His *Grammar of the Hebrew Tongue* presented a succession of self-referential, abstracted rules. His most cogent expression of an underlying purpose and principle for the study of Hebrew came near the end of the book, and for all of its cabbalistic implications, could hardly have ameliorated the thankless rigors of the previous 91 pages. "I would have observed," Monis said with regard to the obscure rules pertaining to certain letters of the Hebrew alphabet, "that the *Stops*, or *Accents*, are not only to give the Reader *Breath* . . . but also to avoid the *confusion* and *obscurity* which otherwise would attend the sense of the *sacred oracles*."[91]

The book ended rather abruptly on this note, which had appended to it a prayer adapted from Zephulon 3.9: "For then will I turn to the People a pure Language that they may all call upon the Name of God, to serve Him with one consent."[92] His ending sounded the long-standing wish of New England's earliest Hebraic proponents—the hope that contact with the "Primitive Tongue" might, in and of itself, instill a graceful transformation. Such things could only be wished for by students who had to labor to get their lessons together. When his methods failed to yield the results that he and his employers sought, but only evoked unruly behavior on the part of his pupils, Monis saw and articulated dire implications. In one letter to the corporation that looks to have been written in the 1740s or 1750s, he warned that Hebrew itself faced "ye Hazard either of Dying, or at least of Growing Wild" at Harvard.[93] In his own way, he was sounding a note similar to the one which the old-line orthodoxy who had originally hired him so frequently used—that of the jeremiad.

By the 1740s Monis was teaching only one day a week, and had long been in the habit of supplementing his academic income with the meager proceeds from the hardware business which he had established in Cambridge in the early 1720s. The fifty pounds he eventually earned annually from Harvard placed him at the very bottom of the College's pay scale.[94] As early as May 1722—within a couple months of his conversion and appointment—Monis had had to resort to the plaintive tones of a supplicant in a note he sent to the overseers.

> However necessary I may apprehend the knowledge of the Hebrew Language to be, and however willing and disposed I may be to teach it, yet Rev'd Gentlemen I, hope, you will give me leave to say, that the salary you have voted as an Encouragement or Reward for my labor is not sufficient to support me. It is not sufficient to sustain me in my single state, much less if I thought to enter into a married state (wch I have some hope of doing . . .)[95]

Monis had either adopted or had imposed upon him the language and tone of a social inferior straining for such regard and treatment as befitted a respected elder. Even as Calvinism lost its influence, the life of a former Jew like Monis would be an enactment of New England's long-standing inability to negotiate the impossible terms of a theology which had deployed the Jewish past as a means of metaphorical, if not literal, communal justification and, at the same time, distrusted all such formulae as presumptuous and corrupt. If Monis could not settle on whether to be obsequious or imperious in his tone, such a result had come about because the New England Hebraism which he had both so fortuitously and so tragically encountered in Cambridge had demanded such ambivalence from him.

It was Monis's misfortune as well to have arrived and attempted a scholarly career in New England during a time at which the clerical profession itself, the necessary training for which had supplied much of the impetus for requiring instruction in Hebrew, began to be supplanted by, among other tendencies, a concentration on law.[96] Monis's letters and Harvard's records limn a steady struggle on his part if not for personal survival than for some measure of respectability in this shifting economic context. An assemblage of less expressive but no less telling records of Monis's financial complaints offers additional insight. Monis was not a perpetual litigant, but his name did appear in Middlesex County court records from 1723, 1729, 1731, and 1736, always as a claimant.[97] In the 1723 case, a civil matter involving a dispute between himself and one Jonathan Willard, Samuel Sewall, who had displayed so keen an interest in Jews earlier on in his life, was the presiding judge. As the end of his career at Harvard approached, Monis submitted petitions, first in 1752 to Harvard, when he was awarded allotments of 8 and then 5 pounds in consideration of "the circumstances of his family."[98] In 1753 and 1759, he submitted petitions to Governor Shirley, both of which referred to his many years of having instructed "the Youth in Ye knowledge of Ye Hebrew Tongue" and not having been afforded a respectable wage for having done so.[99] He had been reduced, his 1750s petitions claimed, to living on less than twenty pounds annually, even though he had been promised a figure much higher than that upon his initial appointment. In one of the petitions, he compared his lot to that "Allowed to Ye Prophesors of Divinity and Mathematicks."[100] He was consistently more than hinting about the monetary value of his contributions, given Harvard's professed interest in "ye Propagation of ye Hebrew Tongue." Neither he nor the overseers of Harvard College, in other words, pretended to inhabit a pristine ivory tower. They coexisted in a rapidly commercializing economic sphere in which bargaining and scheming tactics shaped the discourse.

A complete survey of his actual assets suggests that Monis may not have been as financially insecure as his letters indicate. His intermittent trade as a hardware merchant in Cambridge was hardly lucrative, but it did enable him and his wife to live what looks to have been a stable existence. Early on in his matrimonial life, he had gained a substantial acreage, which ensured him a steady agricultural income. Whether his assets had come to him by way of his own labors, both as a Hebrew instructor and as a merchandiser, or from the Marrett family into which he had married is unclear. His and Abigail's ownership of slaves suggested not only relative economic comfort but an alignment with the elite. Records from the City of Cambridge indicate the marriage intentions in October 1747, of Cicely, "Negro Servant of Judah Monis," to Juba, "Negro Servant of Rev. Pres. Holyoke" (of Harvard).[101] President Holyoke's own diary records his having visited with "Mr. Monis" beginning in 1744 (it is unclear whether the former was accompanied by his slave on these visits) as well as his son's having gone to "Mr. Monis" (to study Hebrew, perhaps?) several times in the years to follow.[102] The marriage between Monis's and Holyoke's slaves probably never took place; the Cambridge record books for December of the same year indicate a new set of marriage intentions between Monis's Cicely and another of his slaves, Cuffe (this same Cuffe had been baptized in Cambridge's First Church, where Monis had undergone his own ceremony, in 1741). While such proximity between a man of Holyoke's station and Monis was not unprecedented (Monis had been ushered into Harvard's fold by none other than Increase Mather, after all), Monis's ownership of slaves in a colony where, though such things were not uncommon, the vast majority of residents did not possess such luxuries, precludes a view of the Hebrew instructor as perpetually cash-strapped and socially excluded.

Moreover, at the end of Monis's life, when he drew up his will, his inventoried assets pointed to something other than a Spartan existence on his part. In 1760, in the aftermath of Abigail's death, he sold a well-appointed Cambridge house and a library that, as advertised, contained "most of the classicks" and also "a variety of books by the best authors, in divinity, history, philosophy, mathematicks, and miscellaneous subjects."[103] Monis's brother-in-law John Martyn provided a comfortable home for the "rabbi's" final years. Monis's will, which he completed in 1761, as well as a codicil he added a year later, stipulated the dispensation of a decent-sized estate, that included acreage, furnishings, his wife's jewelry, and another slave—"my Negro child Moreah"—whom he had either acquired or, perhaps, who had been born to Cicely and Cuffe back in Cambridge.[104] The will's most lasting effect was its inclusion of a provision that was to distribute 50 pounds among the neediest pastors of Worcester County and the seeding of a fund that exists to this day for the widows of Unitarian ministers. More funds were generated after his death upon the sale of Monis's Cambridge house, which had been advertised by his brothers-in-law as "A Good Dwelling House," complete with outbuildings and gardens.[105]

In his material circumstances, then, Monis seems not to have been consigned to the same marginal existence to which his letters pleaded. Those historians who have perhaps, in the spirit of his plaintive rhetorical career, depicted him as a forlorn victim of an underlying conspiracy of anti-Jewish suspicion, have mischaracterized him as a lifelong sufferer of indignities. Monis's life was not free of such cares, but it seems as well to have proceeded in accordance with the social patterns of his day. His learning had served him reasonably well, as had his trading skill. He had, for better or worse, found a family, community, and church life that allowed him to nurture his interest in and commitment to a distinctly New England Hebraism. If his having been a slave-owner did not in and of itself necessarily elevate him into the highest echelons of Cambridge society, it did confer upon him a social status that, until now, historians have withheld from him. Because of his status as New England's most accomplished Hebrew scholar of his day, the attention he has garnered from scholars has always focused on his career's disappointing arc. He has been studied from a theological perspective but rarely seen as a social being whose life took shape in keeping not only with New England's religious life but with its development as an increasingly secular society. By academic standards alone, Monis led a strained existence from the moment of his conversion onward. As an economic being, as a member of a church community, and as a family man, Monis made his way in accordance with the vicissitudes of the age and place in which he lived.

If, as Eisig Silberschlag suggested, Monis poses an enigma to current-day scholars of New England's past and to its Hebraic legacy, he does so for the same reasons that other historical figures often do; he left very little insight into his inner life. If, as Hannah Adams observed in 1812, Monis maintained the Saturday Sabbath up to his death, his having done so does not put the lie to his conversion to Christianity; seventh-day sabbatarianism had had a relatively long history among New England's dissenting sects.[106] Such a practice on his part did not in any way preclude his "true" acceptance of Christ, but it did suggest that that acceptance had not displaced the Hebraism that he shared with so many other New Englanders, if not of his own day then of an earlier time. Monis's relationship to that legacy was certainly more complicated than that of his non-Jewish neighbors, but only because he had inherited that Hebraism upon his birth. Not only does evidence exist to suggest that he never regretted his apostasy, but records from Cambridge's First Church indicate that he was fully accepted as a member of that community. In 1737, he was "publickly declared to be a member . . . and Initiated to all privileges with ye other Brethren."[107] Five years later, he had apparently gained sufficient trust and respect as to be voted a member of the "Committee to Inspect Ye Manners of Professing Christians."[108] All the same, the religion to which he had converted was itself a conflicted one. Monis's life at Harvard provided as profound a testament to that legacy's unwieldiness as New England would ever see.

CHAPTER FOUR

"A HANDSOME ASSEMBLY OF PEOPLE"
Jewish Settlement and the Refinement of New England Culture

THE DEVELOPMENT OF A VIABLE Jewish community in Newport, Rhode Island, in the 1750s coincided with what one historian has famously described as the evolution of religiously pious Puritans into commercially enterprising Yankees.[1] Ironically, this increase in Jewish visibility also coincided with the greatest revival of the Protestant faith to occur during the entire colonial era. Jonathan Edwards, the foremost thinker of this revival, had taken at least passing notice of the growing Jewish presence in British North America. In 1722, two years after he graduated from Yale College and while serving as an apprentice pastor to a group of English Presbyterians, Edwards spent some months living in New York, next door to a Jew. Years later, in his *Treatise Concerning Religious Affections* (1746), he recounted the experience. Edwards must have been something of a nosy neighbor. While studying or resting in his quarters, he "had much opportunity daily to observe [the Jew], who appeared to me to be the devoutest person I ever saw in my life; a great part of his time being spent in acts of devotion, at his eastern window, which opened next to mine, seeming to be most earnestly engaged, not only in the daytime but sometimes whole nights."[2] Edwards's physical encounter with the religious habits of a Jew in North America was an apt illustration of the fact that, by the middle of the eighteenth century, the People of Israel were gaining visibility as practitioners of a living, if divergent faith. For their part, New Yorkers would eventually grow so used to the idea of Jewish worship in the context of an ever-expanding panoply of religious alignments that one of them would include the "Jew's Synagogue" in a panoramic 1771 woodblock print of that city's spire-dominated skyline—the twelfth in an enumeration of twenty-one architectural landmarks, a mere two of which were not houses of worship.

If New England was still a world apart in Edwards's day, it would not be long before its Protestant inhabitants would be forced into an encounter with the inadvertently pluralistic legacy that their forebears' dissenting tradition had wrought. As the influence of British colonial authority and of English culture grew, political expediency had made an expansion of religious tolerance necessary, especially in Rhode Island, whose charter contained no stated impediments to the settlement of "Jews, Turks, and infidels." By 1759, New England would have its first formally constituted Jewish congregation. Four years later the Jews of Newport solidified their claim to permanence in New England by building the shrine to colonial gentility and Judaic heritage that would come to be called the Touro Synagogue. While Edwards and several other instigators of the mid-eighteenth-century Great Awakening had been raised in and had instilled in them the unique tradition of New England Puritanism, their revival far exceeded the geographical boundaries and theological parameters of New England. An expansion of commercial and cultural ties between North America, the West Indies, and the entire British Atlantic resulted in the diminishment of New England's sense not only of its influence but of its own cultural, economic, and religious autonomy. Thus, the very movement whose foremost ministers were poised to import a revitalized Puritanism throughout the colonies was, at the same time, the product and most evident symbol of New England's very eclipse. The formal establishment of New England's first Jewish congregation, though it bore no direct connection to the Awakening itself, manifested many of the same cultural trends that fueled the Protestant revival, and it also offered further evidence of New England's absorption into the larger Atlantic world.

Despite his lifelong devotion to the study of Hebrew,[3] Edwards was no admirer of Jews, and his description of his Jewish neighbor was pointed. He deployed it in order to challenge his audience, reminding them that the most devoted outward show of Christian religiosity, like the Christless davening of a Jew, was devoid of spiritual import and, often enough, a means of concealment as opposed to a demonstration of true piety. In his autobiographical writings and sermons, Edwards had often sounded a similar note, holding out the example of his own youthful "affections" of religiosity in order to confront his hearers with the measure of their own sanctimony. His eventual fame resulted from his role as a central figure in the Great Awakening, the massive revival that both renewed the "faith of the fathers" and, more important, helped to overspread much of the Atlantic world with a new and often electrifying form of pietism. As New England religion gained wider influence, however, it began to lose its local footing and distinct character. The growing impact of itinerant preachers, with whom Edwards was loosely affiliated, was a symptom of a large-scale restlessness that threatened the long-standing integrity and autonomy of individual churches and their parishes.

The Sephardic merchants who created Newport's Yeshuat Israel and built British North America's second synagogue (Jews, who had been present in New York since 1654, had commenced public worship in 1704 and built their first synagogue at Mill Street in 1730) had coped well with life on a cultural threshold. As they sought to establish a formal Jewish community, they confronted their gentile neighbors with their own looming future, in which religious life, even among its most devout practitioners, would, as Timothy Hall puts it, become an adjunct to life in "an increasingly mobile, pluralistic world."[4] The burgeoning of an expansive transnational religious life occurred not in opposition to the era's commercialism but, on the contrary, as an integral aspect of it. Scholars once posited an airtight "declension" model of New England history, in which the descendants of seventeenth-century settlers lapsed at an exponential rate into a religion that lacked both the severity and centrality of Puritanism. The revivals that began occurring in the 1740s, however, were simply too powerful to be dismissed as merely reactionary attempts at reduplicating the lost piety of the past, and to the extent that they were inspired not by an established orthodoxy but by an enthusiastic lower order, the preponderance of evidence shows that the Great Awakening was a dynamic cultural event that encompassed and embraced, rather than shunned, market forces, pluralism, and transatlantic influences.

For obvious reasons, Jews were not participants in the Awakening, but their establishment of a fixed congregation in Newport occurred in the immediate aftermath of Edwards's and others' stirring achievements among not only New England Congregationalists, but dissenters of various denominations and even Anglicans. The development of what Thomas

Kidd calls a "Protestant interest" throughout the Atlantic world was not merely an ecumenical movement, nor was it a compromising gesture toward official tolerance.[5] Because it so effectively dislodged the calcified religious orders at both ends of the New England religious and social spectrum, it heightened awareness of preexisting fault lines. The Awakening fomented, or was perceived as fomenting, a profound social upheaval. It did more than pit the adherents of dissenting sects against the established Congregational—or Anglican—orthodoxy. The activities of itinerant preachers manifested economic tensions between the members of the older merchant class and those of the new. The anomaly of an established Jewish congregation, even in reputedly licentious Rhode Island, called new attention to all of these fault lines.

Leaving aside the culturally exotic nature of Sephardic Jewish worship, the Newport Jews lived out every one of the points of tension that the revivals of the mid-eighteenth century had "awakened." First, by North American standards, the Newport Jews were urbane, and their ties to the network of Jewish merchants on both sides of the Atlantic conferred upon them an extreme form of transatlantic cosmopolitanism that actually exceeded that of the Protestant revivalists. Second, though several of the Newport Sephardim grew to be prosperous merchants, these men had not risen from the ranks of any sort of even pretended aristocracy. Their successful pursuit of wealth and their fashioning of a "new" aristocracy mirrored the rise of New England's "native"-born and newly successful merchant class. Their religious practice, which had both its opulent and its improvisatory, or provincial, sides, followed suit. Although the Newport Jews attempted to achieve orthodoxy in their practice, their *marrano* background and the enormous distance that separated them from other, more established Jewish congregations (not to mention centers of Jewish learning) often impinged on that ability, even as it inspired innovative adaptations on their part that, in their own way, resembled the improvisatory nature of the Awakening.

The Newport Jews exemplified the same profound split that the Great Awakening wrought between a stable, hierarchically ordered, and more often than not *localized* congregationalism, on the one hand, and a globalizing, sometimes commercially inspired if not commercially driven religious fervor that exceeded the bounds of a "specific local network of relationships by ties of kinship and obligation."[6] Though they were mere bystanders to the Great Awakening itself, the Jews of Newport straddled many of the same social and cultural divides that characterized Protestant New England in its aftermath. During their ascendancy in Rhode Island, between the 1740s and the heyday of their congregational life on the eve of the Revolution, the Newport Jews did more than merely illustrate how far New England had come from its early days of religious intolerance. Their many cultural differences from the surrounding Protestant milieu notwithstanding, the Jews of Newport reminded their gentile neighbors of how closely and precariously they themselves were poised at the edge of a new and changing world. A key point in all of this was the idea that New England itself could no longer think of itself as central to God's plan, much less "chosen."

The single force that made such a visible Jewish presence possible in Rhode Island was the growing British colonial interest, which had never looked particularly kindly upon the idea, much less the implementation of New England exceptionalism. As New Englanders Anglicized themselves not only in religious terms but economically, politically, socially, and culturally as well, their religious expression followed suit. Their long-standing preference for local control gave way not to a *decline* in religious observance or affiliation but to a *proliferation* of it. The "illusion of decline," as Patricia Bonomi suggests, masked the new reality, which was that the all-encompassing "veritable utopia" that the founders had sought to create in the mid-seventeenth century had collapsed not as a result of irreligion but as a consequence of a new multiplicity in religious life that its own dissenting tradition had ensured would eventually occur. A growing sense of Englishness among New Englanders of all religious persuasions, from the most cantankerous members of the most dissenting sects, to the established old-line Congregational clergy, to the ever more powerful social and political elites of the Anglican church offset the pre-existing norm, in which New England, if it hadn't exactly been a "New Israel," had been thought to be a special place with a special history.

The merchants who replenished Newport's Jewish ranks in the middle part of the eighteenth century would not have come there if it had been anything less than a promising starting point for fledgling and enterprising commercial endeavors. They certainly would not have made their homes there if it lacked potential as a jumping-off point for the transatlantic and intercolonial trade that alignment with England made possible. Newport was appealing because, while it was a product of the Puritan revolution of the seventeenth century, it was also an exception to the New England rule. Its origins as a haven for various types of religious misfits had a distinctly Puritan, or dissenting cast to it, but—at the same time—its tradition of relative tolerance gave its settlers an early acquaintance and even a level of comfort with the same sort of flux and social mobility that, by the middle of the eighteenth century, was beginning to characterize the rest of New England. Localism and social fixity had been more quickly dispensed within Rhode Island than elsewhere in New England, as the colony's very founding had been an act calculated to create a diverse population of commercially enterprising outliers. From the standpoint of its Jews, in any case, the colony offered an ease of access to markets throughout the Atlantic world. At the same time, and in part because its roots lay in the Puritan movement, by the middle of the eighteenth century Rhode Island was a provincial extension of Britain, a milieu in which the rights and protections accorded British citizens throughout the world were solidified. For Jews, who had only recently escaped the persecutions of the Inquisition, the crown was an attractive and likely guarantor of safety.

As we have seen, Jews had been residents of Rhode Island as far back as the middle decades of the seventeenth century. The exact chronology of their first hundred years has proved difficult to trace beyond a certain outline. Initial, though almost certainly impermanent settlement in the late 1650s led to the establishment of a burial ground in 1677. Less than ten years later, a handful of Jewish merchants in the colony sought and apparently gained redress against the attempts of William Dyer to challenge their right to trade freely. Several decades passed in which no "news" of Jewish Rhode Islanders emerged, save Samuel Sewall's brief 1704 diary reference to the transportation from Boston and burial of Joseph Frazon in "the Jews' burial place" in Newport.[7] The strongest likelihood, in any case, is that even the relatively large influx of Jews from Curaçao that came to Newport in the 1690s was ephemeral, and that that group dispersed within a short space of time. Many of the names associated with the Curaçaoan contingent surfaced later in connection with other Jewish congregations in the Atlantic world, particularly in New York.

Records of renewed Jewish activity in Newport begin in 1705, when a Jew was licensed to manufacture soap in the colony of Rhode Island.[8] A map published in 1712 indicated the existence of a "Jews' Street" in the center of town, but at least one historian claims that in 1712 that street name may have been more of a *commemoration* of a Jewish presence than a label meant to point out ongoing activity.[9] In any case, when a synagogue was eventually built to accommodate a bustling community of Jews in the 1760s, it was indeed built on that same street, which has since come to be called "Touro" in honor of the congregation's leader, or *hazzan* Isaac Touro, as well as his son Judah, who would go on to become one of the antebellum United States' greatest philanthropists and noteworthy Jews. In 1712, the street's earlier name spoke, most likely, to the intermittent presence of a merchant community which had either derived directly from Newport's seventeenth-century Jewish population or was a replenishment of it from other sources than the original ones.

Jacob Marcus suggests the existence of a viable minyan in Newport by sometime in the 1740s, a point by which, according to an earlier historian's count, at least nine Jewish families were residents of the town.[10] Indeed, the arrival of two family groups in particular, the Riveras and the Lopezes, seems to have catalyzed the movement toward the establishment of a congregation. Moses Lopez, a Portuguese *marrano*, arrived in Newport in 1743, having first escaped the Inquisition by traveling to England and then becoming naturalized in New York. He is also known to have earned an exemption from paying taxes by serving as an official translator of Spanish for the colony of Rhode Island (Judah Monis provided a similar service for Massachusetts authorities during the same decade). Abraham Rodrigues Rivera surfaced five years later, and Moses' younger half-brother Aaron Lopez, who would come to be known as the "merchant prince of Newport," arrived in 1752. Rivera is known to have been Rhode Island's first manufacturer of spermaceti candles, starting in the 1740s. In 1753 the colony of Rhode Island granted the elder Lopez a unique license on the basis of his having "made himself master of the true art and mystery of making potash, which is known to few in the kingdom."[11]

Judaically speaking, the arrival of the Riveras and the Lopezes was significant because it was accompanied by several deliberate acts on their part to assert a Jewish affiliation. While in New York, Abraham Rivera is known to have been an active member of the Jewish congregation of that city; on that basis, Marcus suggests that he later became "a guiding spirit" behind the formation of Newport's own Jewish community.[12] The most dramatic story, however, was that of Aaron Lopez, who, along with his brother Moses, had been raised as an observant Catholic in Portugal. How or why Moses came to Newport is unknown, but when Aaron joined him there in 1752, the family began its open assertions of Jewish identity. Aaron was twenty-one when he arrived in Rhode Island. Safe from the Inquisition, he went out of his way to assert a recovered Jewish identity. On August 8, 1756, Lopez wrote to Abraham Abrahams, the *mohel* resident in New York, thanking him for offering to perform a *brit milah*, or circumcision on him and his son Joseph but indicating that he would not be free to travel for a while, "on acct of my prentice being out of his time & gone."[13] One month later, Lopez heard from Abrahams with regard to a mutual friend of theirs, a "Mr. Marks," who was soon to be released from jail and would then be free to attend "Ros Hasana" services at the Mill Street synagogue. Whether Lopez himself traveled to New York for the same purpose or found a minyan in Newport is unknown, but the Shearith Israel rolls for February 1757 indicate the dual circumcision there of Lopez, father and son.[14] The ritual itself ushered in a new identity for the entire Lopez group, as Aaron, whose birth name had been Duarte, took a Hebrew name. His wife, Anna, was renamed Abigail and, several years later, after Abigail's premature death, the woman Lopez took as his second wife, Catherine, became Sarah. As the Newport group would soon be enlarged by the arrival of another contingent from Portugal in the aftermath of the 1755 earthquake and the Inquisition's redoubled efforts to root out all Judaizers, sufficient ground was laid for the creation of a permanent religious community. Marcus suggests that an additional and slightly earlier impetus for the community's establishment was the English Parliament's 1751 decision to ensure the stabilization of New England's paper currency.[15]

Where Protestants of various stripes had developed a long-standing allegiance to New England itself and to the idea of local control over their congregational life, Jews were newcomers to such local affiliations. Their ascendancy as visible and formally constituted worshippers in their own tradition coincided with and, indeed, was a direct outgrowth of a new diversification of religious practice. No claim that the Awakening had the slightest direct effect upon the Jews of colonial America can be made, "except," writes Jonathan Sarna, "insofar as it altered and further diversified the religious environment in which Judaism operated."[16] But diversification was equivalent not only to fragmentation and tumult but to widening, often extra-regional allegiances, especially in parishes whose original establishment had occurred in the context of the region's earliest settlement. For Christians, the development of a worldwide, or at least Atlantic-world "Protestant interest" was something of a novelty. Jews, though their tradition knew no such thing as a grand-rabbinical council, were quite accustomed to participating in the community of *klal Israel* and to communications on all matters of religious interest with their distant brethren. What was new for them, especially given the generations of mobility that the *marranos* had experienced, was the idea of developing local allegiances. For the first time in the lives of most of them, these Jews were poised not only to settle permanently in one place but to assemble a congregational life which would put them, as practitioners of yet one more variety of religious faith, on an almost even footing with Christians in their community.

The apparent disequilibrium between the Jews' tentative status as Rhode Islanders and their much more long-standing mobility and connection to the network of transatlantic trade and Sephardic communal life played out in a similar dynamic to that in which the surrounding Christian community had been experiencing in the Great Awakening. The Awakening, too, had manifested quite contradictory tendencies. At its inception, it had all the appearance of an attempt at retrenchment, of the simple restoration of a long-departed Puritan piety in a milieu that had lost its grounding in the precious tradition of New England's founders. Because of the transatlantic context in which it took shape, however, Puritanism itself had wrought more multiplicity than it had sought, creating what one historian refers to as "a bewildering array of ethnic and cultural enclaves along the rim of the Atlantic."[17] In reaction to the broad and centralizing realm of the established church in England, the Puritans who founded Massachusetts Bay had developed all manner of *decentralized* institutions. Their varying degrees of dissent and their fundamentally anti-clerical theology had, after a hundred years anyway, resulted in an extensive denominationalism and an increasingly powerful system of local control. One parish after the other went to sleep, figuratively, lulled into an ever-deepening provincialism whose effect was to sunder congregants from whatever connections they had once had to the hard-won spiritual and emotional rigors of the earlier days. When itinerant preachers like George Whitfield appeared on the scene, however, their "restoration" of the earlier faith took shape not by recalling auditors to Puritanism's powerful history of decentralization but by conjuring and harnessing a new energy that was drawn from the age's advancing and often commercially based transoceanic tendencies. Whitfield himself, as Timothy Hall points out, "provided personal, representative content with what was soon to become a vast 'imagined community' of saints that transcended geographic and denominational lines through a common experience of the new birth."[18]

Though hardly revivalist in their tendencies or theology, the Sephardic Jews who built a community in Newport certainly shared the Awakening's interest in shaping the sort of Andersonian "imagined community" to which Hall refers. Indeed, though rebirth has never been stipulated in any Judaic practice, the fact that so many of Newport's Jews had undergone the collective *marrano* experience and had survived by *sublimating* as opposed to projecting their Judaism meant that their development of a deliberately Jewish milieu in the New World had about it an air of exactly such a spirit of regeneration. Aaron Lopez and his family had certainly undergone a rebirth of sorts in the tolerant atmosphere or British North America. A key element in his and others' reclamation of their long-hidden Judaism was the existence of and, indeed, the deliberate sponsorship they received at the hands of other already established Jews and Jewish congregations. In this regard, the assertion of a Jewish presence in mid-eighteenth-century Newport had its own version of "internationalism" in common with the Awakening. The trajectories were reversed—Jews were moving *from* a purely transatlantic milieu in the direction of localism, while New England's Protestants were enacting an opposite transition from a localized and decentralized religious life toward what Thomas Kidd calls a "new, increasingly revivalist, decreasingly doctrinaire Protestant interest."[19] Despite the asymmetry of their respective movements, both groups were negotiating the tension between localizing and broadening impulses, and both were subject to the revivifying and potentially fragmenting effects of that split.

A central factor underlying and fueling the Great Awakening had been the growing tendency toward Anglicization, a movement that gained momentum in the wake of the Glorious Revolution of 1689. The broadening commercialism of the early and mid-eighteenth century, leading as it did to participation in the much-disparaged "empire of goods," promoted a thickening as well of economic and social ties to the mother country.[20] New Englanders of the eighteenth century, or at least those who were descended from the original settlers, may have lost any direct sense of what life in England had been like, but they more than compensated for the lack of such memories through their increasing sense of cultural and political affinity for newer English fashions. Provinciality had wrought an odd result, as the Great Awakening redoubled the building sense of transatlantic and Anglocentric common culture. Though perhaps quite inadvertently, preachers like Whitfield and Edwards were encouraging, through such devices as a transatlantic "concert of prayer" that they had organized in the mid-1740s—"an *imported*, transatlantic religious strategy."[21] Their work "contributed to the ongoing integration of New England into an imperial order, even as revivalists excoriated the corrupting consequences of the empire of goods."[22] A deepening affiliation with all such "outside" and apparently modernizing influences, in other words, had ensured that the Great Awakening, far from being any kind of reactionary effort to restore a long-departed "faith of the fathers," would take shape as an adaptive force and as a means not of slowing religion's progress in New England but of accelerating its ability to play a role in the daily lives of its practitioners. Indeed, to the extent that the Awakening has been understood to have been a behavioral and even an ideological precursor and preparation for the American Revolution itself, its embrace of the "Anglo-American consumer market"[23] and its promotion of a broadening sense of extra-regional Protestant affiliations helped to create such a result.

When itinerant preachers were depicted as dangerous disruptors of social tranquility and stability, it was their very itinerancy that instigated such fears. A convergence of seemingly unaligned forces had arrayed against the status quo and given birth to a largely sublimated resentment of imminent change, whether it came in the form of religious fragmentation, excessive "opulence," commercial drive, or various kinds of "leveling" tendencies.[24] Strangely enough, the Jewish settlement at Newport, though it escaped opposition and was quite openly tolerated in a Rhode Island that had long since adjusted to such fluctuations, manifested every one of these potentially fearful attributes. Its unabashedly Judaic worship reified Roger Williams's once entirely metaphorical openness to "Jews, Turks, and infidels," and, short of the allowance of Catholicism, indicated an end to Rhode Island's and New England's singularly Protestant practice. The Jews of Newport also displayed the potentially transformative power of wealth. Though Aaron Lopez was by far more successful and more broadly engaged, commercially speaking, than any of the other Jews in the town, a significant number of his coreligionists were, for a period of time, at least, sufficiently prosperous as to be quite visibly so, and the synagogue they eventually built was a showpiece if not of ostentation then at least of a sublimated aesthetic grace that could have been possible only with their funding largesse. The overarching commercialism that created such wealth and social mobility for the Jews was an instigator behind their strengthening communal and religious ties to one another, suggesting a further connection between a globalizing and expansive force and an enhanced religiosity. Finally, even though some of the Sephardic merchants first arrived in Newport with sufficient capital to advance the cause of their individual and collective wealth, "leveling" was a factor in the Jewish settlement as well, as a heretofore ostracized people of foreign birth were able, in the space of less than two decades, not only to enter the ranks of the town's most prosperous merchants but to collaborate on the building of a handsome and elegant monument both to their shared heritage and to their collective accomplishments in the New World.

Although Jews had been projecting some kind of collective future for themselves in Newport at least as far back as their earliest establishment of a burial ground in 1677, serious talk of creating a fixed congregation and place of worship did not get underway until 1754, when the group began referring to itself in a body as Nephuse (Scattered Ones) of Israel. In 1757 Aaron Lopez went as far as ordering lamps, siddurim, and mezzuzot from a shipping house in London, though, as Jacob Marcus speculates, he may have meant these as furnishings for his family's home.[25] The materials, it turned out, were not available in London, Lopez's English correspondent Abraham Hart wrote, and would have to be sought from Amsterdam.[26] In 1759 a land purchase was made. In March of that same year a group consisting of nine Newport Jews, including both Aaron and Moses Lopez, as well as Abraham Rodrigues Rivera, posted a letter to Shearith Israel in

New York, asking for monetary assistance. The members of the group pronounced themselves "sincerely desirous to establish a regular congregation" in Newport.[27] Even by the late 1750s, however, Aaron Lopez alone represented a significant degree of opulence; the Newport group was not in a position to undertake the cost of the venture without generous assistance. Funds for the building of the synagogue came not only from New York but from Jewish congregants in London, Jamaica, Curaçao, Surinam, and Barbados, and were certainly necessary given the cost of the effort, which Jacob Marcus estimates to have been a total of two thousand pounds from beginning to end.[28]

The future well-being of their religious community was advanced by the Newport Jews' large-scale appeal for help from a loose network of coreligionists, trading partners, and kin on both sides of the Atlantic. The letter that the group had addressed to their New York counterparts appealed in just such terms. The effort began in their own quarters, as the group indicated its already having "raised a small Fund wherewith to Begin."[29] A broader appeal to the larger Jewish world was a necessary piece of their efforts, however. "At present finding our Abilities not equal to our wishes," they wrote, "we have resolved to crave the Assistance of Several Congregations in America."[30] The letter made no pretense of being anything other than a fundraising effort, and its writers explained their timing with complete candor; they knew that Passover would bring more potential donors to their effort into the New York synagogue, and hoped on that basis to garner a larger number of contributions. Their appeal was no "concert of prayer," along Edwardsian lines, but it did contain deliberate references to something like a worldwide effort to build and sustain a sense of Jewish solidarity that was not terribly different from the transatlantic efforts that underlay the "pan-Protestantism" to which post-Puritan New Englanders, especially those who participated in the Awakening, hewed.

Accordingly, the letter concluded by calling attention to a universal Judaism. Notwithstanding the letter's rhetorical invocation of the ancient tradition, its sounding of such themes in the context of a fundraising effort had about it a uniquely modern aspect, one that could only have taken shape in an age of large-scale, highly organized commercial enterprise and the era's burgeoning "print capitalism." Even though some Newport Jews knew some New York Jews personally, the Shearith letter (which had counterparts posted to other contributing congregations as well) invoked just the sort of "imagined community" to which Benedict Anderson refers and Timothy Hall speaks of in direct connection with the Great Awakening.

> When we reflect on how much it is our Duty, to Instruct Children, in the Path of Vertuous Religion; & how unhappy the portions must be, of those Children, and their Parents, who are thro necessity, educated in a place where they must remain almost totally uninstructed, in our most Holy & Divine Law, our Rites & Ceremonies; & from which Place, they may perhaps never have it in their power to depart; when we farther reflect on how much it is our Duty to assist the Distressed; & and when we consider the extensive usefulness of a charity, like this for which we now supplicate assistance, we can entertain no Doubt of your Zeal, to promote this good work.[31]

The letter achieved its desired result, as Shearith Israel's reply, posted after the group had undertaken a collection on the seventh day of Passover, indicated that 149 pounds had been raised toward the building of a synagogue in Newport. When the Newporters wrote to thank the New Yorkers for their help two months later, they once again cited the sense of common purpose that had inspired both Shearith Israel's generosity and their own gratitude by invoking a sense of mutual benefit that could only have taken shape in an atmosphere of extraregional commerce and cooperation. The letter's seemingly perfunctory pronouncement of thanks was, indeed, part and parcel of the discursive context that had inspired it, in which a formulaic social grace was merely the newest instrument by which otherwise disparate selves and communities bridged the gaps between their circumstances. "It is our Inclination," the Newport group wrote, "& we are truly sensitive it is our Duty to return the Congregation at New York our most sincere & publick Thanks for this Instance of their Generous Benevolence towards us."[32]

In every conceivable way, the Newport Jews were tied to their counterparts not only in New York, but throughout the Americas and in Europe as well. The connections that bound them one to another extended beyond the ordinary commercial and kinship networks that predated their building of New England's first Jewish congregation. Even before they had a synagogue available to them, in 1760, they corresponded with Jews in foreign parts on religious matters. Moreover, evidence exists of their having read published Jewish material of general interest. In November 1760, three years before the completion and dedication of the synagogue, the *Newport Mercury* published a notice indicating the availability "For sale, at Shop adjoining Printing office, middle of Parade [Street] of a 'Published Sermon on the death of the English King at the Synagogue of the Portuguese Jews in London.'"[33] Unless the seller was a curious Christian, all likelihood is that both he and the potential buyers were Newport's own Jews, who by 1761 numbered some fifty-six individuals and ten families, according to Ezra Stiles, the pastor of the town's Second Congregational Church (see Chapter 5). The published sermon itself had been delivered by Isaac Mendez Belisario, and by way of commemorating the recent death of George II, it advanced a distinctly modernizing and globalizing sense of Jewish identity vis-à-vis the Jews' recently having gained rights of citizenship as British subjects. In the sermon, which he himself had translated from the Spanish, Belisario paid homage to the man who had been the Jews' protector over several decades, drawing an extended comparison of him to King David. "How much ought we as *Israelites* to reverence his precious Memory," Belisario wrote, "even more than the rest of his loyal subjects, since we Owe to him an additional Mark of Gratuity."[34]

Like their brethren in London, Newport Jews articulated the gratitude of protected subjects, even in the days preceding their legal naturalization. In this way, they expressed allegiance to both their local milieu and the "imagined" or hypothetical surrounding world of such entities as provincial authority and the crown itself. They did so by direct means, through such expressions as their participation in and charitable contributions to common endeavors such as the establishment, in Newport, of a reading library. When the Redwood Library was founded in 1747, Abraham Hart, Moses Lopez, and Jacob Rodrigues Rivera became immediate subscribers to it. Years later, as Moses Brown mounted an effort to create Rhode Island's first institution of higher learning, Aaron Lopez and Jacob Rivera contributed five- and ten-thousand board feet of lumber, respectively, toward its construction.[35] Jews were also active in the city's Masonic order, as fifteen of them were initiated into its membership. Jews also promoted the general interest through their engagement of an international Jewish community which, in its own turn, sought every opportunity to align itself with the protective authority of the crown. This kind of loyalty stood both

the Newporters and their English Jewish counterparts in good stead until
the eve of the American Revolution, when the legitimacy of that authority
was called into question by a growing number of patriotic New England
merchants. In the meantime, from the Jewish perspective, alignment with
the broader and largely abstract and unseen *concept* of the English crown
and Parliament suggested itself as a prudent course. Like so many of their
gentile neighbors throughout New England, the Jews associated not only
their individual and communal safety with English authority but their very
identity.

As Belisario's sermon indicated, Jews had a long and venerable tradition
of seeking the protection of "foreign" kings, stretching back to ancient
times and captivities in Babylon and Rome, among other places. What was
new here was the additional abstract quality that only a modern era could
confer, in which Jewish interest was identical to a larger sense of social
and economic well-being that transcended mere protection and spoke in
more ideological terms to an early Enlightenment worldview. Jews constituted one constituency among many others whose future was tethered
to a political entity much larger than themselves and their discrete interests. "*Morality and Religion are the Soul of Republics,*"[36] wrote Belisario, invoking a newly minted ecumenical perspective that resembled, if it didn't
exactly match, the view that was ascendant among a growing number of
Christians on both sides of the Atlantic and even in fiercely independent
New England, that people of varying religious persuasions, or "societies,"
could, in fact, be common subjects of the same overarching political protector. Though the Great Awakening had borne some of the earmarks of
a localized rejection of such worldly and rational entities as governments
and empires, its greatest proponents rarely hesitated to invoke the abstract
rights represented by and protected by the authority of English identity,
even in the context of their broader rejection of civil authority. As one participant in the movement put it in 1744, "The Rights of Magna Charter
depend not on the will of a Prince, or the Will of the Legislature; but they
are the inherent natural Rights of Englishmen."[37]

By 1764, according to Ezra Stiles's count, the Newport Jews numbered
twenty families. Five years later, the number had increased to twenty-five,
and in 1774, when the minister conducted his final survey, he noted that
Newport, a city of approximately 10,000 residents, had two hundred res-

Touro Synagogue, Newport, Rhode Island. Dedicated in 1763 and named for its first *hazzan*, the Dutch-born Isaac Touro, it is the oldest synagogue in the United States. Photograph by Saul Woythaler provided through the courtesy of Congregation Jeshuat Israel, Newport.

ident Jews.[38] Though he appears to have taken considerable liberties in extrapolating from the handful of existing sources and his broader knowledge of Sephardic ritual, Morris Gutstein's romanticizing description of the new synagogue's dedication ceremony probably doesn't overstate the case for the event's alien quality. New England eyes and ears, unused to any ritual practices outside of baptism and communion, which themselves had engendered a fair amount of controversy over the years, could not but have been struck by what occurred and how carefully choreographed it had all been. The Jews had prepared themselves well, or had at least been sure to enlist the services of a properly trained *hazzan*. Young as he was, Isaac Touro had studied, like many before him, in the "Jewish academies of Amsterdam." He had been in Newport three years, having arrived there from Holland by way of New York at the age of twenty.

> At the appointed time, when the doors of the synagogue were closed and dead silence reigned . . . three knocks were heard . . . After these three knocks, the voice of the Reverend Isaac Touro was plainly heard, chanting in Hebrew, "Lift up your heads, o ye gates, and be lifted up, ye everlasting doors, that the King of Glory may come in." From within the synagogue came the response, also in Hebrew, "Who is the King of Glory?" To which

. . . Touro replied, "The Lord of Hosts; He is the King of Glory. Selah. Open for me the gates of righteousness, I wish to enter them."[39]

As Gutstein depicts the event, the synagogue's doors were then opened, as was the Ark containing the Torah. A procession followed, in which several Scrolls of the Law were carried through the synagogue and a requisite seven circuits were made by the congregation's most prominent members. The attendants, who included Ezra Stiles (his diary constituted one of Gutstein's most important sources on how the ceremony was conducted) and a large party of other visiting gentiles, had been witnesses to one of New England's first, if not most carefully articulated exposures to the outside world of religious and cultural difference.

Stiles, who was the author of the December 5, 1763 announcement in the Newport Mercury of the brand-new synagogue's dedication ceremony, expressed a palpable enchantment that no activity in any Protestant church could have evoked for him. Where Jews would gradually adapt to the Anglo-American tradition of the sermon, the descendants of New England Puritans had not yet acquiesced to the sorts of ritualistic practices that had inspired their initial rebellion against England's all-too popish established clergy. Far from instigating horror, however, the new synagogue's own ceremonialism conjured an appreciation on the writer's part for the elegance of the ancient traditions of the Jews and an attention to the atmosphere of mutuality that they created. The announcement in the newspaper was nothing if not sympathetic, and did not neglect to mention the Jews' gesture of loyalty not only to their own tradition but to the protecting authority of the crown. The writer's words seem to have been calculated to garner the broader admiration of a gentile audience whose members would have been sensitized not only to the practice of an exotic religion but to the display of grace, stability, and elegance—all qualities that New Englanders, of the Congregational variety at least, had long since foresworn.

On Friday last . . . was the Dedication of the new synagogue, in this town. It began by a handsome Procession, in which were carried the Books of the Law, to be deposited in the Ark. Several portions of Scripture, and of their Service, with a Prayer for the Royal Family, were read and, finely sung by the Priest and People. There were present many Gentlemen and Ladies. The

Touro Synagogue (interior). Note the similarity in the decor to that of London's Bevis Marks, as well as the contrast between the staid look of the exterior and the considerably more lavish sanctuary. Photograph by John Hopf provided through the courtesy of Congregation Jeshuat Israel, Newport.

Order and Decorum, the Harmony and Solemnity of the Musick, together with a handsome Assembly of People, in an Edifice the most perfect of the Temple Kind perhaps in America, and splendidly illuminated could not but raise in the Mind a faint idea of the Majesty and Grandeur of the ancient Jewish worship mentioned in Scripture.[40]

Stiles's solicitude toward the Jews' ceremonialism and his lavish description of the event's attention to "Order," "Decorum," "Harmony," and
"Solemnity" are surprising, considering the lack of patience he exhibited
in his many descriptions, or caricatures, of a similarly decorous Anglican
worship. In the broader sense, however, individual loyalties and affiliations would have been moot. The synagogue's enactment of an ancient
tradition whose practitioners could be found engaging in the same exact
practices in dozens of cities throughout the Atlantic world and beyond was
reminiscent of, if not exactly parallel to, the concomitant tendency that
had arisen among even the most unruly Awakeners who chose to meld
their religious practice to the terms set by a "new mobile world of commerce and communication."[41] When New Englanders sought the minis-
trations of visiting pastors, as they did in great numbers during and in the
aftermath of the Awakening, they did so because they had developed what
Timothy Hall calls "an eagerness to reach beyond the confines of the parish for sources of participatory belonging in a way that paralleled long-dis-
tance participation in other areas of social, cultural, and economic life."[42]
The Jews of Newport had managed to bring such a result about largely
by virtue of their preexisting ties to other Jews in other places, as well as
through their evolving awareness, as newly Judaized *marranos*, of the texts
and tenets of their faith.

While the Jews' clear display of a religious faith of an indeterminate
temporal and geographical provenance echoed or even amplified at least
some New Englanders' relatively recent embrace of a similarly transatlantic approach, there was much in their worship to make others among their
Christian neighbors unhappy, even if their denial of Jesus Christ had not
been a factor. Ceremonialism itself, as Edwards and any number his of
Puritan predecessors had pointed out for generations on end, was a dead
letter and comparable in the view of the itinerants and their "New Light"
allies to the "dead formalism" of the Pharisees.[43] It was a Judaic trait that
no self-respecting Protestant could countenance. When Gilbert Tennent,
the Irish-born Presbyterian minister whose regular visits to pulpits
throughout the colonies and especially the Middle Atlantic region gave his
famous and condemnatory 1740 sermon, "The Danger of an Unconverted
Ministry," he pronounced the worst faults of the dissipated and compla-
cent clergy to be their singular resemblance to those Jewish officers who

had rejected the radical teachings of Jesus—men who "were bloated with intellectual conceit, letter-learned but blind to the Truths of the Savior."[44] These were men, Tennent asserted, who "loved the uppermost Seats in the Synagogues, and to be called, Rabbi, Rabbi."[45] Tennent was not the first American Protestant to use the example of the Jews as an occasion for a radical critique of ridicule of established churchmen, but his pronouncement was unique because it came at a time when, indeed, it was possible—or soon would be—for Christians such as himself to witness actual Jews occupying seats in actual synagogues.

Judaism, as practiced in Newport and elsewhere, was quite pointedly uncharismatic, and, at least, in the earliest years of the Jewish presence in America, unabashedly formalistic. The Judaism practiced in colonial synagogues like the one in Newport was a far cry from the often sectarian and cantankerous Judaism of the twentieth century. It "was not . . . something one debated intellectually," writes Jacob Marcus. Rather, "it was something one practiced, lived—and enjoyed . . . the sub-stratum of [one's] life, automatically and spontaneously expressed . . . a socio-ritualistic faith, a culture-religion."[46] As such, and because its advancement was sponsored by men who were themselves not particularly well-versed in its teachings, traditions, or even most basic liturgies, Tennent's points of contention would have been moot. Indeed, to an even greater degree than the most democratized Protestant and dissenting churches, Judaism deemphasized rabbinical leadership by necessity if not by theological preference; the New World contained no place even approaching the status of a Jewish seminary, and only the Jewish communities of cities like London and Amsterdam trained significant numbers of scholars. The first formally trained and ordained rabbi in North America would not arrive until the 1820s.

Like Jews in every other part of the Christian world, the Newport group hoped to build and maintain in-group solidarity that would pose no threat to their hosts. Doing so would necessitate considerable finesse, grace, and good fortune on their part. Even Rhode Island's famously tolerant charter would not protect Jews from whatever social or economic resentment their apartness might engender on the part of neighbors. For all of their considerable efforts to be at once unobtrusive and self-respecting, the Jewish settlers had to have known that their own often mercurial progress up and down the ladder of fortune would not escape notice or fail to remind their neighbors of how precariously they too were poised at the edge of an economic maelstrom. In their own economic endeavors, several of the Newport Jews achieved heights of success that few merchants, Jewish or otherwise, would dream of attaining. Their collective economic achievement, and especially that of Aaron Lopez, offered proof that the Sephardic network, access to ports along the entire perimeter of the Atlantic rim, and good trading skills could transcend every risk associated with the management of such commerce. The immediate witnesses to Lopez's rise might very well have associated his success with his Jewish affiliations.

Lopez and the other successful Jewish merchants in Newport generated interest not so much for their wealth alone, however, as they did for the dynamic means by which they gained it, as well as the overall context in which they managed their financial affairs. If these men had been opulent merchants of a more ordinary sort—if they had inherited their wealth and had been the sons of other rich men—their activities would have lacked interest and borne fewer social implications. New England in the mid-eighteenth century was divided not so much between haves and have-nots as it was by a mounting rivalry between old money and new money. Massachusetts' struggle between 1739 and 1741 over the proposed formation of the Land Bank, for example, had laid bare a stark conflict between those whose interests could be furthered by the decentralization of capital, on the one hand, and those who wished for the maintenance of an older system that had served them well.[47]

At odds in the struggle was not merely the question of how or whether new currency would be issued but how and by whom income would be disposed of. The rather sudden attainment of Jewish wealth in Newport, accompanied as it had to have been by its reinvestment and immediate use, created one more scenario in which New Englanders might see their own unresolved ideas regarding the proper conduct of commerce played out. Not that the Jews themselves had arrived at any kind of uniform condition or attitude of their own. As Holly Snyder points out, the prevailing view among historians has long been that the Newport Jews were uniformly high achievers, economically speaking, and had all come to Rhode Island "with little and proceeded to build a mercantile empire."[48] Her own research has noted the points of social disparity within the community and highlights the stories not only of the women (like Sarah Lopez, Aaron's second wife), but of men like Israel Abrahams, whose tenure in the seaport was interrupted first, in 1747, when he was sent back to New York for indigence and second by a jail term for debt.[49] Abrahams' brother Saul also cut a less than glorious swath through Newport society; upon his death, as Snyder puts it, "the inventory taken of his possessions indicated a certain shabby gentility with a distinctly Jewish bent"[50] (among his possessions were a talus and knives for the ritual slaughter of livestock). Aside from estate inventories, records regarding the community's administration of charity, or *tzedakah*, constitute an additional source of insight into the varied economic profiles of the Newport Jews. In 1761, the Newporters evidently sent two men "who had come to them from Jamaica" as "objects of charity" on to the congregation in New York, claiming themselves to have "contributed as much as the Nature of our affairs would admit of at this time."[51] One historian notes at least two instances of the Newport congregation's having debated whether or not to administer tzedakah to several dark-complexioned overseas visitors who claimed to be Sephardim but were suspected by them as being mulatto impostors.[52]

The Jewish merchants of Newport were not uniformly prosperous. In addition, and despite their concerted efforts as a formal community to avoid all appearance of infighting and dissent, they "quarreled among themselves," writes William Pencak, "and took their disputes to the courts and newspapers in an effort to obtain vindication and keep themselves respectable in the eyes of gentile society."[53] Two members of the Polock family, Myer and Isaac, found themselves accused of slander and of skipping out on a debt, respectively, by their fellow Jews.[54] When the conservative merchants and clergymen of Massachusetts and Connecticut had opposed the issuance of paper currency, they had attempted to scare their fellow New Englanders off from doing so by suggesting that so broad and irresponsible a distribution of wealth would bring about just such a result, and that the decentralization of commercial activity and its extension to men who might otherwise not be so engaged would only promote social tumult and discord among people who had once been genial neighbors to one another. The litigiousness of these Newport Jews, even among themselves, confirmed such a view.[55] The generation of new wealth could be dangerous to the social fabric, not to mention to the religious climate.

Rhode Island was already a lost cause, from such a standpoint, and Jews might only be expected to behave in such a manner. If the members of the ever-shrinking congregational orthodoxy had been paying attention to such goings-on, they would have gained one more powerful basis for the issuance of additional jeremiads on the subject of New England's swift moral decline and the social cost that had been wrought by the sort of religious tolerance that had allowed Jews entry in the first place.

Despite his large profile and ever-increasing wealth, no such aspersions seem ever to have been cast upon Aaron Lopez, the "merchant prince" who amassed a brilliant commercial empire within a few short years of his first arrival in Newport in 1752. His accomplishments have defied any historian's ability to enumerate them, but included retail merchandising, the manufacture and sale of spermaceti, and shipping enterprises that took the over thirty vessels he owned at various times on hundreds of voyages to the West Indies, South America, Canada, the Middle Atlantic colonies, the Carolinas, and ports throughout Europe. He traded all manner of goods, including fish, lumber, tobacco, rum, spermaceti, and slaves. Nonetheless, had he been unlucky or developed into anything less than an upstanding gentleman over the course of his Newport years, potentially hostile and judgmental Christian critics might well have cited his example as further evidence if not of Jewish "guile" then at least of the moral dangers attendant on the proliferation of credit. At least one modern historian, with the bene-fit not only of hindsight but of total access to Lopez's voluminous business correspondence, notes that his accounts, particularly in the years immedi-ately preceding his sudden death, by drowning, in 1782, suggest anything but permanent prince-like status,[56] and that his passing at a premature age may very well have rescued his reputation from ruin. To his good fortune, Lopez was spared the fate of his father-in-law, Jacob Rodrigues Rivera, who had at one point in time in his Newport career to declare bankruptcy.[57] Few question either Lopez's personal rectitude or his business savvy, but as an exemplar of the precarious and risk-maximizing practices of the era's new merchants, Lopez did distinguish himself. His daring business ventures helped to establish him as one of the most successful Sephardic merchants of his day, not only in Newport but in British North America.

At the same time, Lopez and his empire constituted a telling illustra-tion of the potentially destabilizing effects upon an ordered and formerly devout society of great wealth finding its way in to the hands of new men. His example offered illustration of how far New England had come. Lopez's career and business undertakings were sufficiently complex to defy any simple summary. "For honor and extent of commerce," wrote his contemporary and friend Ezra Stiles in the aftermath of Lopez's death, "he was probably surpassed by no merchant in America."[58] "His genius," as Jacob Marcus sums it up, "lay in a marvelous capacity for organization—the ability to carry on dozens of operations simultaneously, to send ships out to every part of the Atlantic world."[59] Indeed, the folk history of Newport itself contains at least one reference to an actual physical remnant of the brilliance to which Marcus refers. Writing in 1873, Thomas Wentworth Higginson paid homage to Lopez's scheme, describing one of the remnants of the merchant's warehouses and the presence in it, along the crossbeam, of "the pigeon-holes once devoted to [Lopez's] different vessels," each of which bore the vessels' names—"Ship Cleopatra," "Brig Juno," and so forth.[60]

Lopez's archived correspondence contains not only hundreds of his own letters, but thousands of letters written to him by debtors and creditors alike, and it is in these papers that we find the strongest evidence not only of his considerable innovation but of just how much of an improviser he was. One of his many apparently formulaic sets of shipping orders, issued on July 2, 1766, instructed Captain Thomas Brown "to embrace the first fair wind and proceed directly to Bristol [England]."[61] From here, as they so often did in just about every other set of orders he issued, the instructions grew more complicated and were based almost entirely on contingencies. Arriving in Bristol, Brown was to submit another set of Lopez's orders to the latter's agent in that city, Henry Cruger, Jr. Brown was further advised by Lopez that he would be expected, based on Cruger's judgment and market conditions as he found them in England, to return to Newport for November or to sail first to Cork, report there to another of Lopez's agents, and then, following upon that agent's instructions and depending on what freight had been added to the vessel in Ireland, sail for Jamaica to conduct additional trade there.[62] The trader's papers are replete with similarly wrought instructions, and it seems remarkable on the basis of such dealings that he was able to sustain such a steady and, indeed, expansive commerce on so many fronts simultaneously.

Though few of the letters that Lopez received, even from his most demanding creditors, ever struck a note of anger or even impatience, there is more than a sufficient body of evidence to suggest that his ventures were risk-filled and, often enough, strained his ability to keep them under control. The same Henry Cruger, Jr., who handled Lopez's business in Bristol sent one letter, in February 1767, attesting plaintively to his approaching desperation as he awaited payment from Newport. "I do not upon my word, Dear Sir," wrote Cruger, "doubt of your ability . . . but I repeat, if you cannot pay, how can I pay?" Two years later, Cruger was worried about another of Lopez's debts and how it endangered his own status, as the "*friendly* creditors" to whom *he* owed money would lose faith in him. "The cords of Friendship and Indulgence is strained so tight," Cruger warned Lopez, that they would surely break, barring the Newport merchant's offsetting his debt with a new and bountiful cargo from *somewhere*. "Would to God it were in my power ever to forgive your Debt," Cruger continued, "I would do it rather than any longer to wait upon you and myself for it."[63] A long view of Lopez's career, and even one that takes his frequent indebtedness into account, will still see the genius and, for that matter, the apparent honesty and integrity behind his ventures. But as we lift our gaze from the career of this single and exceptional man and apply it to the broader implications of his and his fellow Newport Jews' ambitious enterprises, something of a pattern becomes evident.

Lopez was only the most powerful of at least a dozen Newport Jews during the period spanning roughly 1760–1775 who helped transform Newport from a relatively small seaport to a bustling center of transatlantic commerce. The introduction of new capital ventures that occurred there, particularly in the absence of any centralizing religious authority as even post-lapsarian Massachusetts still had, suggested a strong parallel between the Rhode Island port and its nearest truly urban counterpart to the south, New York. In her geographical survey of the business undertakings of the Newport Jews, Holly Snyder mentions a shop owned by Lopez on Thames Street that was such a landmark that four other local merchants identified the location of their stores in relation to it.[64] Jews did not settle in one area but located their businesses and homes throughout the town. Other establishments owned by Nathan Hart, Moses Isaacks, Samuel Moses, Naphtali Hart, Moses Lopez, and Joshua Isaacks ensured that, during this fifteen-year period at least, no resident of or visitor to Newport could possibly have failed to note the Jews' prominence and broad provenance, despite the fact that, using Stiles's census figures, they accounted for only one percent of the town's total population. We have little record of any large-scale resentment of their collective presence. Nonetheless, their participation in and leadership of so many business ventures offered powerful evidence of a changing world. As market-savvy and enterprising Bostonians had been finding out as early as the late seventeenth century, and as Newporters were now learning, wealth took shape not so much as merchants concentrated their capital but as they extended their speculative risks and willingness to strain credit.

No group exemplified this trend more brazenly than the Newport Jews. They succeeded, in large part, owing to their skill, their market connections, and the fact that all of New England was undergoing a profound transformation at the time. The "mystery" of their rather sudden appearance in the period immediately preceding the Revolution is no greater than the "mystery" of why one of the greatest religious revivals in American history swept the colonies during those same decades. Over a hundred years of failed and anxiety-driven attempts to create a religious utopia (or, in Rhode Island, a utopia from another religious utopia) had led to one form after the other of communal and social fragmentation. As the often unwitting participants in these endeavors grew more frustrated, they created new structures and ways of life, including, by the mid-eighteenth century, a world in which commercial enterprise replaced church-going as the primary basis for social interaction. In the meantime, as the Atlantic Ocean seemed to shrink in size, New England's exposure and permeability increased. As a movement fomented in large part by itinerants, the Great Awakening was less of a reaction against such changes than it was an adaptive embrace of their transformative implications and a transformation, on that basis, of a static, provincial religiosity into a dynamic form. The Jews' ascendancy in Newport was a sign that wealth itself was an itinerant force and that New England's religious future would be an outgrowth of a dynamic, if unpredictable, economy.

Between 1761 and 1774, Lopez is known to have sent fourteen vessels to the slave coast of West Africa. Close attention to detail suggests that slave-trading was, indeed, one of many diversified means by which Lopez maintained his "empire," and that he thought nearly as little of burying cargoes of blacks in the holds of his vessels as he did casks of rum or fine English goods. Research by Virginia Bever Platt shows that less than half of these voyages turned a profit.[65] Platt estimates that over the span of his career, Lopez imported over one thousand slaves. Her broader conclusion is that slave-trading was a mixed venture for the merchant and that, on the whole, he gained relatively little from it. In this respect, slave-trading was one more means by which he undertook and lived with financial risk. Indeed, Platt shows in another article that Lopez's Carolina commerce, which he conducted in connection with many of his West Indies voyages and which included slave-trading but also the shipping and sale of such staples as rice, sugar, and molasses, was also only intermittently remunerative.[66] Moreover, much of that Carolina trade involved another kind of risk-taking: smuggling. In short, Lopez was an exemplar of increasingly ubiquitous New England trading trends. If he stood out among his peers or if his dealings suggested anything unsavory to his gentile neighbors, he was merely among the most visible practitioners of a new kind of trade which, while not incompatible with localism or even strong religious affiliation, was based on risk, mobility, contingency, and easy credit. A nascent movement to end the slave trade had been underway in England for some years, but it had not gained sufficient force to exert the sort of cultural pressure that would have been necessary to cause Lopez, or any number of other Rhode Island–based slavers to cease operations.[67] Likewise, though New England itself would come to occupy center-stage in the struggle to end slavery by the nineteenth century, as it still lacked the influence of the Enlightenment era's rhetoric of natural rights, whatever rhetorical basis that would have been necessary for such a movement in Lopez's day did not exist. In 1706, Cotton Mather had asserted the strong possibility that black men and women had souls and could be saved, but his voice on this particular matter was not the dominant one.

Lopez did not live ostentatiously, and neither did the other Jews of Newport. Owing to their own history as Jews in the Christian world, and more particularly as people of *marrano* origin who had learned to sublimate their separate identity with care and skill, the merchants avoided calling an excess of attention to themselves, both in their home life and as a collective body. Even a brief survey of Lopez's correspondence, however, or of the various estate inventories of other Newport Jews, suggests a standard of living that, if it wasn't luxurious, was at least comfortable and most certainly comparable to the status of the genteel. As early as 1759, Moses Lopez had established himself handsomely "in a large house on Marlborough Street . . . consist[ing] of 'four rooms on a floor, and four Fireplaces, a large snuff-mill, a commodious Stable, a Spermaceti House, a good Pump, and a large Garden . . . with many other conveniences.' "[68] Even in his incidental correspondence, Aaron Lopez showed himself to have been someone who partook unself-consciously of the good life. He did not own a large number of slaves, but his home was sufficiently populated with "servants for life" to afford a degree of comfort for his immediate family and a fairly constant stream of houseguests. In July 1766, Henry Cruger, Jr., sent him, by way of his agent "Osborne," "five Game Fowls," which, Cruger hoped, "would prove very welcome to [Lopez's] friends who love Cocking."[69] Lopez's reputation as someone who lived well preceded him. Relative strangers could be counted upon to be aware of his status, as was suggested by a letter he received from the loyalist Samuel Ward, who had never written to Lopez before. Ward lived just across the bay from Newport in Westerly, Rhode Island, and wrote in September 1772 to advise Lopez that "some persons have taken upon my Beach a cask of wine which," as his letter explained, he ought to have been able to claim by right.[70] The Westerly man thought and acted otherwise, however, not only on the basis of Lopez's high standing but as one gentleman merchant might be expected, in a somewhat conspiratorial tone, to write to another. He surmised that a member of one of Lopez's crews had intentionally tossed the cask overboard with some others in order to avoid detection by customs agents. As the sea had proved, as he put it, "more merciful" than the agents would have been, Ward wrote that he "should be glad of an opportunity of alleviating your loss in a small degree," and happily offered to restore the recovered token of Lopez's lost wine upon Lopez describing the cask and, incidentally, remitting a modest reward.

For all of his apparent status and respectability as an individual, Lopez could not single-handedly establish a reputation for all the Newport Jews, if for no other reason than the fact that the community was home, as Holly Snyder has shown, to a significant number of members who were, as best, only "shabbily" genteel.[71] No other attainment of Lopez's or of the other

Newport Jews of the mid-to-late eighteenth century approached the building and establishing of their synagogue in 1763 as a single gesture by which the community sought and, until the coming of the British in 1775, secured its reputation as prosperous and respectable. As New Englanders pursued refinement in all of its forms, and as religion, even in Rhode Island, still existed as a primary form of public display, the effort that culminated in the creation of New England's first permanent Jewish community and house of worship bore great significance and adhered to a larger pattern. Throughout the formerly Puritan colonies, ecclesiastical architecture underwent a transformation during this period. As ministers donned wigs, the parishioners and benefactors who built and maintained the churches around them carried refinement into the one setting that, in the seventeenth century at least, had resisted it. When the Newport Jews added their synagogue to their city's already existing houses of worship, they were making a statement about their own collective achievement. Because their building and what went on in it was different from what happened in the surrounding churches, their gesture invited (or forced) their gentile neighbors into a renewed reckoning of the larger stylistic and cultural shift that was underway. William Pencak goes so far as to say that the edifice that would eventually come to be called the Touro Synagogue was built "not to honor God, but to establish a symbolic superiority over the Christian churches."[72] That the Jews had waited so many years, having been at least intermittently present in Newport since the 1650s, before building their house of worship, in Pencak's view, was indicative of their desire to wait until they had acquired sufficient funds and social capital to do just such a thing.

Until the beginning of the eighteenth century, ecclesiastical architecture had been a last bastion of Puritan thinking. During the first generations of settlement, as Richard Bushman writes, churches—or "meeting houses," as they had been referred to—were "boxy" buildings lacking in all exterior adornment.[73] On the interior they presented an egalitarian setting by which "people entered from all sides and surrounded the preacher from left to right."[74] In keeping with their rejection of the Church of England and their perception of it as a fetishizing context in which ceremony had upstaged the unadorned word of God, they avoided the sort of balanced "longitudinal" symmetry that might separate ministers from parishioners. New England churches in the seventeenth century also lacked a central feature that has since become associated with them; until the turn of the eighteenth century and the building of the Brattle Street church in Boston (where parishioners also engaged in public worship practice that diverged from the Puritan precedent by deemphasizing the spiritual confession that had once been required by all who would take communion), no New England church had a spire. The broader cultural trend toward Anglicization and refinement, however, had engendered a shift toward an architectural style that, if not ornate, replaced minimalism with a measured gentility. The change spanned public and private life. Where New England houses had once been uniformly spartan and oriented around the maximal use of shared central space, the homes of both established gentry and small land-owners grew, by the early eighteenth century and in accordance with how close people lived to the more populous settings, to be symmetrical, larger in size, multi-storied, and also more inclusive of private spaces.[75] Even the orientation of houses changed, so that homes that had once been aligned with magnetic north were now set up to face streets and in such a way as to present a public facade to passers-by.

Even as such stylistic changes occurred, however, the vast majority of New England builders of both houses and churches continued to be practitioners of what Bushman calls a "vernacular gentility." Architectural style and interior design occurred in accordance with folk memory, for the most part, and comparatively few buildings were designed by formally trained architects. The Newport Jews were not the first New Englanders to enlist the services of a architect who possessed classical knowledge (and their architect, Peter Harrison, seems never to have received formal training in his acquisition of architectural skill, but he had had a sufficient immersion in the subject to be able to replicate European styles), but they were among the first to do so in Newport. The two thousand pounds that it cost to build the synagogue was a significant expenditure and, significantly, was expended on materials and labor only; Harrison himself charged no fee. According to one writer, the English-born Harrison was "the most academic [architect] in the colonies before Jefferson."[76] Harrison was closely linked to the same general trend toward gentrification of churches, having been the designer, in 1749, of Boston's King's Chapel, an Anglican church. Though no formal alliance ever existed between the Newport Jews who hired him to design their synagogue and that town's Anglican community, a stylistic affinity between the two groups is obvious. Until the Revolution, the Jews' security and stature was a function of their participation in the larger trend toward Anglicization. Indeed, as one architectural historian has pointed out, Harrison's design of the synagogue had been based quite closely on his measure of or what he knew by reputation about the Bevis Marks synagogue in London. Although Bevis Marks had little in common with its closest counterpart, the 1675 Portuguese synagogue in Amsterdam, it does seem to have borne a close resemblance, in both its exterior and interior features, to several Anglican churches in England, including Christ Church on Newgate Street (1675) and St. Peters (Cornhill) (1607–1681) in London.[77]

The Newport synagogue certainly stood out among that city's other architectural landmarks. Although its exterior has often been referred to as having been deliberately unremarkable and unostentatious, it did own the distinction of being the town's only brick house of worship.[78] Despite its stylistic affinity with Anglican churches in England, it followed a trend that extended well beyond the parameters of the Anglican church, which still held minority status in New England. As with the Brattle Street church, as well as several other successive New England Congregational churches, the synagogue's builders "revealed a willingness to embrace English ecclesiastical architecture," regardless of their theological alignment.[79] The building itself was not enormous but, by local standards, it was commodious enough. It was Georgian in style and stood two stories in height. Situated on a lot that was 91 by 102 feet, the structure itself was 35 feet in width, 40 feet in length, and 48 feet in height. Residents of Newport evidently took a certain pride in the building which, in the words of Walter Channing, who grew up there during the period of its most concentrated use, "being the oldest of the Temples of India and Egypt, deserve[d] the first place."[80] Passers-by and visitors to the town routinely noted its handsome profile and dignified aspect. From the outside, it did not differ greatly from any number of other public edifices, and the committee who arranged for its construction and had consulted with Peter Harrison had evidently wanted it that way. In one respect, however, the building's calculated unobtrusiveness was offset by one noticeable point of divergence. Unlike surrounding buildings that faced for the most part directly on the street, the Jewish synagogue was set off at an angle, owing to the necessity of aligning its ark properly toward Jerusalem. Even this most cultivated and genteel of public edifices presented one departure from the local norm.

Despite its formidable exterior, Jews and gentiles alike gained their fullest impression of the synagogue upon entering the building. Whatever his influences, Harrison had evidently thought carefully about achieving a result that would be both unique, at least by New England standards, and similar enough both to existing Sephardic synagogues and to certain churches. It was designed to strike the perfect balance between the Jewish stricture against including anything remotely iconic in a synagogue, on the one hand, and the gentility and elegance of the new sort of church interior, on the other. The synagogue's interior eliminated the obstruction that existed at New York's Mill Street, at least, between the women's viewing gallery and the sanctuary, suggesting an idea of openness and access that would have been commensurate with the earlier model of New England church, in which the segregation of the congregation, both from the minister and from their fellow parishioners, was discouraged. At the same time, the synagogue's lower level was ornamented by a series of twelve Ionic columns that supported the women's gallery, creating three concentric spaces: a perimeter underneath the gallery, a central seating area, and a *tebah*, or reading platform, which, in the Sephardic tradition, stood at the center of the building and was set off by a high balustraded fence. During services, as David de Sola Pool wrote in his history of the synagogue, the "seats [were] arranged not facing the Ark but along the north and south walls at right angles to the Ark, so as to keep the space between the reading desk in the center and the Ark at the east end."[81]

The result would have been a use of sanctuary space that would have seemed both exotic and oddly familiar to visiting gentiles, whose own church officials, while shunning ceremonialism, sought nonetheless to strike a balance between hierarchy and egalitarianism as methods for the use of interior space. A corresponding number of Corinthian columns ran between the upper gallery and the building's ceiling. The columns on both levels have been interpreted as representing the twelve tribes of Israel and, in that way, suggest a distinctly Jewish representational scheme. Indeed, Bevis Marks, which had been built over sixty years earlier, had the same number of supporting columns. The use of columns, per se, however, and their creation of a complex, hierarchical, and demarcated space spoke as

much to changing architectural norms and standards and the congregation's desire to create a material enhancement of their worship experience. The synagogue's interior, like its outward appearance, suggested the
congregants' seemingly dual loyalties both to the idea of a simple worship
in keeping with the ancient practices of their forefathers and, at the same
time, a fairly enthusiastic embrace of the material comfort that they had
found in the New World and, indeed, within the British Atlantic. In this
regard, the synagogue could not itself have been more "indigenous" to
New England, whose entire population was engaged in the vexing task of
negotiating its experience of material plenty with the austere legacy of its
founders.

In its architectural mirroring not only of London's synagogue but of several of its churches, the Newport synagogue also appears in large part to
have been the product of strong "foreign" influence. The Jews could hardly
be blamed for relying as they did upon English and Dutch models, and the
fact that two of the torahs contained in its ark in 1769 came from London
and Amsterdam would not have surprised anyone, as proper torah scribes
were not available in the colonies. Why it might have been necessary for
the builders to construct the building out of bricks sent from London, on
the other hand (and, indeed, whether or not they actually did) remains a
mystery. Mordecai Gutstein claimed in the 1930s that the bricks had been
shipped in 1760, largely on the basis of the oral traditions that had been circulated among Newport's residents in the nineteenth century and recorded
by its memoirists. Despite a contemporary historical archaeologist's inability in recent years to ascertain whether or not the story could be corrobo-
rated, the tradition's broader implication is of no less value than its possible veracity. Newporters evidently associated the Jews with foreign goods
and a sort of material enchantment that spoke to their own fascination with
such things. Nineteenth-century commemorators of the town's glorious
pre-Revolutionary age, many of whom either remembered it firsthand or
had been spoken to about it by their elders, were quite taken by the cosmopolitan mantle that the town's Jewish history had afforded them. "We boast
that Newport was once the metropolis of the colonies," Thomas Vernon
had orated at one commemorative event. "Our noble harbor once bristled
with forests of masts; here lived merchant princes . . . whose influence and
correspondence were solicited by European houses; here, too, the thrifty

Jews . . . filled their Storehouses with the merchandise of every clime."[82] Accordingly, congregants and Newport natives alike shared the oral tradition that one of the synagogue's five hanging candelabras had once hung in a Spanish monastery.[83] Another tradition held that a secret vault that the Jews had build under the synagogue's *tebah* had been put there for fear of the Inquisition somehow finding them in Rhode Island.

If Yeshuat Israel had been conceived and built at any other time, its outward patterning after so many European precedents and its inclusion of so many features whose origins lay across the ocean would have suggested an entirely alien architectural provenance. Because its establishment coincided with the transformation of so many Christian houses of worship, however, the synagogue's apparently alien trappings can just as easily be ascribed to its congregants' receptivity to local, or at least New England–based trends. The transformation of church architecture that resulted in the adding on of spires, the rearrangement of interiors along a longitudinal design in which newly gentrified pastors—sometimes wearing wigs—held forth, and the increasing decoration of church walls, for all of its apparently Anglicized origins, was now a distinctly New England, or at least British North American phenomenon. It had as great an impact (if not a greater) upon Congregationalists as upon Anglicans, for whom no leap had been necessary.[84] As eager as nineteenth-century memorialists had been to associate the Jewish synagogue of Newport with exoticism and romance, its development along "foreign" lines had occurred in keeping with the entire region's transformation and adoption of a largely contrived English look. Newporters who witnessed the development of the Jews' synagogue and considered it to be an outpost of cosmopolitan style and taste could not but have noticed its uncanny resemblance to their own places of worship. The building and its contents, like the merchant activity that made its construction possible, were the products of the same confluence of new and old, as well as foreign and domestic economic and social influences.

What actually went on in the synagogue once it was built adhered to a similar pattern, in which the force of tradition, on the one hand, and the force of change and adaptation, on the other, converged. For New England Protestants, the Great Awakening had created a similar dynamic. On the one hand, the revival was an apparent reaction to what Joseph Conforti calls the "advancing rationalism and gentility in religious life."[85] That retrospective force operated concurrently and in tension with an equally powerful adaptive element that exploited the rapidly changing world and used such burgeoning developments as newsprint and itinerancy to its greater benefit. The Jews of Newport were no revivalists, and they neither clung to their traditions nor raced toward the future by relinquishing all connections to their Jewish or *marrano* past. Instead, like the New England Protestants whose own divergent practices were also transformed by the transatlantic context of the Great Awakening, the Newport Jews found themselves negotiating a varied path toward the establishment of a Jewish future in New England. They had already taken several steps in such a direction. Having openly declared their Judaism and, at least in Aaron Lopez's case, undergone adult circumcision, they had eliminated all pretense of being anything other than Jews (besides, as Catholics, they would have been even more unwelcome in New England).

Over the years, their repeated, if somewhat inconsistent efforts to adhere to dietary laws and holiday practices, as well as to engage in acts of Jewish charity, suggested as well a visionary outlook toward the future. In engaging in all of these acts and in establishing a formal community and synagogue, they had by necessity both to recover Judaic practice that, at best, could only be informed by reports and very occasional visits from abroad. Despite their eagerness, in other words, to fortify and legitimize their Judaism, the Jews of mid-to-late eighteenth-century Newport practiced a religion that was every bit as susceptible as New England Congregationalism was to the modifying tendencies imposed by a changing world. Their synagogal practice was not transformed by the Great Awakening, except insofar as it had in common with the Protestant revival the tendency, based in large part on simple expediency, to call "into question the power of mimetic tradition that earlier generations of colonial Jews held sacred."[86]

Newport Jews in the middle and late eighteenth century sought as urgently to *recover* a religious life as to devise or invent one. In Newport, at least until the 1770s when a series of visiting rabbis came to the congregation, knowledge and use of Hebrew was limited to its most basic liturgical uses, except in the case of Isaac Touro, the Amsterdam-trained *hazzan*. Lay members of the congregation might refer fairly routinely, although just as often by means of transliterations into English as with actual Hebrew letters, to approaching holidays. Joshua Hart did so in two letters he wrote to Aaron Lopez from Charleston, South Carolina, sometimes mixing English, Hebrew, and Portuguese in the process: "I wish you and everyone of your family a Merry Pascua de Pesah . . ."[87] Indeed, the business correspondence of many colonial-era American Jews quite often contained such gestures, typically as the writer approached his salutation. In keeping with their efforts to fashion a discourse in English that might render a Judaic perspective comprehensible in a New World context, sometimes the writers might referred in fairly abstract terms to such phenomena as "inestimable blessings"[88] and "Smiles of Heaven."[89] The merchants' acquisition of English was unquestionably more important to them than their recovery of or retention of Hebrew, even in the correspondence between fellow Jews. As the High Holidays approached, David Lopez, Jr., expressed a wish that his uncle Aaron would "enjoy the approaching festivities, and be written and Seal'd in the Book of long Life and Felicity."[90] What was remarkable about the Newporters' expressions of Judaic interest was their consistency and perseverance in the face of so many obstacles. In November 1767, Abraham Abrahams of New York wrote Aaron Lopez announcing his enclosure of "four Double sets Tsits'iths . . . being a present from Mr. Isaac Alolphus," who would also have supplied "Tephilim" but had none to spare.[91] The Newporters also went to considerable lengths to ensure the availability, at least on holidays, of kosher foods. In March 1762, with Passover approaching, the merchant prince received a shipment from Sol Marance of New York of "one barrel which contains . . . 2 _ch. Water Matzot" (250 pounds), accompanied by the shippers' wishes that Lopez and his family "may with health and happiness enjoy the ensuing Passover."[92] Lopez, most likely because his relative wealth made it possible for him to indulge such practices, is known to have avoided launching his ships on the Sabbath.[93] He kept his shop closed from Friday evening until Monday morning. When James Sheldon came at one point to settle a debt he owed Lopez, his visit was refused as the Jews in the merchant prince's house were busy observing Passover that day.[94]

The Newport synagogue's earliest operation coincided with the tenure there of Isaac Touro as *hazzan*. Touro had been recruited for that purpose from his home in Holland, and he served in that office from his initial election until his Loyalist leanings made it necessary to flee to Jamaica. He

seems not to have distinguished himself as any kind of exceptional authority on Jewish knowledge, but was sufficiently learned as to have served in
the late 1760s as Ezra Stiles's Hebrew instructor (see Chapter 5). Although
Touro's Anglophilia eventually cost him his standing in Newport, it stood
both him and the congregation in good stead during his earlier years. He
was not alone; he followed in the footsteps of several other Jewish religious leaders in the British Atlantic in enthusiastically embracing the
opportunity to express his appreciation of British protection. Like Rabbi
Belisario of London, Touro adapted Jewish history and Jewish practice to
modern use. In November 1765, in a pronouncement that made a sufficient impression upon its hearers as to have been translated from Touro's
Hebrew rendering into English, the Newport *hazzan* delivered a prayer of
thanksgiving to accompany the general holiday that had been declared for
that day by the governor of Rhode Island. Touro's oration of 1765 went
down in history not only as one of American Jewry's earliest published
prayers but, owing to its timing, as the first official act of Jewish affiliation
with New England tradition.

Touro's prayer asked God's "Compassion and Mercy" and wished for
both an "internal Peace in the Land" and a peace between "all States and
Potentates." After asking God to protect and "prosper" "our most gra-
cious Sovereign, King GEORGE the third, and all the ROYAL FAMILY,"
Touro went on to wish as well for the preservation of "the whole British
Empire."[95] Although the Jewish religion had imposed no strictures upon
such expression of political or worldly opinions, and although Touro was
only doing what countless generations of grateful—or merely obsequious—Jewish leaders has been doing for millennia, his pronouncement of
the Thanksgiving Prayer was of particular interest not so much for its content, which looks to have been fairly typical, but for its extremely public
nature, which may or may not have been the result of either Touro's wish
or his efforts. That a Hebrew prayer delivered by a Jewish "minister," and
especially in connection with a public holiday whose initial adoption had
come about in order that New Englanders might properly commemorate
the original settlement of their home would be published in a newspaper
is a compelling testimony as to just how adaptable Judaism, at least in this
period, had become. Gentile readers of Touro's prayer, who had by necessity to have constituted a substantial majority owing to its appearance in

the town newspaper, would have been encountering a profound reflection of New England's overall religious transformation. Not only was a Jewish prayer rendered in as plain a fashion as might have been the utterance of a Congregational minister, but the prayer itself was being deployed in the context of a public, colony-wide holiday whose very application spoke to the region's newly tolerant religious atmosphere of ecumenical compromise. Jews in this case were among the first religious practitioners to enter this new territory. Centuries of experience at the margins of European society and as central players in transatlantic commerce had acculturated them to such eventualities. Among Jews they were pioneers as well, "among the first," writes Eli Faber, "in the modern world to explore the combination of Jewish tradition with contemporary culture."[96]

Newport's Jews would experience one more decade of even greater economic prosperity and religious revival. Their initial accomplishments, including the establishment of a viable congregation and the creation of a synagogue that would eventually become one of American Judaism's most important historical shrines were unprecedented affairs, even in the context of Rhode Island's distinctive history as a haven for religious tolerance. The congregation had taken shape around a discrete set of historical circumstances which had an equal bearing both on the rapidly evolving status of Jews in British North America and on the changes that all New Englanders had undergone in the immediate aftermath of the Great Awakening and its ushering in of an expansive cultural and commercial atmosphere. The earliest settlers of the region had established their commonwealth by virtue not only of their religious fervor but of their commercial initiative. A hundred years after the founding, intercolonial and transatlantic contacts had been maximized and New England's chosenness, as Thomas Kidd suggests, "was supplanted by a British chosenness."[97] The arrival and social ascendancy of the Newport Jews, who themselves were exemplars of mobility and ease of access to the entire Atlantic world, had coincided with New England's newfound receptivity to the concept, and the Jews' development of a congregational life in Newport offered a particularly vivid dramatization of these new exposures. Likewise, and in keeping with a post-Puritan embrace of an overall Anglicization and pursuit of gentility and refinement, the Newport Jews also offered a case in point regarding the dynamic infusion of "new" money and an adventurous entrepreneurialism into the previously staid economic atmosphere. The merchants' prosperity, in turn, enabled them to develop a small but influential Jewish community whose substantial impression upon the surrounding population of gentiles offered further confirmation of New England's long-standing Judaic fixation. With the growth that the Newport congregation experienced in the 1770s, its increased visibility among Jews and gentiles alike, and the cataclysmic events of the Revolution lying in the near future, the Jewish convergence and encounter with New England's distinctive history would reach its culmination.

CHAPTER FIVE

"AN OPENNESS TO CANDOUR"
Scholarly Ecumenicism in Pre-Revolutionary Newport

Isaac Touro, the *hazzan* of Yeshuat Israel, was not the only member of Newport's clergy to deliver a Thanksgiving sermon on November 28, 1765.[1] Two short blocks from the new synagogue, Ezra Stiles addressed Newport's Second Congregational Church on the same occasion. Born in 1727 in North Haven, Connecticut, Stiles had served as a minister in Newport since 1753, settling there after completing his studies and then serving as a tutor at Yale. Stiles's strident pronouncement on the nature of religious liberty, freedom, and political power suggested that its author, like his townspeople and like Isaac Touro, was wrestling with a newly dawning cultural reality: in the wake of mid-century religious revival and economic tumult, spiritual affinities were becoming increasingly politicized. While the Jews of Newport were in no way responsible for such an outcome, Stiles's long-standing interest in their affairs and the relationships that he developed with one Jew in particular would be a spur to his education in discursive cultural politics, an education which, according to one twentieth-century biographer, would help to make him "one of the most learned men in America."[2] The ten short years between Touro's and Stiles's Thanksgiving sermons and the coming of the American Revolution brought about a transformational intermingling of religious and political affairs, and Newport's Jewish community would prove to be an agent of that change, particularly in and through its relationship with Ezra Stiles.

Within two decades of his arrival in Newport, Stiles would become one of the most steadfast and articulate ministerial proponents of the American revolutionary cause, but in the remarks he delivered in his 1765 Thanksgiving sermon he spoke his unstinting approval of and appreciation for the blessings of life in the British empire. Like Touro, Stiles emphasized God's sovereignty over all the affairs of men. The public thanksgiving had been declared by Rhode Island's governor, and had specified the colony's debt to King George III, among others, but Stiles reminded his auditors that "a perfect Government" could only be found in God's nature. "The sacred Scriptures," he observed, "refer to the Dominion of God as a wise, good and perfect Being."[3] A public thanksgiving might afford a proper opportunity for clergy and laity to acknowledge the advantages of good and just human government, but such acknowledgments could be articulated and justified only under the rubric of God's "Controll" and "Supreme Wisdom."[4] In 1765, Newporters were becoming aware of political events and changes, but they still imagined and described a world in which God, through the medium of His various religious institutions, reigned entirely supreme. Touro, Stiles, and a host of other religious leaders in Newport would certainly have disagreed with one another as to the exact nature of divinity, and within ten years they would also part ways politically. In 1765, what they shared, however, was their mutual linguistic disorientation in the face of change, as Jews and Christians alike vainly sought for the proper terms by which they might translate their religiosity within an increasingly politicizing realm. Stiles's entire career, as one recent historian has put it, demarcated the "changing relationship among religion, learning, and politics that reshaped Revolutionary New England."[5]

As a font of religious pluralism with no equivalent anywhere else in New England and, indeed, in British North America outside perhaps of New York, Newport provided an environment that, while not exactly ecumenical, supported a wide range of viewpoints on religious matters. As Jews and Christians encountered one another in Revolutionary-era Newport, they engendered one more discursive legacy of New England Hebraism. In their actual interactions, as well as in what they spoke and wrote about one another, the Newporters inadvertently fashioned a newly politicized body of expression. The Jewish presence in the town afforded an unprecedented occasion for the immediate descendants of New England Puritans to witness a living Judaism at firsthand. That this ecumenical encounter coincided with the coming of the American Revolution and its myriad political and social upheavals both enriched and imposed limitations upon the resulting discourse. Judaism was no longer an abstraction, and Jews were no longer mere figments of the gentile imagination. On the contrary, their physical presence and their public deployment of an apparently exotic religious tradition in a modern, New World setting necessitated the expansion of a heretofore hypothetical Christian paradigm.

Newport's atmosphere of religious pluralism between 1765 and 1775 did not ensure common cause among its various constituencies. Nor, as one recent historian suggests, could "houses of worship . . . become politicized so easily [i.e., in a single cause]," even as war with Britain approached.[6] If anything, the dialogue among the town's various religious groups, including its Jews, merely exacerbated tensions and, in some cases, actually created new ones that precluded unity. In the charged political atmosphere in which clergy and laity either took sides with Loyalists or Whigs or, as best they could, attempted to stake out neutral positions, religious affiliation constituted a sometimes inadvertent platform for an increasingly fractious political discourse. The Great Awakening had deepened rifts and rivalries. Jews had not sought this result; among all the town's "sects," they could least afford to assume even slightly controversial political positions. Nonetheless, in the years immediately preceding the Revolution, as one historian writes, "American Judaism adapted—and contributed—to the pluralistic character of American religious life."[7] Although their achievement of full civil rights still lay in the future and would be established only in fits and starts several years following from the creation of the American republic, the pre-Revolutionary era in Newport saw their informal but collective establishment as one more among the town's several religious "societies."[8]

When Ezra Stiles and Isaac Touro delivered their respective Thanksgiving Day prayers and sermons in November 1765, they had known each other for several years. Stiles had taken an early interest in the *hazzan*, and in Jewish affairs generally. Touro's arrival in Newport apparently gave Stiles the impetus he needed to pursue the advanced study of Hebrew. While "most Christians in the eighteenth century" viewed "the study of Hebrew and the study of Jews as a living community" as "unrelated enterprises," Stiles had seen past the doctrinal stumbling blocks to opening up a dialogue with practicing Jews and engaged what Jews he could find in such conversations.[9] He found in Touro a willing and competent instructor in Hebrew, a man who though he lacked the expertise of a rabbi,[10] possessed considerable skills as an experienced and "native" Hebraist. Stiles himself exemplified a lifelong "ambivalence" regarding the Jews and their apostasy.[11] In his own private writing, he often betrayed his theological frustrations with Jewish "blindness." Nonetheless, his receptivity to Jewish instruction and, as his relationship with Jews in the ten years leading up to the Revolution proved, his personal magnanimity and friendship appear quite often to have overridden his doctrinaire objections to their practice and his prejudicial suspicions of their motives. When Touro arrived in Newport, and as the Jews went about establishing their synagogue community, Stiles knew that he had "an excellent laboratory in which to observe Jews" and "learn first-hand about their customs and traditions."[12] His apparent willingness to suspend disbelief and his own theological objections to their errors was entirely new, and it spoke not only to his own qualities of openness but to the newly pluralistic cultural climate in which he, the Jews, and every other resident of Newport lived.

Stiles's arrival in Newport coincided with the Jews' establishment in the town in the early 1750s. An obsessive recorder of the town's demographic developments, he wrote in 1755 that they numbered fifteen families and that, at the time, they lacked a "minister."[13] His interest in their affairs was sufficiently broad as to exceed the immediate geography of Newport itself, and his access to specific information about their "Society" indicates that he must have enjoyed at least some contact with the as yet unaffiliated Jews who lived around him. He knew enough, in any case, to be able to write of their existence in New York, where, as he also noted, they were able to avail themselves of an "Alhazzan."[14] Stiles's familiarity with Jewish culture and the Hebrew language grew considerably as soon as Yeshuat Israel was permanently ensconced in its own synagogue. When the *Newport Mercury* ran its notice describing the opening of the town's newest house of worship (see Chapter 4), Stiles was the correspondent who provided the eyewitness report. Indeed, while the newspaper notice rather abbreviated the story, in his own writings Stiles had lavished great and admiring detail on his description of the proceedings, as well as of the interior architecture of the building itself and its ritual contents and appurtenances. He was particularly impressed by the "three Copies & Rolls of the Pentateuch, written on Vellum or rather tanned Calf Skin," one of which was, as Touro had apparently told him, was "Two Hundred Years Old."[15]

Stiles's evident admiration for the Jews was tempered by what one historian has referred to as his "ambivalence" and also by what appears often enough to have been genuine antipathy. When Aaron Lopez and Isaac Eliezer were refused in their attempt to gain the rights of naturalized subjects from the Rhode Island Supreme Court, Stiles recounted the occasion by recording, among his private papers, both the contents of the petition and his telling judgment upon the court's verdict. The judges had cited Rhode Island's adoption, in 1663, of a charter specifically precluding the rights of any "person who does not profess the Christian Religion."[16] When the court dismissed Lopez and Eliezer's case, it did so on the same day that it passed judgment in three felony trials. The symbolism was not lost on Stiles, who could not resist such a fine opportunity to invoke the divine judgment implied in a negative ruling upon their case having been handed down in a scene reminiscent of Christ's' crucifixion among the three thieves.[17] "Providence seems to make every Thing to work for the mortification to the Jews & to prevent their incorporating into any Nation," he wrote.[18] If nothing else, the Rhode Island jurists' interpretation of parliamentary law was intent on preventing such an eventuality. Stiles noted this fact himself, as he went on to write that "Tho' the Naturalization Act passed Parliament a few years ago, yet it produced such a national Disgust towards the Hebrews, that the Jews themselves joined in Petition to Parliament to repeal that Act, & it was thereupon repealed, for Britain."[19]

The next ten years would bring about a fascinating transformation, not only in Stiles's attitude toward the Jews, but in his sentiments regarding Britain itself, to which, in 1762, he was still referring as an arm of Providence in its judgment against the Jews, as well as for its preservation of Protestant integrity. In this respect, he did not differ enormously from many other New Englanders who, right up until the eve of the war and even after hostilities had commenced, could not conceive of themselves as anything other than loyal British subjects, wishing only to be granted the rights that they associated with such status. Newport in particular did not display the militancy of Boston and, indeed, any of the other major American seaports whose merchants and mobs alike undertook overt acts of resistance in the face of mounting taxes and a centralizing British colonial authority. For a combination of reasons, Newport had experienced a "golden age" in the 1760s and 1770s that set it apart from the rest of New England. The town's economic prosperity had come about because of its enterprising merchants' vigorous pursuit of the famous "triangle trade" and, in particular, its production and importation of molasses. Where Boston merchants resorted to ever more strident acts of resistance in the face of such punitive Parliamentary acts as the Sugar and Stamp Acts, as well as the duty on tea, Newport sea captains and vessel-owners often succeeded in feigning acquiescence to such laws and relying instead on smuggling and bribery in order to circumvent British trade restrictions. Newport's clergy, though some few of them would evolve into steadfast American patriots, were widely enthusiastic in their praise of the crown well into the 1770s.

In his Thanksgiving sermon of November 1765, Stiles offered no obvious hint of his eventual partisanship toward the American cause. Although his remarks left no doubt as to his vestigial Puritan loyalty to New England's distinct ecclesiastical mission, as well as several reminders that all political power had been granted by virtue of "the present attention & control of Supreme wisdom . . . ,"[20] he devoted the closing portion of his sermon that day to celebrating not only the blessings of English heritage but the joys of life under the protective and magnanimous royal authority of George III. British citizens, Stiles asserted, experienced "a liberty unknown to any other Kingdom on Earth." Their ancestors had achieved such heights as the drafting and acceptance of the Magna Carta, the defeat of the Spanish Armada in 1588, and the adoption of the Bill of Rights following from the Civil Wars of the mid-seventeenth century. The founding of New England marked an additional high point, at least for those who placed a premium on "pure & undefiled Religion."[21] Precious as they were, however, such liberties could be guaranteed only at the benign behest of the king himself. "The Happiness of the British Empire from the Accession under the mild & just Dominion of the illustrious house of Hanover," Stiles declared, was a special gift proffered by the king.[22] Stiles's praise for the king was more than perfunctory, as his entire theme in the Thanksgiving sermon concerned the thanks that were due a sovereign under whose dominion the free exercise of dissenting Protestantism had prospered, especially as Parliament itself seemed bent on impinging upon those and other colonial liberties.[23] In a sermon he delivered in 1766, Stiles went even farther, designating George III the "divine Benefactor" and the head of a worldwide "system of liberty."[24] The religious atmosphere of the day stipulated an equation of the crown with liberty. To the extent that Stiles, or any other religious leader, engaged political subject matter in sermons, their primary vehicle for doing so was their profession of an unquestioning gratitude for the freedoms granted them by the English sovereign.

As Benjamin Carp has remarked, Newport's "golden age" coincided with a hitherto unprecedented atmosphere of religious pluralism,[25] or what another chronicler of the town's revolutionary-era years refers to as "an underlying harmony of interests."[26] As long as the town's economic picture was bright, otherwise debilitating religious rivalries and rifts could be deemphasized or even ignored. What looked like tolerance could just as easily have been a species of insidious indifference.[27] A superficial calm, in other words, reigned during the pre-Revolutionary era, in which future enemies on the question of loyalty to the British or American causes *appeared*, as they conducted their religious affairs, at any rate, to harbor little or no ill will toward one another. The pluralistic atmosphere prevailed in the relative absence of economic and social tension. Public religious discourse, as a consequence, tended to uphold a mutuality of interest, in which the minister of the Second Congregationalist Church conveyed a similar gratitude for the gifts of English liberty to that which was being articulated by the Jewish *hazzan* and a host of other leaders in the town. Beneath the surface of such pronouncements, particularly the ones uttered along the wide spectrum between, say, that of the town's Anglican minister and its more radical dissenters on the religious "left," such as the Quakers, lay something other than openness to foreign or radical doctrines, let alone mutual appreciation.

If any one of Newport's religious practitioners would have been likely to be an exception to such a rule, it would have been Ezra Stiles. Although he had been born into a thoroughly Puritan milieu (his maternal grandfather had been the pietistic poet Edward Taylor), Stiles struggled early on with Calvinistic doctrine and seriously contemplated a career in law so that he might avoid having to come to a final reckoning with his spiritual doubts.[28] Before 1755, as Christopher Grasso writes, Stiles had "been a skeptic in the study, a Calvinist in the pulpit, and an Arminian by reputation."[29] If nothing else, he knew that his parishioners would not take well to his expressions of doubt. When he finally committed himself to the ministry and assumed the leadership of Newport's Second Congregational Church,

Stiles began at once to study the religious beliefs and practices of others. He sought to accumulate spiritual knowledge in the style of an anthropologist or, more specifically, a sort of "participant observer."[30] Granted, he was a lifelong skeptic with regard to any practice that even remotely resembled those of papistry; Anglicans rarely received anything but unmitigated scorn at his hands. In his 1765 Thanksgiving sermon, for instance, he exerted little effort to disguise his contempt for such opulent practitioners as the Anglicans across town, who were wont to engage in "solemn acts of religious praise, with the debonair and jovial Disposition, as they would mix in a Ball or a military Triumph."[31] The Revolutionary War would only deepen Stiles's opposition to Anglicanism. For all of his expressions of skepticism and contempt, however, Stiles lost few opportunities to engage the adherents of rival faiths.

That Stiles became as personally affected as he did by his encounter with the town's Jews, about whom suspicions, even on his part, abounded, was a testament to his eagerness for candor. His apparent receptivity to Jewish knowledge and, more important, to establishing and maintaining meaningful personal friendships with individual Jews would have a transformative effect on his ministry. It also exemplified a broader cultural change and the evolution of an inter-religious dialogue, by which a deeper acceptance of unbridgeable spiritual gaps (such as the divinity of Christ, as a starting point!) would become an expedient accessory if not to the experience of fighting a revolution then to the establishment of a republic. Though it was initially inspired by what had by then evolved into a fairly standard form of Puritan Hebraism, Ezra Stiles's burgeoning interest in Judaism as a living religion was part and parcel of his growing acceptance of a new order in the relationship between the affairs of church and state. Though Stiles may have single-handedly constituted the vanguard of such ecumenical tendencies, the rest of New England would follow suit. During the first decade or so of their congregational existence in Newport, the Jews of that town had dramatized New England's economic evolution and transatlantic exposure. Now, as the Revolution itself approached, their presence might help to usher in a previously unthinkable transformation in the public discourse concerning religion and its place in the organization of social and political life.

Stiles's initial interest in the Jews, like the more intimate contact he sought and found among them in the years to come, derived from his practical scholarly interest in learning and then perfecting his Hebrew. As well as the linguistic study which had served as a spur to his visits to the synagogue and to the homes of such men as Touro, Aaron Lopez, and Abraham Rivera, Stiles seems to have pursued a deepening of his knowledge of Jewish ritual. In a diary entry from March 1769, he noted the celebration of Purim.[32] He watched on May 19th of that year as two new torahs, one of which had been donated by Lopez and the other of which had come from Bevis Marks in London, were placed in the ark for the first time.[33] Stiles also noted the observation of the major Jewish holidays, including Rosh Hashanah, Yom Kippur, and Passover.[34] His diary included extended descriptions of circumcisions, based on a long conversation he had with Touro, other Newport Jews, and the sequence of six visiting rabbis who came to the synagogue between 1770 and the first years of the Revolutionary War. He paid attention as well to the female purification ritual, the *mikveh*, as well as to the Jews' regular recitations of the *kaddish* and their mentioning of the names of the dead during services. Frequent visitor and participant that he was, he seems on occasion to have balked at certain rituals. One wonders, for instance, why at a dinner that was served at Isaac Touro's home ("the only Time I ever happened at Meal with a Jew"), Stiles chose not to wash his hands ritually with all the other diners.[35]

For the most part, Stiles's ethnographic observations of Jewish rituals and practices passed without extensive commentary on his part; his primary interest seems to have been in simply recording what he saw and heard among the Jews. The content of the entries suggested a deep curiosity on his part and a lack of any inhibition about making bold inquiries. When Stiles attended a synagogue service on February 8, 1770, he approached "a little Jew boy" (Aaron Lopez's son?) and asked him about the significance of "the strings at the corner of the White Surplice" (tallit).[36] The boy explained the ritual of gathering the shawl's four corners and kissing the *tsitsits* in preparation for each recitation of the *shema*. Evidently, inclement weather was a spur to one of his most telling realizations, which came on July 31, 1769. As a raucous thunderstorm raged outside the synagogue, Stiles noted, "The Jews in Newport threw open their Doors, Windows, and employed themselves in Singing and Repeating Prayer for Meeting Messias."[37] That Stiles showed any interest at all in Jewish practices was already an indication of his receptivity. That he displayed curiosity regarding their belief in the imminent arrival of a messiah other than Jesus Christ suggests a deeper level of interest on his part, a way in which the Jews and their synagogue rituals spurred his Christian practice. For while Stiles certainly would have delighted in the prospect of perhaps converting, or at least *witnessing* the conversion of Jews, the largest motivating factor behind his inquiries about Judaism was his belief that his *own* religion might be enriched or enhanced by a fuller understanding of its Jewish roots. Where earlier Puritan Hebraists' interest in Jewish messianism had been part and parcel of their eschatology and their overriding hopes of securing conversions in the interest of advancing Christ's return, Stiles—especially as the years passed and as he met new Jews—merely sought to gain additional insight into the Christian tradition. His ecumenical endeavors suggested a certain capitulation, in other words, to the novel idea that Jews, while they were quite likely destined for a bad end in the afterlife, could be fairly counted upon in this life, at any rate, to persevere in their religious practice. Moreover, as he established fuller relationships with these Jews, he learned as well that their very perseverance, mistaken as it was from a divine perspective, could sometimes be a sign of their decency and even nobility as human beings.

Stiles was the first New England Puritan, in other words, to describe an encounter with Jews whom he believed to be virtuous and theologically sophisticated, and to describe their virtue without dismissing its relevance to Christianity. In a broader perspective, his engagement of Jews and of the living Jewish religion bespoke a lessening of Calvinistic fervor. It acknowledged the contemporary reality of errant religious practice, and it did so without at once condemning the practitioners or dismissing their practice as unworthy of sustained attention. While Stiles was hardly free of anti-Jewish prejudices and while he would never have acknowledged Judaism as anything but misguided, he was nonetheless able to speak and write about it in such a way as to grant it a certain discursive dignity. Although only the Revolution and its aftermath would see Jews awarded the rights of citizens, the Jewish religion could no longer be looked upon as a mere dead letter, as far as New Englanders were concerned. The Protestant Reformation and the Puritan removal to New England had opened the door to "the idea of religious liberty,"[38] but colonial Americans could not conceive of that idea as anything other than the freedom of Protestants to dissent. After a century and a half of Protestant experimentation had established the necessity of acknowledging and accommodating doctrinal differences, however, and as the earlier force of Calvinism waned, the time of "Jews, Turks, and infidels" was approaching. A first step, as Ezra Stiles was demonstrating in Newport, was the acceptance of contemporary facts, the recognition that, despite their hopeless damnation, Jews and other non-Protestants had entered the public fray. Stiles was a pioneer of such previously unthinkable admissions. As far back as 1769, and on a day when he had already spent the morning at the synagogue, he recorded an even more startling meeting he had held that afternoon: "Spent several hours in discourse with a romish priest."[39]

Stiles's discourse with Jews differed from earlier interactions between New Englanders and Jews because it was indeed, a discourse, a communicative process that was open at both ends. Nearly every entry in his diary that recorded an encounter with Jews made plain that he was a participant in an exchange. On March 15, 1770, he was "visited by a Jew from Lissa in Poland and had much *conversation* with him."[40] On February 16, 1771, "Mr. _____, a Jew," visited Stiles "to *converse* upon the New Testament" (my italics).[41] As Stiles indicated in his diary, the man was not necessarily planning to convert; he was courting a young Jewish woman who herself had been considering Christianity and wished to equip himself for that eventuality (in the end, neither Miss Pollock nor her suitor converted).[42] Even when he evinced an automatic interest in the prospect of conversion, his writing on the subject suggested an interest that was more ethnographic than theological in its origin. In September 1771, Stiles heard that the brother of Moses Michael Hays (a Jew from New York who came to settle in Newport and, eventually, Boston; see Chapter 6) was considering converting to Christianity. When Stiles asked Hays about it directly, the latter replied that "he knew nothing of it; & did not believe it."[43] Moreover, Hays added, any Jew who converted was unlikely to be sincere in his or her new profession. Whether or not Stiles agreed with Hays's cynical assessment, he (Stiles) was fascinated by the apparent ubiquity of Jews and Judaism, so much so that he shared his opinion with Hays that "there were more covert Xtian Jews in Spain & Portugal—& that the Jew blood was spread among them all—that it might be proved that the King of Spain or Portugal was of Jew extract."[44] If conversion was a subject of interest to Stiles, it was so not only as he followed his forebears in contemplating the apostasy of Jews to Christianity but the reverse as well. He was fascinated to learn, for instance, of the conversion of an English couple to Judaism, which included the husband's undergoing a circumcision. In 1772 he wrote in his diary about "one woman in New-England who was a Hebrician, perfectly understanding the Hebrew Bible . . . [who] was taken off a wreckt vessel . . . near Plymouth." Upon her eventual return to England, she "lived in a Jew family which taught Hebrew."[45]

The more Stiles interacted with the Newport Jews, the more aware he became, or the more aware he sought to become, about modern Judaism. On a visit to England in 1772, the Newport clergyman went out of his way to attend worship at Bevis Marks. There he noted the inclusion of "chaunting and Singing," as well as the Jews' expressed intention, the following night, of featuring "the reading [of] the Treble by the Leone, a most celebrated Singer in Imitation of the flute."[46] Though he never reached the point of arguing in favor, even in his diary, of Jews being naturalized or of Judaism becoming a legally protected religion, Stiles had, as Shalom Goldman suggests, "forged something new" in his Hebraism.[47] The new equation was not equivalent to tolerance because Stiles stopped well short of relinquishing any claim for Congregational Protestantism's status in his view as the true religion. Nor did it profess the value of anything remotely like the disestablishment of that church. The novelty in Stiles's attitude toward Judaism was its unprecedented *avoidance* of any finality in its judgments. Stiles was less interested in converting Jews or even in resolving the mysteries of early Christianity than he was in pursuing untethered scholarship. Though he was more staunchly religious and sectarian than the Boston firebrands or the Virginia Deists whose writings and agitations would soon help to instigate the Revolution, he was a willing participant in a free exchange of ideas from which there could be no turning back, especially as Newport and the rest of formerly British America set out to establish a new kind of authority in the war's aftermath.

If such an endeavor could take shape anywhere in New England, Newport would have been the place. Its very foundation had been an act of dissenters. By the middle of the eighteenth century, even stalwart Boston had gained its share, if not of outright freethinkers, then of heterodox skeptics on religious matters. In Newport, however, the combination of a dissenting tradition and an atmosphere of acquisitive opulence had helped to create an outpost of energetic speculation—a veritable marketplace of ideas. For a man of Stiles's temperament, whose "curiosity followed every path it came to,"[48] New England's second city offered all manner of exposures. Not that a man of his serious disposition would have cared for such things, but the city's atmosphere of tolerance had, by mid-century, opened its residents to several un–New Englandlike pastimes, including dancing, theater, card-playing, and horse-racing.[49] Those of a more scholarly persuasion, while they were unlikely to care about or dabble in such activities, found other ways to pass their leisure time and to assuage their restless curiosity. The town's relative wealth, or the wealth of certain townspeople, made possible the establishment of a subscribers' library. In 1747 Abraham Redwood, whose fortune had been made, like so many others, in the West Indies trade, donated an initial five hundred pounds toward the creation of the Redwood Library, whose building, like the synagogue, was designed by Peter Harrison and is still in use. In the library's founding documents, Redwood made clear his motives and purpose—"whereas Heaven has blessed him [Redwood] with an ample Fortune," he wrote, he wished to improve "the Place of his Residence in knowledge and Virtue."[50] Years later, Stiles himself would prefigure Emerson's exhortation in praise of "The American Scholar" by rendering his ideal scheme in which farmers, laborers, and mechanics in small New England towns might avail themselves of a resident philosopher who might, in the spirit of Redwood, supply all manner of intellectual stimulation to enrich their evenings.

Though an initial fee of one hundred pounds was required and members needed as well to pay an annual subscription of fifty pounds, Redwood expressed an ideology that spoke directly to the Enlightenment tendencies of the age. He wished the library to serve the common good, so that "the bewildered Ignorant might freely repair [there] for Discovery and Demonstration to the One, and true Knowledge. . . . "[51] His constituents would be "those Gentlemen" who possessed the foresight to appreciate the "beneficial Consequences that would accrue . . . of diffusing Light and Truth to Places far and wide . . . " Stiles was just this sort of gentleman, and he would soon serve as the official librarian there. The library supplied an ideal alternative pulpit for "the man who sensed God's presence in the joy he felt when gleaning knowledge from books [and] wanted to enlighten those who had little time for reading."[52] As the library's founding document had not stipulated any sectarian intention, and as its sole stated membership requirements concerned the payment of subscription fees, the town's two most prosperous Jewish merchants, Aaron Lopez and his father-in-law, Abraham Rivera, were also early members. Their participation could not but have helped to guarantee the Redwood Library's establishment as a refuge for unencumbered scholarly exploration in a range of subjects. Although the library was not brimming with Judaic materials per se, it did contain some, including a book that its catalogue referred to as A Treatise in Hebrew, by David Nieto, who had served as the hacham at Bevis Marks in London from 1701 until his death in 1728, and had himself been enough of a scholar of the natural world to have been the first Jew to calibrate the times of the sabbath's beginning and ending to England's northerly latitude.[53] More important, the library's holdings supported the study of Greek and Latin classics, the exploration of the natural world, including Newtonian physics, and a wide range of historical scholarship. Its existence helped to establish a larger atmosphere of inquiry in which a man like Ezra Stiles could sally forth from his pulpit and engage in open-ended dialogue with a broad range of interlocutors.

Newport was not the only town in British North America to support such tendencies. Nor were its Jews the only Jews along the seaboard who interacted socially, or at least on an intellectual basis, with gentiles. For Sephardim especially, so many of whom had been not only in but of the Christian world for centuries, such passage had been quite commonplace, and a ghettoized existence would have been not only unnecessary but unthinkable. Stalwart as they may have been in their religiosity, their ties to Judaism had been forged only rather recently. Jewish life in the Atlantic world, and especially on its American shore, was a "world in motion,"[54] in which communities were constantly expanding and contracting, the synagogue was not the only locus for Jewish communal engagement, and an extreme geographic mobility precluded an even remotely hermetic existence.[55] Accordingly, Jews like the ones who settled in Newport were often quite receptive to opportunities for social interaction and intellectual dialogue with non-Jews. Despite the name of the street where their burial site was located, the Newport Jews did not live all together on Jews' Street, but were widely dispersed throughout the town.[56] Moreover, at least for those few within the Jewish community who enjoyed broad business connections and the high living standard that went along with them, cordial encounters with non-Jews would be frequent. Places like the Redwood Library offered an ideal setting for sustained discourse. As the library's gatekeeper, Stiles not only partook of this openness, but served as the guarantor of it.

A starting point for Stiles was his conviction that even though God was unknowable, all attempts to learn about His world would be of potential value toward developing a deeper relationship with Creation. The reputation that he eventually gained as New England's most learned man had had its initial inspiration in his doubting tendencies. In a sermon he gave on May 7, 1758 (and then repeated, according to his notes, in 1763), he asserted quite brashly that "The religions of the world abound with Folly" and that even "The true religion" was so infected by "human invention, as to bear the Aspect of Vanity & Folly . . . if not Wickedness."[57] A year later, Stiles reminded his parishioners "That God is incomprehensible as to his being," especially "by Intelligences of such limited Capacities as Man in his present State."[58] None of Stiles's doubts were sufficient to challenge his adherence to Protestant Christianity, however. On the contrary, they seem to have inspired him to pursue deeper understanding through enhanced knowledge. His appetite for intellectual exposure was voracious. And in pursuit of shoring up his faith, he worked toward establishing a reasoning basis for a full and complete acceptance of the scriptures. This practice slightly scandalized his colleagues, one of whom worried in 1758 that Stiles's having "called up such a host of supporting evidence" for his belief in the scriptures might easily backfire and betray him as a skeptic.[59] In the mid-1760s Stiles actually entered a "hellfire" phase in his preaching, perhaps, as Christopher Grasso speculates, in order to refute rumors that his scholarly skepticism had outrun his commitment to the idea of divine grace. His concerns regarding his public reputation may have inspired him to adjust his pulpit rhetoric, but they only sublimated and intensified his pursuit, in private, of deeper insight. As Grasso puts it, a "veil between the truth a man perceived in his study and what he was willing to proclaim in public" was central to Stiles's evolving theology and worldview.[60] In his endeavor to ground his religion in a fuller knowledge of the scriptures and their sources, Stiles knew that the study of Hebrew would provide a useful entry into a more comprehensive grasp of scripture. Isaac Touro's arrival in Newport in 1759 coincided with Stiles's search for a rational basis for the scripture, but it wasn't until the late 1760s that the Congregational minister set about learning the language he had neglected while he had been a student at Yale.

As late as May 1767, Ezra Stiles knew only ten letters of the Hebrew alphabet. He put before himself the goal of translating entire books of the Bible, and to that end, began studying with Isaac Touro, whom he knew from his increasingly frequent visits to the synagogue. Before long, the two might be found walking together along Newport's busy Parade Street, with Stiles conning his lessons and Touro, presumably, correcting errors and providing steady guidance. Before long, as Stiles's diary makes clear, he was reading "ten pages of Psalter every day before breakfast."[61] His attendance at the synagogue picked up, and he was more frequently drawn into, or the instigator of, extended conversations on various scriptural and Judaic arcana. His sermon notes for these years, however, betray little evidence of a spillover from his Hebrew study to his ministry, aside from a few references to "Cabala," a subject which had long been a favorite topic of Puritan clergy with an interest in eschatology.

Stiles's study of Hebrew and his engagement of Jews on points of religious interest was a private matter, not so much in the sense that he wished to hide it from parishioners or townspeople, but in the sense that it informed his own fairly solitary spiritual pursuit. If Ezra Stiles's study of Hebrew and his encounter with Jewish tradition represented a new chapter within New England's long-standing Judeocentric history, it did so precisely by abstracting the pursuit from any prescribed theological agenda. Such an endeavor could only be undertaken in private, where Stiles would be able to allow for a range of implications. In the 1770s he developed an interest, for example, in locating the most reliable version of the Hebrew Bible, which he assumed could be found only among practicing Jews, who still had access to texts whose provenance predated the days of the early Christians. His was the "scholar's quest . . . to recover the scattered fragments of that primeval knowledge hidden in the archives of the world's great civilizations and among its scattered peoples."[62] Stiles was fascinated as well by the exact terms by which the Jews projected the arrival of the messiah. His encounter with the Jews of Newport seems only to have deepened his commitment to his Christianity, but it did so by opposite means from those employed by a range of New England clergy from the seventeenth century to Stiles's own time, for whom such learning might be employed only in strict and narrow accordance with preexisting precepts.

If private inquiry was the central basis upon which a man of Stiles's temperament might most readily explore a fledgling ecumenicity, his introduction to and developing friendship with Haim Carigal, who visited Newport between March and July of 1773, served as his most profound means of achieving it. Although the Newport synagogue had a paid *hazzan* in Isaac Touro, it could not hire a permanent rabbi, as men of such high Judaic scholarly achievement simply did not live anywhere in North America. The congregation did, however, enjoy a sequence of temporary visitors from abroad, each of whom, at least as Stiles had written about them, had the requisite training to be known by the title of "rabbi." Carigal was neither the first nor the last of the six rabbis whom Stiles met during his years in Newport, but the impression he made upon Stiles far exceeded those of the other five men combined. The basis for this impression was, at least in part, Carigal's level of erudition, especially given his relative youth (his age during his stay in Newport was 40). Stiles also noted Carigal's exotic personal aspect; he had been born in Hebron, of Sephardic parents, and his style of dress accorded with his "Oriental" origins. More important than any of Carigal's personal achievements or inherited traits, however, seems to have been his deportment, in which "Dignity and Authority . . . mixt with Modesty,"[63] as Stiles described him in his diary. Both men developed a mutual admiration early on (although Carigal kept no diary, his letters to Stiles plainly demonstrated his fondness for the minister, and Stiles's diary also recounted many of the rabbi's expressions of fondness for its writer), and while that mutual admiration may have had its origin in their respective scholarly achievements and shared interests, its strongest foundation lay in their fondness for each other. What made Stiles and Carigal's relationship different from previous personal relationships between Puritans and Jews (Menasseh Ben Israel's embassy to Oliver Cromwell comes to mind, as well as Samuel Sewall's and Cotton Mather's acquaintance with the Frazon brothers) was that friendship and strong mutual admiration, regardless of their respective theological positions, constituted the central basis for their interaction. This foundation of mutual admiration helped, in turn, to bring about one of the most profound ecumenical discursive exchanges in the history of colonial America.

When Carigal arrived in Newport, he had, according to Stiles's thumbnail biography of him, been traveling for nearly twenty years with little pause. He had been born in Hebron in 1733. After studying with the rabbis in Hebron, where he was "entitled Hocham and Rabbi" by the age of seventeen, he set sail for a succession of Jewish communities throughout the Middle East and North Africa. In 1757, at the age of twenty-four, he visited several cities in Italy, as well as Vienna, Prague, Nuremburg, Amsterdam, and London, among others. By virtue of such exposures, he had become an exemplar of the Jewish cosmopolite; though he was of Sephardic origin, his trips throughout Europe had exposed him at a young age to the Ashkenazic rite and to a broad range of rabbinical scholarship. He also gained a significant acquaintance with the various gentile communities with whom he had lived and a concomitant linguistic ability in German and English. In 1761, his mission to raise money for the small Jewish community of Hebron launched him on the first of his two extended sojourns in the New World. He served as the rabbi of the synagogue in Curaçao from 1761 until 1764, whereupon he returned to Europe and then Hebron, where he remained for four years. Before embarking on his second trip to America in 1772, which was the occasion for his visit to Newport, he spent two years teaching "at a London yeshiva."[64]

Although the original impetus for Stiles's synagogue visits and interactions with its *hazzan*, congregants, and visiting rabbis was his quest to anchor his own spiritual unease about the reliability of the Bible, his diary treatments of his friendship with Carigal were distinct not only for the high level of admiration that they expressed for the rabbi but for the way that they so frequently conveyed a certain kind of idiosyncratic detail. Stiles, who could be quite reserved and even sharply judgmental in his descriptions of people, expressed his admiration for Carigal in no uncertain terms. "I shall wait and expect [you] at my house, untill you come to me this day at III o'clock Afternoon," wrote Stiles to Carigal (in a heavily stilted biblical Hebrew) on June 7, 1773, and "at that Time, if thy Servant hath found favor in thine Eye, he will rejoyce to see thy face, that he may sit at the feet of a man of God . . . & be delighted with the Sweetness of thy wisdom."[65] Early on in their acquaintanceship, the minister wrote that Carigal was "learned and truly modest, far more so than I ever saw a Jew," and in later entries, he referred repeatedly to the rabbi's "modesty" and "elegance." No attribute of Carigal's seems to have been as important to Stiles as the former's "Candor," however, to which the minister referred on more than one occasion. Given so many religious adherents' tendency to avoid jeopardizing their founding doctrines, candor was a quality that would have been in relatively short supply even in a place like Newport, where Congregationalists, Baptists, Quakers, Anglicans, and Moravians were constantly vying for one another's memberships and defending their separate turf.

Although his diary did occasionally address stories of Jewish converts to Christianity (and vice-versa, as we have seen), Stiles evinced no particular interest in converting any of his Newport Jewish friends. The mere facts of life in the Holy Land were of sufficient interest to hold his attention. A typical interaction between the two men occurred on April 26, 1773, when Carigal and Touro paid Stiles a visit in his study, where the three men remained "till evening." Stiles recounted the encounter:

> We viewed a large sheet of antient Character of the oriental Paleography; & examined some medallions or coins with Samaritan Letters . . . upon which a Dispute arose, whether Moses wrote in Samaritan or Chaldee? The Rabbi said he wrote in the present Letter of the Heb. Bible— . . . . He had never seen these Sheckels and Coins & was unacquainted with the Reasoning upon them. He attempted to consider them as spurious, but at length seemed to grant them genuine, yet knew not how to account for Inscriptions in Samaritan with *Jerusalem the Holy*, which a Samaritan would not say after the Return from Babylon. He was puzzled yet spake like a Man of Candor, & disputed in such a manner as was Pleasant and Noble.[66]

Carigal's letters to Stiles suggested a similar appreciation on his part for the Newport minister, though they provided considerably less detail pertaining to their actual interactions. In characteristically effusive terms, Carigal's first letter to the minister, which he also wrote in Hebrew, spoke warmly of Stiles's knowledge *and* kindness: "A learned man thou art," he wrote, and then, invoking a passage from Job, continued, "Thy love is engraved in the innermost thots of my heart that Volumes of Books would not suffice to write a thousandth part of the eternal love with which I love you."[67]

Stiles evidently relied on Carigal for information and insight on a range of scripturally related subjects, ranging from the distance between Hebron and the Dead Sea (Stiles also asked his friend if he had ever seen the pillar of salt believed to be the remnant of Lot's wife) to "the Antiquity of the Hebrew Letters," to the question of "whether a man might Marry his wife's sister's Daughter" after becoming a widower.[68] Stiles had been impressed to hear from his new friend that "one may breakfast at Hebron and dine at Jerusalem."[69] Throughout the diary entries that spanned Carigal's time in Newport, Stiles commented on the rabbi's spontaneous responses to his many questions. Often enough, the minister's curiosity was more practical than theological in nature. Knowing that Carigal had crossed the River Jordan on many occasions, he wished to hear, for instance, "if the stones Joshua put on the Bottom of Jordan were still in being—adding that if they were there they might easily be found, as the water was so shallow" (Carigal answered that he had not thought to look for the rocks but that he also "believed the place of the Passage was a little higher up" on the Jordan).[70] Many of Stiles's inquiries seem to have been similarly motivated by his interest in reifying his scriptural knowledge and in anchoring biblical narratives in the landscape that his new friend had inhabited from birth. Carigal's knowledge, which was occasionally of an offhand variety but often enough the result of his long years of rabbinical study, was a welcome influence upon a man for whom matters of faith had been a cause for intense inner questioning. As a Jew and especially as a modern-day inhabitant of the Holy Land, Carigal had knowledge of many biblical antiquities that was experiential as well as abstract. The rabbi contributed to Stiles's evolving sense of Judaism as a living religion being practiced in the modern world. When Stiles had asked him about the salt pillar thought to be Lot's wife, for example, Carigal explained to Stiles that he had never seen the pillar because local regulations under Ottoman rule forbade Jews from traveling to the Dead Sea.

For men whose public personae had been fully formed in the context of their respective leadership of their own religious communities, both Stiles and Carigal experienced a unique rapport and intellectual affinity as they spent the spring and early summer in each other's frequent company. Personal fondness and candor eclipsed all other currencies. Neither man wished to convince the other to abandon his beliefs. The closest that

Stiles ever came to doing so, in writing at least, was in clearly identifying—in the context of a twenty-nine-page Hebrew letter he wrote to the
rabbi on July 19, 1773—the points of divergence between their faiths. In
the course of an extensive exposition on the names of God and the Judaic
roots of Christian belief in the Trinity, Stiles sought to explain his "opinion of the person of the glorious Messiah."[71] In the slightest digression
from his lengthy dissertation on Jehovah's component parts, the minister
offered the following clarification, in a purely factual mode: "Your opinion
of him [the Messiah] is that he is the great Angel above all Angels yet and
not eternal, but that there was a Time when the Messiah was not." Before
returning to his objective rendering of Christian doctrine, Stiles continued,
"In my eyes he is infinitely greater & far more glorious than he is in your
Eyes."[72] Both men easily embraced a mutual spirit of inquiry. When Stiles
remarked on Carigal's candor, he noted as well that his new friend was
"most remote from a disposition to obtrude his own assertions without
being ready to offer the Reasons."[73] They enjoyed a unique opportunity to
disagree with perfect amicability. Shortly after Carigal had departed from
Newport, Stiles said as much in a letter to his friend, who was sojourning
in Surinam at the time. The minister knew that Carigal would be less interested in the idea of a "suffering Messiah" than he; nonetheless, he had
sent his friend a rabbinical commentary on the subject, on the assumption
that Carigal would be "happy to agree" with its author's emphasis on the
"future glory of the Messiah's Kingdom."[74] Most important, he asked for
Carigal's honest reply; "it will be agreeable to me," Stiles wrote, "if you
will please communicate your remarks . . . to me with Freedom and liberal
sentiments."[75] Stiles was imagining and inviting his friend to join him in
a discursive climate that, by prior New England standards at any rate, was
entirely new. "For Gentlemen of letters," he wrote, "there is an openness
to Candour in the disquisitions & communications of the learned not to be
found among others."[76] The remark echoed many of his pronouncements
on one of his favorite subjects: the "unbiased openness of mind for Liberal
Inquiry" that had motivated his private studies, his work at the Redwood
Library, and his prolific correspondence with a range of interlocutors.

Perhaps their respective status, clerical achievements, and the professional security that went along with them constituted a firm enough basis
upon which they could both afford, at least in private, to be so unguarded.

For his part, Carigal represented a late generation within a distinguished family of Sephardic scholars whose progenitors had left Portugal for Salonica in the seventeenth century before making their way to the Jewish enclave in Hebron. Haim Carigal's father, Moshe de Carigal, had himself been an industrious author and the administrator of two *yeshivot* in Jerusalem. The extent of Haim Carigal's travels, as well as his erudition and his considerable success as a fundraiser, distinguished him from other rabbis of his generation. Well before his arrival in Newport, while serving a three-year term as the rabbi and teacher of the synagogue in Curaçao, he had earned an unheard-of 750 pesos annually—more money than one of Amsterdam's most important rabbis was earning at the same time.[77] Carigal's teaching in the midrash was spoken of decades after his passing, and his ability to inspire gift-giving from congregants outdid all expectations; upon his return to Amsterdam in 1764, he is known to have deposited 3700 florins in an account he held in that city, having also traveled there in the company of two servants, whose passage had been paid by the parnassim.[78] Though Stiles had not yet earned his place as the president of Yale College, his position at the helm of the Second Congregational Church easily made him one of the most influential ministers in Newport, if not all of New England. Both men could afford to take intellectual risks.

Carigal's letters bore no obvious evidence of their writer's self-consciousness regarding his participation in a ground-breaking sort of "amor intellectualis" (Stiles's term), but Stiles took note of the novelty and told at least one of his friends about it. A letter to the minister from Benjamin Gale of Killingsworth, Connecticut, suggested just how excitedly Stiles had shared tidings of his new friendship among his fellow ministers. For his part, Gale was just as enthusiastic: "I am told he [Carigal] is a Man of Learning among the Israelites," he wrote Stiles, before asking the Newport minister to inquire of the rabbi "whether [the Jews] Expect the Messiah will come Immediately from Heaven," among other questions.[79] Each time Stiles remarked on Carigal's "candor," he was silently invoking his own prior experiences, or at least perhaps his established prejudices regarding Jewish stubbornness. He evinced an appreciation for the efforts that Carigal was evidently making to venture into foreign spiritual realms. Carigal was aware of the tradition of Puritan Hebraism and could not but have been familiar with the many Protestant theologians who, like Stiles, sought wisdom and corroboration in the writings of both ancient and not so ancient "rabbins." When the appropriate opportunity showed itself, therefore, the rabbi produced a "Passage of St *Austin de Civitiae Dei* in a Hebrew book of David Neito" for his Christian friend to see; as Stiles indicated in his diary, Carigal was "much pleased that he was able to shew me something out of our Fathers for my Extracts out of his Rabbins."[80] Both men were eager to demonstrate their openness to each other's traditions and to show, indeed, that such mutualities and borrowings as they were themselves performing already had a history within both of their respective traditions.

Although their friendship was forged in the relative privacy of their studies, Carigal and Stiles also undertook another sort of discursive exchange whose terms were enacted from the pulpit. On May 28, for Pentecost, Carigal delivered a sermon from the *tebah* of the synagogue, with a full complement of congregants and visitors, including Stiles, in attendance. A few months later, when Aaron Lopez funded the publication of Carigal's sermon, it became the third Jewish sermon to be published in British North America, and the first one to be published that had also been *delivered* in North America. Stiles's diary notes on the sermon asserted that, because his friend had spoken in "Spanish,"[81] he had only understood a mere half of what he heard, so it is all the more remarkable that the minister's comments came as close as they did to touching on Carigal's main points. One month later, in a mind to return the favor, Stiles delivered a sermon at the Second Congregational Church with the rabbi in attendance. Stiles had apparently gone out of his way to make his friend at home, arranging for his son to welcome the rabbi to the Stiles home before meeting time and then placing him and his companion (an unidentified Newport Jew) in his own pew in the church. It is difficult to resist the temptation to interpret both sermons, which were delivered less than two years before the outbreak of the rebellion against Britain, as commentaries on the looming crisis. Whatever their respective political implications may have been, however, both sermons spoke volumes about the transcendent importance of personal friendship. Stiles's remarks were more obviously calculated to affirm the worth of Carigal's spiritual tradition. The rabbi gave voice to a spirit of adaptation, in which the practitioners of an ancient tradition were called upon to continue their practice of that religion but, at the same time, to find practical means of extending its life, given the changing conditions of life in the Diaspora of the Enlightenment age. As one recent scholar points out, Carigal felt an urgent need to counsel his fellow Sephardim toward a unity of purpose.[82]

Stiles's sermon does not exist in text form beyond the outline of it that he recounted in his diary, but his notes there made clear that his preaching that day had been deliberately calibrated to the interests and tastes of his Jewish guest who, as Carigal evidently told him, "*had never heard a Christian preach a sermon before.*"[83] None of Stiles's sermon notes for the period before or after Carigal's visit suggest that he was in the habit of preaching on the subject of the Jews. Thus, though he was delivering his remarks for the benefit of his parishioners, his special focus on the Jews that day was out of the ordinary. For Carigal's part, since the Newport sermon is the only one of his ever to have been published, it is difficult to know whether its contents reflected the rabbi's typical subject matter or something out of the ordinary. Knowing what we know about Carigal's own history and of his involvement in so many Atlantic world synagogue communities during his short lifespan, however, the subject of his sermon suggests that it contained a message for Stiles about the unique nature of their friendship and, at the same time, that it was meant to strike or establish a receptive chord on the part of his other listeners.

The starting point for both men was the "chosenness" of the Jews. As the seventeenth and eighteenth centuries marked the earliest manifestation of an emancipated Jewry, at least in the British Empire, both men were cognizant not only of the Jews' history as a persecuted "race" but of their emergence as a people whose lineage had been forged in ancient times but whose status in the world could be understood only in a modern context. In this way, Stiles at least was departing from the predictable path of Puritan Hebraism, in which the Jews existed as the sum total of their biblical experiences and of their unfortunate commitment to perdition. It is easy to understand why Carigal would have argued vociferously against the idea of the Jews constituting a "cursed" race, but the fact that Stiles's sermon, at least as he recounted its structure and contents in his diary, made no mention of Jewish cursedness is striking, given the centuries-long precedent for such a formulation. In his own remarks, Carigal set about "disproving" the ancient Christian argument concerning God's eternal judgment against the Jews. To that end, he cited several instances within world history in which God had called down enormous acts of destruction against gentiles, including the eruption of Mt. Vesuvius, in which "thick clouds of smoke and darkness" replicated the experience of an eclipse and "burning lava and ashes . . . caught up aloft and hurried by the violence of the winds, were carried to distant places."[84] The eruption was a hell on earth that spewed "torrents of liquid fire," and Carigal pointed out that it occurred in Rome shortly after the Roman legions had burnt and destroyed the Second Temple in Jerusalem in 70 C.E. It was the *persecutors* of the Jews, after all, and not the Jews, who were being made to suffer. Had the Jews been singled out as the beneficiaries of God's judgments upon their enemies, or was God simply acting inexplicably, punishing both the victims and the persecutors of those victims? Carigal's rebuttal of the traditional Christian doctrine of Jewish cursedness would not have discomfited Stiles, whose lifelong devotional to rational inquiry as an adjunct to spirituality had never favored the Puritans' earlier formulations of a divine sanction and retribution as overarching explanations for the patterns of human history.[85]

Of the two men, it was Stiles who made the more voluble case for Jewish chosenness. Carigal cited the volcanic eruption and other natural disasters that had befallen the gentiles in order to disprove any idea that the Jews had been singled out by God for an especially large share of suffering. Stiles, with his new Jewish friend seated in his own family's pew that day, swept the history of Jewish suffering aside in order to make an even bolder case. "The Seed of Jacob," he asserted, "are a Chosen and favorite people . . . [and notwithstanding] God's Chastisement of their Iniquity & Imperfection . . . [He] hath not forgotten his Covenant with Abraham . . . and his posterity . . . but intends them Great Happiness."[86] Stiles's sermon was remarkable for its consistent use of the present tense in association with a people who, for successive generations of Puritan Hebraists, had been associated solely with their storied past as the betrayers of Christ or with their fabled future either as eternally damned or as reconciled converts to His kingdom. In Stiles's sermon, the emphasis was on a current state of affairs. Moreover, Stiles counseled his parishioners that they had a role to play in God's plan for the Jews, not necessarily as proselytizers but as men and women who, in order that they might "partake hereafter with

Israel," ought to "share & rejoice in the Gladness of God's people & the Glory of His Inheritance."[87] In other words, notwithstanding Christian hopes regarding the eventual conversion of the Jews, the immediate task was simply to witness them, and to celebrate with them, as they observed their own distinct traditions.

Besides the personal example set by Carigal, Stiles may as well have admired the theology of Carigal's May 28 sermon which, within a few weeks of its delivery, had been translated from Spanish into English, published, and distributed in Newport. Though the sermon's ultimate message included, as Lee Friedman puts it, an "acceptance of the revealed word of God," Carigal's remarks also suggested that such acceptance could come only as the result of study which, in turn, was an act of free will. At the outset, the rabbi quoted the Talmud and the words of Rabbi Ismael: "If there arise within thee an evil desire, the best remedy you can get to subdue it is to proceed directly with it to the sacred colleges."[88] "The ability of Torah study to erase sin," as Laura Leibman puts it, would have rung true for Sephardic conversos who had recently renounced Christ, but no kind of biblical study, from a Christian point of view, could suffice as a substitute for divine mercy.[89] As long as the individuals concerned were of Stiles's and Carigal's scholarly inclination, however, they might reach an unstrained agreement on the matter. Throughout his sermon, Carigal counseled his hearers to study the law, arguing that only as they did so would they stand the slightest chance of repairing the wrongs of the world. God was mysterious and powerful, he reminded his listeners, but mere capitulation to His greatness would merit little. Rather, "the ardent and vehement desire of unvailing and comprehending the truth," as Carigal put it, would in itself result in a virtuous outcome.

These were daring words which could have been uttered only by someone of an Enlightenment temperament to an audience whose members were prepared to hear them. Although the sermon "defend[ed] traditional Judaism and its values against modernist incursions,"[90] its author did not hesitate, as Stiles must certainly have appreciated, to cite several classic Roman texts as he made his case. Only a person who had a certain faith in the innate goodness of humanity would suggest, as Carigal did, that knowledge and study of *anything* could in themselves drive away evil tendencies:

Such is the force of truth, such the efficacy inseparable from the sacred study, that even when the meditations applied solely for curiosity and ostentation, or even when the wicked intention may be used only for the purpose of finding something to censure, yet its excellence & perfection is so great, that the critics themselves soon find their malevolent dispositions subdued, being unable to give any solution to the false ideas they have formed, and gradually opening the eyes of their understanding, acknowledge their error, and admit the unconquerable impression of truth.[91]

From what we know of him, it was characteristic of Carigal to hold up the ideal of truth but to avoid imposing his own version of it upon his listeners. His correspondence and interaction with Ezra Stiles had been a case in point.

How Carigal's sermon affected the Newport Jews we cannot know, but it struck a chord in Stiles. The minister's summary of its contents, as he noted in his diary, suggest that he had been able to comprehend more than his mere "Affinity of the Spanish and Latin" ought to have taught him. He also described the rabbi's appearance, which conveyed a "fine and Oriental" version of "Oratory, Elocution, and Gesture." As Stiles found out in subsequent conversation with Carigal, though the rabbi looked at times as he was standing at the reading table as if he had a script before him, he had in fact, "*seald* it first in his head and so deliver[ed] it."[92] Most important, the Christian minister expressed his approval of Carigal's sermon and of Carigal's persona by preparing and delivering his own sermon, a month later, on the worthiness of the Jews and more particularly on the gift that God had conferred upon the entire world by "preserving a Remnant of this people, that of this seed he may make a glorious Nation hereafter."[93]

Stiles and Carigal were forging a new path past the old Puritan Hebraic usages and in the direction of a less secure but more durable mutual affinity. Again, though we may only go by Stiles's diary notes for his sermon, the minister's studious avoidance in his own remarks of *naming* the savior but, instead, of maintaining a consistent focus on "the Messiah" suggests that he had gone to deliberate lengths not only to avoid discomfiting his two Jewish audience members but to posit a final jubilee in which Jews and Christians would be indistinguishable from one another as they reveled in their first appearance "in one glorious Body before the Throne of God."[94] The line was remarkably reminiscent of one that Carigal had evidently spoken to him when, on his last night in Newport, Stiles had asked him "If a woman had more Husbands than one, which wife would she be" in Heaven? The rabbi had answered with his usual modesty and candor, saying "God Almighty could only determine" and that "he was contented to know that the Resurrection state would be happy and glorious, though he did not pretend to know and solve all questions and mysteries" concerning the afterlife.[95] For many years to come, Stiles would continue to harbor an overall "ambivalence" regarding Jews, especially in the tumult of the Revolution and the British takeover of Newport. Nonetheless, his time with Carigal proved to be so transformative that it enabled him to suspend his prejudices at least provisionally. And even as his suspicion of Jews continued to surface, he could not reverse the course of the larger epistemological change that his Jewish encounters had helped to inspire.

In addition to Carigal's influence, it was the political events of the early 1770s that prevented Stiles from maintaining a more strident, spiritually doctrinaire congregationalism. Although dozens of Newporters, including the Jews, tried to hedge their bets and avoid demonstrating a fixed allegiance either to Britain or to the patriot cause, Stiles was far from a neutral party, and his investment in the American rebellion ensured the further evolution of his religious sensibilities. Like everything else, religious expression became an instrument of and for political change. As more than one historian has pointed out, Newport's atmosphere of tolerance was effectively shattered by the Revolution, but this outcome resulted not from a lessening of diversity or from any deepening of the Calvinistic doctrine that had once united some New Englanders and held others apart from each other. Rather, as Newporters underwent the tumult of revolution, their religious ties became the primary vehicle by which they expressed their political affiliations. Thanks in part to Carigal's influence, Stiles's adoption of a point of view that could indulge in an ecumenical search for the truth did not mean that he was no longer a steadfast Congregationalist. Despite his many private caveats, Stiles had spent much of his career agitating in favor of what Grasso refers to as a "union of New England Protestants based upon liberty of conscience and polity."[96] The battle lines being drawn among Newport's churches—among which the town's tiny synagogue occupied a sort of no-man's land—would have less to do now with the degree of a given minister's or congregation's arminian or antinomian leanings than they did with their stance on non-importation agreements, their opposition to the Stamp Act, or whether they continued to drink tea in the aftermath of the same boycott that inspired the Boston Tea Party in 1773.

When the Revolution began, Ezra Stiles, who had been so completely won over by his relationship with Haim Carigal, expressed a fundamental distrust of the Jews resident in his town. In 1777 he observed in his diary that "the Jews [of Newport] are very officious in informing against the inhabitants."[97] Even more disconcertingly, Stiles subscribed to a unsubstantiated and paranoid theory that the Jews of London operated a "secret intelligence office" whose purpose it was to monitor reports on Whiggish behavior among the American colonists[98] (he later noted in his diary that the rumor had been proven false). When, in the midst of the war, Stiles recorded one of his periodic surveys of various demographic phenomena of Newport, he kept close track of who might be counted as a supporter of the Revolution and whom he believed to be a Tory. By Stiles's reckoning, Jews never figured into the first category and frequently found their way into the second. In actuality, though the Jews were fairly widely suspected of being "less trustworthy patriots,"[99] the divisions among their ranks merely reflected the entire town's divided state. If the number of Jews associated with the patriot cause appeared to be scant, it was because those among them who had decided to take their chances with the rebellion had left Newport to escape persecution at the hands of the English, who had begun a naval bombardment of the town in July 1775 and were threatening to burn it in its entirety.[100] A year later, with five hundred of the town's houses in ruins, its population had decreased by nearly half from its prewar high of ten thousand.[101]

For all of his suspicions of Jews, Stiles did not completely vacate his sympathetic interest in their affairs even when the immediate benefit of his fellow Congregationalists was in question. In October 1780, a letter from Moses Seixas to Aaron Lopez recounted the Congregational pastor's role in counseling the town's remaining Jews that they had a right to refuse the use of their synagogue—one of the town's few remaining religious sanctuaries that hadn't been either destroyed or commandeered by occupying British soldiers—to a "Mr. Channing," who had applied for and been granted the right to use it in order to conduct a Congregational service there. Seixas wrote that he had "availed [him] of the impropriety of letting him [Channing] have it,"[102] perhaps in order to forestall whatever accusations of disloyalty might have come to him and his fellow Jews. Since that time, however, he went on to inform Rivera that

> Doct'r Stiles is come here on a visit . . . and . . . he expressed much concern and amazement at the application, assur'd me it wou'd not have been made had he been here, that he was well convinc'd we cou'd not accede to it, without violating our religious principles, and all that lay in his power shou'd be done to remove any unfavorable impressions that a refusal might create amongst his congregation, and on the whole express'd a very friendly feeling for us . . .[103]

As one historian frames the subject, Stiles had acted the part of a consultant on halachic matters for a Jewish congregation that was either too intimidated or too uninformed on Jewish law to respond properly to Channing's application. In his responsum to the question of whether or not Channing ought to have been granted or denied the use of the synagogue, the Talmudic scholar Alexander Gutman, writing more than two hundred years later, concluded that Stiles had been "entirely correct in stating that the use of the synagogue for Christian services was prohibited by Jewish law."[104] Stiles's loyalty to his own sect, in other words, could be trumped by principles he had formed in the spirit of free inquiry and loyal friendship. Moreover, in the absence of a qualified Jewish authority on such matters, Stiles was more than willing to serve as a proxy for the departed Isaac Touro in passing judgment on the legality of his fellow Congregationalists' request.

Although Haim Carigal had come and gone before any of these events had transpired, his friendship and interactions with Ezra Stiles had acted as a catalyzing agent in the development of the minister's newly politicized rhetoric. More than one historian has suggested that Carigal himself was an agent or prophet of revolutionary change. On the one hand, his sermon of May 28, 1773, was an "exhortation (to Jews) to remain true to their religion."[105] But as his audience had included two of Massachusetts' most identifiably Loyalist judges and as he spoke repeatedly about the dangers of men "pretend[ing] to be angels while we are only men," he might just as easily have been exhorting those Whigs among his listeners (among whom Stiles would certainly have been a sufficiently subtle listener as to comprehend such a larger purpose, if he were able to follow along in the Spanish) to resist English tyranny.[106] The question of whether or not Carigal had absorbed enough knowledge about the patriot cause to have so strong an opinion about it is unresolvable (his friendship with Stiles could very well have swayed him in this direction, but he might just as easily have been influenced by his frequent companionship, while he was in Newport, with Isaac Touro, the *hazzan* whose Toryism was sufficiently steadfast as to cause him to flee, once the war was underway, to Jamaica). Carigal's influence upon Stiles was not ideological; the minister would scarcely have needed persuasion, let alone from a foreign Jew, of the justness of the patriot cause. Where the rabbi exerted a powerful influence was in inspiring a shift in Stiles's willingness and ability to dispense, once and for all, with merely abstract doctrinal arguments as a basis for his sermons. Now that he had fully grasped the advantages of free inquiry on spiritual matters and the transcendent importance of worldly relationships regardless of their participants' respective religious beliefs or practices, he could devote himself to developing a fully politicized clerical discourse.

More broadly speaking, the presence of Jews and their active pursuit of a lively religious and communal life had itself played a significant role in shaping Newport as a pluralistic, if unharmonious setting in which separate sectarian interests contributed to an overall climate of agonistic rivalry. Despite its long history of apparent tolerance, Newport was a tumultuous microcosm of all the American colonies, in which "dissenters formed the majority of the inhabitants,"[107] and uniformity of political opinion was unheard of. While the debates in the town between Anglicans and Congregationalists and other dissenters was particularly rancorous, the Newport Jews, whether of Loyalist or Whig leanings, more or less melted away with the coming of the war. In 1774, Newporters who suspected them of disloyalty to either the Loyalist or Whig cause desecrated their cemetery.[108] For his part, Stiles was one of several Newporters who maintained strong suspicions, well before the war began, that Anglican authorities in England intended to impose a "Bishop of America" on the colonies. Once the war was underway, he kept a close watch on Newport's

Anglicans, most of whom did not bother to disguise their loyalty to the crown. "I find the Chh. of Engld in America espy N. Engld inspired with such a secular principle," he wrote in 1777, "unanimated with the Love of Jesus so much as with the Love of Dignities and Preeminence."[109] He worried as well about Baptists, whom he believed to be "guilty of this Absurdity that if the World . . . was already Xianized & in the opinion of Baptists regenerated . . . —[they] would consider all this as nothing" on the basis that prior paedobaptisms disqualified so many would-be communicants.[110] For good measure, Stiles also dismissed Quakers for all of their worldly renunciations. In the larger context of his almost blanket condemnation of so many religious sects, Stiles's skepticism regarding the Jews' loyalty to the patriotic cause seems at least slightly less malicious.

Even the broad approval that Stiles expressed for Congregationalists and Presbyterians, whom he judged to be "the most truly Charitable & Catholic of any part of Xtiandom" was tempered by his deepening politicization, which kept him from swearing "any kind of doctrinal allegiance to *any* orthodox interpretation of the Scriptures."[111] The Age of Reason had coincided with the coming of Haim Carigal, and it turned Stiles, who when he "first set out in Life . . . had a much better opinion of Mankind & of the different Sects," into a skeptic on matters of religious loyalty.[112] "I was never *particular & exclusive* eno' for a cordial & close Union with any Sect even my own," he wrote.[113] He had resisted the New England tendency to "Condemn all as Arminian & Arians in N Engld whom the Minister and Chhs. In general tho't such."[114] Indeed, as Edmund Morgan writes, as Newport's other Congregationalist minister, Samuel Hopkins, was attempting to "drive the unregenerate out of his church, Stiles tried to sweep them in."[115] Most important, Stiles had learned to place more faith in acts and in the quality of humanity and less in the entirely abstract notion that, in the Calvinist vein, "a man may be regenerated in his sleep."[116] Nothing could have been more indicative of Carigal's and, indeed, of a wider Judaic "influence" upon Stiles than his realization that something was intrinsically wrong with a theology that argued that "for an unregen. Man to be Killing his father & mothr was a less sin than to pray to God for Pardon."[117]

Stiles had never been a fully committed Calvinist anyway, and for all the changes that it ushered in, the American Revolution did not itself cause other New Englanders to develop an entirely new theology. The impact of the Revolution, in which New England's few Jews once again found themselves to be inadvertent participants and witnesses, was its urgent politicizing effect upon religious discourse and, in that respect, Stiles found himself promoting a view that, whether it was Calvinist or anti-Calvinistic at its base, was built upon the principle of free inquiry and the value of personal integrity. He had no more jettisoned his Puritanism than New England had shed its founding emphasis on the right of dissent. As Edmund Morgan puts it, Stiles—like several generations of New Englanders after his time—had "transformed [the Puritans'] reverence for Scripture into a platform for liberty of thought."[118] Stiles's Puritanism "was . . . a compound of the old piety and the new enlightenment,"[119] and to the extent that his friendship with Haim Carigal, as well as other Jews in Newport, had contributed to it, Stiles was going a long way toward illustrating New England theology's long, complex, and ever-evolving relationship with Jews and Judaism.

Although Haim Carigal left Newport four months after he arrived there, he did not disappear from Stiles's life. When the two men took leave of each other, on the evening of July 18, 1773, they expressed their mutual affection quite openly, and Stiles himself, who had generally been the less effusive of the two, said that he was saying farewell "with a great Reluctance, and should ever retain an affection for him[;] that it was probable we might never see each other in the Land of the Living and wished we might after Death meet together in the Garden of Eden and there rejoice with Abraham Isaac and Jacob, and with the Soul of the Messiah till the Resurrection."[120] Carigal answered in kind, saying that he "loved [Stiles] from the Heart, and had [his] Name in his Book, and should soon send it to Jerusalem, where I should soon be known as I was here."[121] Though the rabbi never did publish "his book" in Jerusalem or anywhere else, he did maintain a written correspondence with his friend in Newport, which the two managed to continue—quite often in Hebrew—until Carigal's premature death, at Barbados, in 1777.

If nothing else, the rabbi was eager to send immediate word of his welfare to his friend in Newport as soon as he arrived at his first destination in the Caribbean, which was the Dutch colony of Surinam. He wrote to Stiles in the vein of their earlier acquaintance: "My fervent prayers to the Allmighty to grant you his Blassing that you may enjoy Your Life with health

& prosperity for many years."[122] For whatever reasons, he had decided to spare Stiles the full account of his misadventures, which he did relay to his coreligionist Aaron Lopez in a letter that described stormy seas, a shipboard epidemic, and dangerous shortages of food and water. One year later, Carigal told Stiles of his arrival in Barbados and his installment there as "Rabbi of this place."[123] Stiles maintained a faithful correspondence as well, as the extant letters show, especially given the strain that composition in Hebrew, which he had learned less than ten years earlier, would have required. His diary referred repeatedly to lengthy letters he posted to his friend in Barbados.

The extant letters displayed the degree of Stiles's voracious Hebraism and his eagerness to keep up a dialogue with his rabbinical confidant. No one in Newport, including the Jews who were permanently resident there, could have responded meaningfully to his questions on "the Subject of the Patriarchal Chronology," for instance, about which he posted a five-page Hebrew letter to Carigal in March 1774. In that letter, he indulged in some verdant biblical phrasing, telling the rabbi that his memory of their conversations "was more sweet to my taste than Honey, & much more pleasant than . . . Excellent perfume."[124] From this starting point, the letter marked out Stiles's desire to locate a reliable, integral version of the scriptures. He outlined a phase in the earlier history of Christian biblical scholarship that followed from the absorption of "the Jewish Christians among the Gentile Christians" during which few of his coreligionists had pursued the study of Hebrew. "In this space of about a thousd years," he wrote, "all the copies of the Bible except the only one left in the hands of the Jews perished."[125] Like the previous generations of New England Hebraists, Stiles knew and appreciated the Jews' longevity and lineage. In his letter he asked Carigal if he remembered having once told him that he had "seen a copy of the law 900 years old."[126] Stiles's fascination with Jews, as well as his evident fondness for Carigal, was more than mere antiquarian reverence. From Carigal in particular he craved a response that would have been based on the rabbi's lifelong immersion in a dynamic Judaic scholarship that few Christians could appreciate. He recognized that there were often acute differences of opinion among Jewish scholars of his own day, and he wanted Carigal's opinion on such matters. In his correspondence with Carigal, Stiles was seeking insight into a scholarly debate which, although it may not have borne any obvious doctrinal implications, might have served to fortify his hopes of resolving his own doubts and dilemmas. His questions for Carigal took for granted the latter's intrinsic right to uphold beliefs and traditions that were entirely incommensurate with those of a Christian. As always, the relationship trumped any potential points of contention.

When Stiles wrote to Carigal to inform him of his own wife Elizabeth's death, the fighting in Massachusetts had just begun. The latter portion of his July 1775 letter contained a detailed description of the Battles of Lexington and Concord, the ensuing organization of an American army in Cambridge under the command of George Washington, and a narration of the events at Bunker Hill, which he accompanied with a map that referred to both armies' positions in and around Boston. The letter included Stiles's estimate, based on reports from both British and Continental sources, on casualty figures from both sides, as well as the numbers of men who served. Why did Stiles address Carigal in such extreme detail on a matter that would appear to have been so remote from the rabbi's immediate concerns or interests? Had the two discussed the colonists' growing resistance to British authority during Carigal's time in Newport? It is difficult to gauge the level of Carigal's interest, not to mention his comprehension (this letter of Stiles's had been written in English, not Hebrew). In his reply to Stiles's "Bunker Hill" letter, the rabbi went on to devote the bulk of his remarks to the subject of Elizabeth's death, and restricted his comments on Stiles's reportage to the following sentence: "I thank you for the words concerning the American affairs and I hope that may soon be accommodated."[127] At best, Carigal was deliberately misreading the minister's letter, which made no pretense of wishing for resolution but, instead, assigned biblical significance to the war and associated the Americans with a just cause. In their efforts to resist the British military, the Americans were "neither intimidated nor despaired," Stiles had written. Having been "animated by their Generals with the same spirit as that which the Patriot Nehemiah animated God's People of Old," the American soldiers might have been an eighteenth-century version of Cromwell's New Model Army, as far as Stiles was concerned.[128]

When Carigal died in 1777, Stiles was coming and going from Newport periodically in the aftermath of the British takeover there. In 1778, which was a low point for the American cause, he left Newport and his congregation permanently, having been invited to serve as the president of Yale. Among the many executive decisions that awaited his attention over the succeeding years was the question of whose portraits he might enshrine in the College's library. Four years had passed since Carigal's death, but in 1781, Stiles began the process of commissioning a portrait of the rabbi, which would soon share space there with images of King George I, Connecticut's Governor Saltonstall, John Davenport (the founder of New Haven), and a handful of other New England stalwarts from ages past. Soon he was writing to Aaron Lopez, in hopes that he would provide some of the necessary funding for the portrait of "that great & eminent Hocham, the Rabbi Karigal" that he wished to install at Yale.[129] In this way, the merchant prince could ensure Jewish participation, as he had already done in contributing to the founding of Moses Brown's College, in the furtherance of New England's institutional future. Stiles invited Lopez to decide as well upon an appropriate Hebrew inscription to be included at the portrait's base. The merchant was more than willing to do Stiles's bidding and arranged, on Stiles's suggestion, for a rough crayon portrait of Carigal that had been completed during the rabbi's stay in Newport to be reinterpreted, in "oyls," by the Rhode Island artist Samuel King.

The portrait was completed in 1783, and Stiles immediately placed it in the library at Yale, where it remained until his term as president ended upon his death in 1795.[130] It bore a striking contrast in its simplicity to Samuel King's portrait of Stiles, which had been completed in 1770. For while Stiles labored through his entire career to affect a balancing act that might alleviate the "public incongruities that could exist between personal belief and public doctrine,"[131] his friendship with Carigal had afforded him a brief but precious acquaintance with an alternative, though practically impossible harmony of theological and scholarly interests. In commissioning the portrait of his dear and departed Jewish friend, Stiles seems almost to have wished to enshrine Carigal's apparently imperturbable elegance and tranquility as a man of learning who managed, at the same time, to be a man of unimpeachable moral and spiritual rectitude. Stiles, by contrast, had required a sprawling group of accompanying "Emblems" in order to articulate his complicated attempt to bring about the balance between the "inner realm and his public image"[132] that, to all appearances, Carigal had projected so effortlessly.

Ezra Stiles (1727–1795). From the 1771 portrait by Samuel King. Image provided through the courtesy of the Yale University Art Gallery.

When Stiles had hired King to prepare his own portrait, he must have gone to great lengths to prescribe its almost dizzying array of iconographic figures. Stiles's portrait presented a field of denotative and connotative possibilities, including a shelf of books, a numinous floating sphere (which, in turn, was inscribed with the tetragrammaton), and a carefully arranged representation of his face and torso. In his journal, Stiles devoted two pages to a full annotation of King's portrait of him. The books alone, which happened to include a disproportionate number of Judaic voices, merited the following description: "A Folio shelf with Eusebio, Hist. Ecc, Livy, Du Halde's Histry of China, and one inscribed Talmud By Aben Ezra, Rabbi Selamoh Jarchi in Hebrew Letters and a little below R. Moses Ben Maimon Morela Mevochim."[133] In Stiles's portrait, space was carefully compartmentalized. The book that Stiles held in his hand (his diary identified it as a Bible) was prominently displayed and held out toward the viewer. The black of his gown contrasted sharply with the ruddiness of his complexion. The books' authors and titles were rendered with all possible precision and, as Stiles indicated in the journal, their very placement spoke to an almost hierarchical ordering on his part, by which he "denote[d] his taste for History, and the Mythology of the Fabulous Ages," among other interests.[134]

Counterbalancing the books that King had depicted to Stiles's left was the "private hieroglyph for the spiritual universe,"[135] by which Stiles had hoped to denote his belief in the "Tendencies of Minds to Diety," or his lifelong effort to employ and to justify scholarly inquiry as a fitting path toward union with God. The spheroid image included several pinpoints of light (presumably representing individual seeking souls) who were being drawn toward the blinding light of Yahweh by means of a webwork of tethers. A black cross near the bottom of the sphere served as a reminder of the crucifixion. Such complex and multivalent iconography practically required the accompaniment of a critical apparatus, which Stiles supplied at least to those members of future generations who might care to know about such things, in the form of his diary entry on the subject. The overall effect wrought by the portrait's overlapping fields of visual, linguistic, and iconographic statements suggested that Stiles was eager to be understood on his own terms, even as he knew that those terms were almost impossibly opaque to his parishioners. That he wished for King to depict not only the clarity of expression conveyed in his public face but the complexity of his inner thoughts, as intricately relayed by means of the portrait's myriad compartments, hierarchies, and hieroglyphics, suggests as well that he had felt the strain incumbent on anyone who had so long attempted to negotiate the difficulties of a dawning age in which Puritan conviction and a nascent spirit of inquiry, which he meant to combine, so often seemed to be operating at cross purposes.

Rabbi Raphael Haim Isaac Carigal (1733–1777). From the portrait by Samuel King, completed in 1783. Image provided through the courtesy of the Yale University Art Gallery.

The Carigal portrait, by contrast, completely unencumbered by any concerns regarding either the public persona or private self of its deceased subject, was a study in relative simplicity. One of its most striking features was the expression of what Stiles would perhaps have called "absolute Candour" in the rabbi's face. The painting lacked the slightest reference to any abstract or carefully denoted background details. Carigal too held a book in his hand as an assertive prop, but where Stiles held his book out toward his viewers, King depicted only the upper right-hand corner of the rabbi's volume, and the positioning of the book was such that only its holder would have known its contents. Where Stiles encountered his viewers from a seated position, with his torso bent slightly forward as if in anxious eagerness to convey a particular sentiment or truth, Carigal's portrait presented a standing figure. Both men appeared in what Stiles referred to as "a Teaching Attitude," but Carigal's "Effigies," or physical figure, was the sum total of his curriculum. Where Stiles glanced sidewise at his viewers, with the back of his hand carefully positioned over his midriff as if to contain a myriad of inner complexities, Carigal's glance at the viewer was direct, and he held his hand away from his body in mid-gesture, as if pausing in the middle of a disquisition.

What Carigal's portrait lacked in iconographic complexity and background material. it displayed in its striking use of its reds and blacks. The rabbi's exotic physical appearance had made an early impression on Stiles, who many years earlier, upon first meeting him, had described his appearance and clothing in enormous detail, as if to say that the outward show, at least in this case, was a sign of inner light. In particular, Stiles had noted "a *scarlet outer garment* of Cloth, one side of [which] was Blue, the *outside scarlet*, [that] reached down . . . near the Ankles."[136] Likewise, Stiles had noted Carigal's "White Cravat round his neck," his "long black Beard, the upper lip partly shaven," and "on his Head a high Fur Cap, exactly like a Woman's muff, and about 9 or 10 inches high."[137] Since King had only an early crayon sketch to go by as visual guidance for his depiction of Carigal, the rabbi's appearance in exactly the same clothing as Stiles had recounted him wearing in his diary entry of April 8, 1773 (the day happened to be Passover), suggests that Stiles had shared his visual depiction with the artist and, on that basis, that he had hoped that the portrait might capture his earliest fond impression of the man whose "modest" and "reverent" behavior had struck him so powerfully. The scarlet robe, beard, and tall cap all suggested an exotic elegance that was the exact counterpoint to what Stiles had already identified as an admirable and uncompromising candor on the rabbi's part. In an oration he had delivered at Yale before the portrait's commissioning, Stiles had in fact referred to Carigal as having been "like Joseph of a comely aspect and beautiful countenance."[138] As Arthur Chiel points out, the new president of Yale had evidently "wanted for that countenance to look down on his youthful students in the library."[139]

Accordingly, in King's portrait, Carigal's image constituted a univocal utterance which necessitated minimal accompaniment. Whether Carigal's own peripatetic and hectic existence at the center of a dynamic transatlantic Sephardic community was as free of conflict and complexity as Stiles's impression of him suggested, the portrait's only appurtenance was a single inscription at its upper right-hand corner which read, "Rabbi Raphael Haym Isaac Karigal, born at Hebron. Educated at Jerusalem & Died at Barbadoes—Aetat—MDCCLXXII."[140] Haim Carigal's brief sojourn was not the "subject" of King's portrait even if it supplied the sole occasion for Ezra Stiles's friendship with him. As a complete outsider to the culture of New England and perhaps the only man Stiles would ever truly know who could be entirely dispassionate on the vexing theological concerns that had marked his own career as a man of the cloth in post-Puritan New England, Carigal had given his Christian friend the most cherished gift imaginable; firsthand knowledge of what scholarly enterprise and personal virtue, detached from doctrinal concerns, might actually look like.

CHAPTER SIX

"A MOST VALUABLE CITIZEN"
Moses Michael Hays and the Modernization of Boston

MOSES MICHAEL HAYS SOUGHT a private transformation when he quoted "The Great Mr. [Alexander] Pope" in his 1770 letter to Aaron Lopez and Jacob Rod Rivera,[1] but the words he borrowed from the English poet's "Essay on Man" spoke as well to cultural changes that were ascendant throughout New England in the revolutionary era. Born in New York in 1739 and part-time resident and merchant in Newport by the late 1760s, Hays hit a low point in 1770 when he was sentenced to a term in New York's debtor's prison. Hoping to clear his name even in anticipation of his time in jail, he wrote a series of letters to several business associates, including a few to Newport's merchant prince and his father-in-law. As Hays invoked Pope's aphorism that "An Honest Man is the Noblest Work of God," he affirmed a principle whose truth, however self-evident it is to us today, was not necessarily native to New Englanders of his own day. Although the strictest Calvinism had long since waned in church practice, many New Englanders still rejected any equivalency between human virtue and divine sanction. In the New England tradition, neither "Honesty" nor any other human virtue had been a guarantor of a saved or godly man. In business endeavors, however, personal honor would soon grow to be of greater importance than adherence to any particular theological precept (especially for Jews), and Hays's eventual redemption as a financial pioneer and civic leader in postrevolutionary Boston would prove the point.

Particularly as revolutionary-era New Englanders would soon find themselves having to invent entirely new political and civic institutions, Pope's wisdom was apt. If God was to be of any assistance in this new milieu,

Moses Michael Hays (1739–1805). From a copy of the Gilbert Stuart portrait made by Miss E. M. Carpenter in 1883. Provided through the courtesy of the Grand Lodge of Masons in Massachusetts (Boston).

it would have to be as He invested His human agents with the virtue and fortitude they would need in order to fashion a republic in the aftermath of their rebellion against the king. Moses Michael Hays's letter to Lopez and Rivera represented his best attempt to restore his personal reputation as a merchant who could be trusted with credit, but in the wider scheme, it also adapted both the communitarianism and the individualism of the Puritans to a newly secularizing purpose. Although Hays, as a Jew, had never known a Calvinistic past, his redemption and his rise to prominence and stature in the years between his release from jail in 1771 and his death in Boston in 1805 manifested a new sort of self-actualization that went hand-in-hand with New England's broader cultural transformation. That Hays was unapologetically Jewish *and* committed to the present and future prosperity of New England was not lost on his admiring neighbors.

Hays's letter to Lopez and Rivera, written in December 1770, followed in the aftermath of his having been unable to furnish debts he owed to several New York merchants, including "Mr. Charles Mr. M. Bayard Mr. Thos. Backe Mr. Lewis Pintard & many other People of the first integrity . . . "[2] His immediate concern, and the primary subject of his correspondence not only with Lopez and Rivera but with several other Newport merchants, was the wrong that had been done to him by his business partner, Myer Polock. Knowing that he and Polock faced an uncertain future as they came to terms with their New York creditors, Hays recounted in one letter that they had nonetheless "Determined to bring our unhappy Matters to Issue & Accomodation."[3] Hays and Polock had left Newport with the intention of achieving some sort of reckoning with the men to whom they owed money. Upon their arrival in New York, however, Polock, who had defamed himself ten years previously by uttering libelous allegations about another Newport Jew, deserted his partner. He headed south by water to Sandy Hook, New Jersey, and thence back to Newport, taking with him Hays's remaining assets.

As Hays subsequently related the chronology to his friend Samson Mears, once aboard the Newport-bound ship (a vessel that he co-owned with Hays), Polock had sent belated word of his whereabouts: "I am on board the *Mermaid*," he told Hays; "you shall hear from me and I will do you all the Justice [and] many reasons, you shall know for my sudden departure."[4] Polock's side of the affair is unknown since he seems never to have delivered either the "Justice" or the "many reasons" he had promised. Nothing had so upset Hays as his partner's impugning of his honor. On December 31, 1770, he sent the first of two letters he would write directly to Polock and his brother "Jack" (Jacob), in which he pressed his case in no uncertain terms. Hays claimed that in the course of his open communication with their common creditors, Polock had sullied his (i.e., Hays's) reputation: "I never objected to your going to Newport," Hays wrote, "so [long as] you went with consistent Honor."[5] Whatever Polock had wished to do would have been acceptable, in Hays's view, "so that it was agreeable to our Creditors & that you could be justified, and . . . on my own part I wanted nothing but that every Creditor we have both [in New York and] Rhode Island . . . should receive equal Justice."[6]

Hays sought every opportunity to if not to clear his name then to show his correspondents that he knew exactly what was at stake. To Solomon Simpson he wrote on December 10, 1771 that he was bound to remain in New York and could leave that place only with the approval of the creditors, "to whom we both [meaning himself and Polock, presumably] Engaged and Pledged our word that we would not [leave]."[7] He told Simpson how eager he was to convince one creditor in particular that he had "timely and Seasonably fix[ed] on certain measures to Prevent any Injury arriving to him, and that what Ever may Happen He shall never be Suffering from any part of my Conduct."[8] To the creditors themselves, Hays began by explaining that Polock's misdeed had created the present "unhappy matter," but that in his eagerness to bring about "the Justice I could sincerely wish," he wished to offer "Some Proposalls."[9] Nothing was so important to him as achieving proper redress for the creditors and redemption for himself, and the language he used centered on a concept of personal virtue which had less to do with divinity than it did with a human attempt to bring about Alexander Pope's dictum. His schemes for restoring his creditors to their funds, he wrote, "flow from me with firm attachment to Integrity as well as to Extricate myself from my uncertain state."[10] As extreme as his condition was, he did "not wish to pay one farthing less than we are justly indebted."[11]

His business reputation notwithstanding, Hays's eagerness to achieve resolution, both between Polock and himself and with the New York creditors who were awaiting payment, inspired the merchant to seek and achieve new heights of social respectability. That he was a Jew must certainly have played a role in instigating such efforts on his part. Though he may not have been subject to a great deal of overt anti-Jewish prejudice, Hays knew well enough that his vulnerability before his expectant creditors—at least those of them who were gentiles—was increased by virtue of his being a Jew. Whatever inspired it, his rise from 1771 onwards occurred in conjunction with the transformation of New England into a place where men of the world were increasingly understood to be shapers of the future. As they advanced toward political autonomy, New Englanders had no choice but to invest more cultural capital in human virtue and worldly relationships.

By the time that the colonists drafted their Declaration of Independence in 1776, the spirit of the times and mere expediency had quieted the voices of those whose public expressions were of an exclusively religious tenor. Although Protestant Christianity and even Calvinism had hardly gone dormant and had done much to shape the rebellion and to influence its discourse, the unifying document of the American Revolution, as one recent historian points out, "never mentioned Christ" and, for that matter, 'never cited Old or New Testament verses to support the American cause."[12] Instead, it "referred to 'the laws of nature and nature's God . . .' [and] then moved to issues of common concern—taxes, troops, and tyranny."[13] In the context of such a rapidly changing cultural milieu, it ought not to have been surprising that a man like Moses Michael Hays, Jew that he was, might make his way, not only within Newport's merchant circles but, upon the commencement of the war and the invasion of Rhode Island by the British, in the formerly Puritan bastion of Boston itself.

Hays had been born in New York on May 9, 1739, the son of the Dutch-born Judah Hays, who had come to New York in 1720 from The Hague, along with his brother Isaac (Isaac would go on to be the father of one of Philadelphia's most prominent early Jews, Samuel Hays).[14] Judah Hays was naturalized in New York in 1729 and, on the basis of his being a "naturalized citizen of Hebrew nationality" named a Freeman in 1735. Like so many other Sephardim, Hays engaged in the West Indies trade. He also built his name by gaining a commission for his ship, *The Duke of Cumberland*, as a privateer in the French and Indian War.[15] Judah married Rebecca Michaels and fathered six children, of whom Moses was the fifth and the second son. The parents had evidently cared enough about their Judaism to affiliate closely with Shearith Israel as far back as 1728 (the Mill Street synagogue was only built in 1730). Judah and his son Moses appeared twenty-five times in the minute books of that congregation. Moses himself signed the synagogue rolls as one of the *yahiddim* in 1759, at age twenty, and also served as *parnas* there from 1767 to 1769. Throughout his life, even when his family constituted the only Jewish family in all of Massachusetts, Moses Michael Hays retained strong connections to Judaism. His adherence to the religion of his forebears would prove, especially in the years following the Revolution, to be a means by which he also fashioned a new identity as a Bostonian, New Englander, and American.[16]

His ability to do so seems to have followed from his apparent determination to make a name for himself as a dutiful citizen. While his origins and early career might easily have allowed him to distinguish himself as a man of extensive wealth and refinement with no particular interest in or loyalty to a larger civic body, Hays seems to have been moved by the spirit of the times to make a name for himself as a publicly minded businessman who happened to be a Jew. His journey toward this kind of respectability may not have been eased or accelerated by the fact of his Jewish affiliation, but neither was it hampered. As Hays moved incrementally deeper into a New England milieu, by relocating first from New York to Newport and thence to Boston, he managed to retain his Jewish ties and, at the same time, to establish new ties to a newly formed *American* context. Throughout the course of his evolution along that trajectory, his adherence to a Jewish identity, which he also passed onto his children as well as his nieces and nephew, served to distinguish him in the eyes of his neighbors, who could not help but take notice that he had established himself in spite of his being an obvious cultural outsider. That he could achieve such a result without having to relinquish his religious difference was a testament to two emerging actualities: 1) an individual's Jewish origin, in an American context, might not necessarily detract from his participation, on a civic, professional, and social level, in the life of the new nation; and 2) individual identity, at the dawn of the American republic and even in the formerly Calvinist bastion of Boston, could now be shaped by proper and exemplary behavior, as opposed to through "faith alone."

Hays's debut as a merchant occurred in keeping with his having been born in the New World and as a part of a fairly well established Sephardic family there. His father was the owner of a store in New York that "specialized in broadcloth, velvets, linens, and general supplies."[17] After returning from a trip to London (his father is on record as having paid his return passage aboard the Jewish-owned *Prince George* in 1760),[18] Moses Michael worked with his father. The Hays receipt book constitutes the clearest guide to their merchandising during the period between Moses' return from London, his father's death four years later, and his flight from Newport in 1776.[19] Haym Salomon, whose financial assistance of the revolutionary cause would go down in history as the most momentous Jewish contribution to the war effort, made one of his few documented appearances in the

Hayses' records.[20] Hays father and son also engaged several non-Jews in business, including members of the Van Wyck, Van Deussen, Beekman, Jay, De Lancey, and Livingston families of New York. Their receipt book also indicates that, for all the business they conducted with noteworthy customers, the Hayses were tenants as opposed to landowners, and that upon the death of the father, the remainder of the family moved to even cheaper quarters. In his early years as a businessman Moses Michael Hays, in other words, was neither impoverished nor opulent. In 1766, he married Rachel Myers, the sister of the noted silversmith Myer Myers, whose torah crowns adorned the torah at Yeshuat Israel in Newport. The two would go on to raise five daughters and one son. In 1769 Hays was admitted, as his father had been before him, as a Freeman in New York, and listed in the city directory as a "watchmaker." His solo business debut was anything but auspicious, and it hardly distinguished him from any number of other middling Jewish merchants of the eighteenth century.

Two letters from Hays to Jonas Philips, a prominent Sephardic merchant in New York, from 1769 and 1770 suggest that, by that time, though he retained significant connections in the city of his birth, Hays had established himself in Newport. In September 1769, immediately preceding the episode during which Hays and Polock were sent to the debtor's prison, Philips wrote to Hays that he and his wife "pray that the almighty May Reward your Children for your intended Goodness to a poore, but honest family."[21] His condition was apparently intensified owing to Rachel's having recently given birth to two children who had to be "clothe[d] from nakedness" and fed. Some one of their kin had also sent them an orphaned infant to care for as well, and in August 1769, Hays wrote to his cousin Joseph Pinto in "Stanford," Connecticut that he needed to pass the infant onto him. "It really makes me unhappy," he wrote, "that my ability would not admit me the keeping of it."[22] Months later he wrote to Solomon Simpson of his fear of leaving his family "Penny less." Philips's second letter, dated April 1770, indicated that goods he was expecting to receive by packet from Newport had not been delivered. Whether Hays's inability to deliver was the result of his partnership with Polock or, as one granddaughter later wrote, merely the result of "various losses at sea and other inevitable misfortunes," financial disaster set in.[23] The crisis occurred in the late autumn of 1770. At that time, Hays wrote to several of his associates and fellow Sephardim in New York and Newport, desperate in the face of Polock's desertion, to regain his former stature as a gentleman who might be trusted in business.

Regardless of whom he was writing to, the central currency and subject matter of Hays's letters following upon the Polock affair was honesty. In his appeal to Samson Mears, another member of the New York Jewish merchant elite, Hays alluded as well to his having the "Highest & Greatest Confidence" in his addressee as "my Real friend, and a man of unblemished integrity."[24] Especially as he wrote to the Polock brothers—the very men by whom he believed himself to have been betrayed—Hays made clear his intention of acting with the utmost rectitude and even in a spirit of forgiveness. Aside from a single reference to his having been left "so much like Jacob did Laban" and "Laid . . . under necessity to vindicate [myself] to the Gentl[men] here," Hays's letter did not contain the slightest nod or reference to God or even to his and Polock's shared Jewish heritage.[25] Rather, Hays placed emphasis on what he viewed as proper gentlemanly behavior. "I never was averse to anything Reasonable," he wrote the Polocks, long after the affair had already caused him considerable mortification and familial distress. "If I had been less compliant I should not have had the reproach I now labour under," he continued, as he proposed, finally, that "If you will convince me that you mean still to go hand in hand & resume our former Friendship, you will reply to the contents of this letter."[26] Hays invested meaning in friendship. A year earlier, he had written to another of the Newport Jews who owed him money, Samuel Hart, that he expected "the very Serious Promises" Hart had given him to be honored in the spirit of their "Good Friendship."[27] To Lopez and Rivera, Hays had written as well with regard to his "own vindication" and his need, in pursuit of such an end "to lay before you every of our transactions and every part of both Mr. Polocks conduct & Behavior," but only once he was "well convinced [that] they are determined in their unfair channel."[28] Even in his private correspondences with disinterested parties, in other words, Hays was determined to avoid any implication of libel against a partner whose word he had once been willing to trust.

Exactly when and where Hays served his term as a debtor is unknown, but the weight of the existing evidence points to New York, as it was a New York newspaper that published the notice that announced his appeal for redress. In June 1770, several months before Polock's flight to Newport, an advertisement appeared in *The New-York Journal* indicating that Moses and his brother Benjamin were seeking to be declared insolvent debtors and thus released from all responsibility to their creditors.[29] In his letter to Lopez and Rivera, Hays expressed his willingness to "suffer in a Dungion my life time" if his attestations of the truth regarding Polock's behavior were proven false. Both Hays and his partner were jailed, in any case, but only until December 1771, when a debtor's relief measure was passed and the two were released. In May and in October 1771, notice of Hays's and Polock's petition to have their insolvency declared before the Rhode Island General Assembly had been announced.[30] By July 1772 the two had evidently not only been released but had also resolved their debts, because Hays was advertising his own store "on Point, near Holmes Wharf" in Newport and the goods he had available there—"Raisins, salad oil, Irish beef, Burlington pork, gin, brandy, bar iron, and flour."[31] One year later, he contacted the Boston bookseller Henry Knox with a request that he might be supplied with a stock of books and stationery on six months' credit, based on the "Enquiry" that he invited Knox to make into his reputation as a "reliable and timely debtor."[32] The partnership with Polock had been dissolved, and Hays entered a new phase in his business career.

Whether he was seeking to establish a new profile or whether he was merely caught up in the events of the age, Hays found himself rather quickly at the center of Newport's attention. As Jewish merchants faced ever-increasing pressure in the face of new political developments either to sign non-importation agreements or to take their business elsewhere, Hays was asked to sign a loyalty oath. Like that of the other Newport Jews, his position was unenviable. The protection of the crown had been instrumental to his and his father's establishment as New York freemen, and it had also made it easier for Sephardim in Newport to be fairly unimpeded in their prosperity, not to mention their freedom to worship as Jews. Aaron Lopez had finessed the loyalty issue, prolonged the period of his neutrality, and, by 1775, moved his entire family and entourage to the safe haven of Leicester, Massachusetts, as soon as Newport had grown too dangerous for him. Isaac Touro, a confirmed Tory, fled as well, seeking the protection of royal authority in Jamaica. Hays was daring and ideologically adventurous enough to take a third course and declare his support for the American cause, though he did so by gradual means. In 1769, he told one correspondent that, notwithstanding a shipment of goods he was expecting from London, his operation in Newport had sought to avoid any infringement "on the Resolution of non-importation."[33] All the same, as the letter made clear, he had chosen to conduct that particular transaction from Newport because New York, which was still the center of his operations in 1769, had also adopted a non-importation pact. He would support such measures if he had to but, at least in this case, proved his willingness to work around them. In July 1775 he signed his name to an oath in which he asserted his loyalty to the American rebellion against Britain and his belief that the "War Resistance and opposition in which the United American Colonies are now engaged against the fleets and armies of Great Britain is . . . just and necessary." The pledge also indicated that Hays would "not directly afford assistance of any sort or kind whatsoever to the . . . [British] armies and navies."[34]

Though Hays's signing of the 1775 oath ought to have sealed his safety from any continued prosecution for Toryism, it did not. In the immediate aftermath of the Declaration of Independence, the Speaker of Rhode Island's Lower House brought forward a list of seventy-seven Newporters, four of them Jews, who were suspected of being "inimical" to the nascent United States. Each of the four, in keeping with the extreme social vulnerability that such accusations brought them as Jews, responded differently to the accusation. Isaac Hart, who would later be brutally murdered in an American mob's attack against the Loyalist stronghold on Long Island to which he had fled from Newport, declared that he would not sign the new loyalty oath until it was forced on all Newporters. Myer Polock, Hays's erstwhile business partner, refused because oaths, he said, "were contrary to the custom of the Jews."[35] Isaac Touro, the hazzan of the synagogue, would not sign for three reasons: 1) he had never been naturalized in the first place, 2) like Polock, he claimed that the oath violated his religious principles, and 3) he was still a Dutch subject.[36] The three had all stood on principle, but in doing so they had also assumed defensive positions. For his part, Hays offered another sort of resistance altogether, in which he took the bold step of confronting his accusers directly. His reaction to the demand for a new loyalty oath, though it contained its fair share of rhetorical affirmations of the American cause, was testy. Hays argued strongly in defense of his worth and honesty, as well as his belief in the inherent value of an individual's virtue. He went so far as to invoke the rights of citizenship that such virtues ought to have conferred upon him.

On July 17, 1776, Hays presented his own petition to the Rhode Island General Assembly. Where Hart, Polock, and Touro had each attached his defense to or cited his rights as members of one or another collective body (i.e., all the citizens of Newport, "the Jews," "the States of Holland"), Hays asserted a right was that he based on his own personal integrity, on his assumption of "freedom," and on the guarantees that he believed these qualities ought to have ensured him. He was pioneering a new order of qualifications, one that would take shape in keeping with the emergent and secular values of the new nation, in which free citizens were to be accorded their "self-evident" rights. In demanding to be treated in accordance with the same rights that were outlined in the Declaration itself, Hays was acting the part of an American patriot, by confronting governmental authority with its own ideology. After pointing out that he "hath ever been warmly and zealously attacht to the rights and Liberalities of the colonies," Hays presented a narrative of his recent experience of having been "sighted by the sheriff to appear at the court house." He wanted to know who his accusers were and asked that the Rhode Island legislators grant him "the Rights & Privileges due other free citizens when I conform to everything generally done & acted."[37] Hays wished to be treated in accordance with his actions and not his beliefs or affiliations. His sentiment had a long history as a counter-tradition in New England thought. As early as Roger Williams's founding of Rhode Island and as recently as Ezra Stiles's critique of pure Calvinism, dissenting voices had argued that rightness in action trumped proper belief, whether in religious principles or political ideologies.

In addition to the petition that he presented on July 17, Hays had already proffered a written statement in which he also asserted his refusal to sign the test on the basis not only of his support for the war but of his having been denied voting rights on the basis of his identity as an "Israelite." He wanted his loyalty to merit respect, in other words, and not merely act as a hedge against persecution as an unfairly suspected Tory. Though there is no direct evidence to suggest that Hays's assertive reaction to the loyalty oath had any broad reverberations beyond his own case, he was in fact left alone after he pleaded his case and not asked to furnish any additional signed loyalty oaths. In November 1779, when another list of accused Loyalists was issued in Rhode Island, Hays's name did not appear on it.[38] Though Hays had not been so bold as to demand equal rights as a Jew, his petition had nonetheless broached the subject from the opposite point of view. If he *weren't* to be granted voting rights as a Jew, what difference could his loyalty make in the first place? Those who wanted to make political demands upon him—and political demands could only bear acute economic consequences—would have either to leave him alone or grant him equality. Here was an outsider who, in his own small way, was not afraid to employ his status as a kind of test case for an entire polity, all of whose constituents would, sooner or later, seek to define their role and status within the new political reality.

Moses Michael Hays was not a pioneer for Jewish rights in the ordinary sense. Although he appeared on record as a proud and forthright "Israelite," his petition before the Rhode Island General Assembly had not been intended as a defiant act meant to secure Jewish civil rights. His refusal to sign the loyalty oath had more in common with the revolutionary cause itself than it did with any desire on his part for Jewish redemption. It was contiguous with the same effort by which six years previously he had sought to restore his good name in the wake of Myer Polock's betrayal. Nor could Hays have known, especially as early as 1776, that the war would eventuate in the gradual enfranchisement of Jews. Where he had gambled effectively was in seeing an opportunity to gain individual rights on the basis of individual behavior. In the years to come, as the Federal Constitution and a succession of new American states granted Jews equal rights, they did so because compelling arguments had been made in favor of the rights of minorities and dissenting individuals to exercise or not exercise religiosity in the ways that they saw fit. Jews like Hays counted as individuals, and not as representatives of a larger, communal order. Religious freedom in the newborn United States was the result of an effort to ensure the disestablishment of churches as opposed to the affirmation of the rights of the communities they represented. If Hays "represented" the Jews, he did so not by demanding collective rights for his people but by establishing his own worthiness as an individual who also happened to be a Jew.

That Hays, like Aaron Lopez, ended up choosing the revolutionary cause might also have spoken, simply enough, to his economic interests. Most

Sephardim, not only in Newport but in other North American seaports as well, sided with the Americans. Jews of German origin, who incidentally included the Hart and Polock families of Newport, tended to be less unanimous in their loyalties; on the whole, their economic status tended to be more marginal, perhaps because they lacked the benefit of the trans-atlantic Sephardic trade network and perhaps because they were more recent arrivals in the New World. The Polock family, in fact, would soon be singled out for praise by none other than Edmund Burke, who gave a speech in Parliament praising the sacrifices that certain Jews had made to the Loyalist cause. The most illustrious of the Newport Jews, Aaron Lopez, who had previously expressed somewhat tepid support for the American cause, left town in the face of the English occupation. From his new home in Leicester, Massachusetts, he was able to conduct business both as a shipping merchant, although in considerably compromised circumstances owing to the British naval blockade, and as a store-owner. Lopez's eventual historical association with the American cause resulted from his having financed privateering operations. Fully 6 percent of the money that was raised by American privateering operations had been gained under the auspices of Jewish ship-owners like him. If economic self-interest lay at the heart of such contributions, so too had it underlain the very premises upon which the rebellion had taken shape and motivated the anti-British mobs of Boston and other North American cities in the early 1770s.

Hays seems not to have remained in Newport for many more weeks beyond his encounter with the Rhode Island General Assembly in July 1776. As late as June of that year, he was still advertising his groceries and wares in the *Newport Mercury*, to be sold "At the House lately occupied by James Robertson, and opposite where the late Martin Howard, Esq. lived."[39] Though he was not listed as a permanent resident of Boston until 1782, at least one historian dates his removal to the Massachusetts city to 1776, a time which does, in fact, coincide with his disappearance from Newport. Whatever residential connections he may have retained to New York came to an end that same year, as the Continental Army was driven from that city in the aftermath of George Washington's unsuccessful engagements with the combined British infantry and naval forces at Brooklyn and Manhattan. Only Boston, of the major northeastern seaports, remained free of British occupation. Having cast his lot with the Americans, Hays brought his family to the font of the American rebellion and set about establishing himself there permanently.

What exactly Moses Michael Hays was doing at the height of the Revolutionary War, between 1776 and 1781, is unknown. Like Lopez, he did outfit some privateering vessels that raided English commerce for the American cause. Though he seems always to have been measured in his allegiance to the Americans, we can scarcely doubt where his sympathies lay, if only on the basis of who his primary business associates were. Moreover, his choice to settle in Boston was as incontrovertible a statement of patriotic affinities as might be imagined, as that city was a hotbed of American sentiment and had driven out its last Loyalists when Thomas Gage had evacuated the city in 1775. Hays had certainly not gone to Boston to get closer to other Jews.[40] Although he would go on to become the first unconverted Jew to choose that city as a permanent home for his family, Boston supported no Jewish community and, indeed, would not do so until the arrival of a significant group of German-Jewish immigrants in the 1840s. What Boston could support, however, was an independent-minded purveyor of merchant goods, an enterprising ship-owner, and an imaginative entrepreneur. The city had come a long way since its founding, and although its citizens were still highly churched, a newer faith in civic obligation and economic self-sufficiency had all but replaced or, at least, subsumed the church-centered communitarianism of earlier decades. The great political transformations of the 1770s had introduced a new and largely secular discourse into public life, and an apparently self-made and economically secure man like Moses Michael Hays, even if he was a Jew, could now establish a base there.

In part because there was nothing even approaching a Jewish community in Boston, Hays was able to achieve acceptance, build stature, and even garner admiration as an individual who happened to be a Jew. After his petition to the Rhode Island General Assembly, there is no evidence that he ever uttered a word in public regarding his rights as a Jew. While various spokesmen on all sides of the revolutionary-era debates on religious freedom were arguing their points regarding establishment, a new kind of civic religion was taking shape, a religion within which Hays was well disposed to gain recognition. As rebellion against Britain evolved into an increasingly coherent, if often volatile republicanism, personal stature and civic virtue gained unprecedented cultural importance. In one important respect, the new "religion" would, indeed, closely resemble a spiritual practice—Freemasonry, in which Hays would develop into Boston's most prominent mover, was an important outlet for republican expression. But even outside or at least alongside of Freemasonry, the cult of manly virtue gained stature. It took shape in part as Bostonians collectively jettisoned their earlier fealty to George III and to the idea of a directly sanctioned "idea of a king."[41] By the late 1780s, and especially in the aftermath of the Constitutional debate, this new cult coalesced around the persona of George Washington in particular, but its development had as much do with a larger cultural shift favoring human virtue as it did with popular admiration for Washington per se. For one thing, where a previous association had existed between the king, divine right, and the king's divinely sanctioned display of ostentation and splendor, newly republican "Americans" sought to minimize such displays. When Washington came to Massachusetts on his way to accept the American presidency, he made his first stop in Cambridge, where fifteen years earlier he had accepted the command of the Continental Army. After putting on his army uniform and forgoing his horse, he entered Boston on foot. "He knew enough," writes Richard Bushman, "to shed the trappings of his office, anything that hinted of elegance or grandeur, and to present himself as a simple soldier."[42] The city that welcomed Washington in such a manner and erected an eighteen-foot-high triumphal arch across the street that bore his name was a city that had developed an appreciation for men of civic virtue.

The Hays family's settlement in Boston occurred in stages. Hays had been conducting business there since his days of apprenticeship with his father, and had increased his profile there as he entered the Newport market and established a home in that city. On December 24, 1781, however, Hays established a permanent place for himself by announcing in the Independent Ledger the opening of a new office. The new venture would go a long way toward improving the common lot, though its primary purpose, of course, was to enrich its proprietor. "The Public are informed," read the announcement, "That an office is this day opening, in the front room of the American Coffee House, in State Street, for Intelligence, foreign and domestick, Insurance of every kind effected on best terms, purchasing and disposing of Bills of Exchange of every denomination, Merchandize bought and sold, on easy terms, Bills and Notes discounted, vessels bought and sold, as well

State Street, Boston (1801). Moses Michael Hays's office is pictured in the foreground, on the right-hand side of the street. Oil on canvas by James Brown Marston. Courtesy of the Massachusetts Historical Society.

as Chartered . . . lands purchased and disposed of."[43] The location could not have been more central, as the American Coffee House was adjacent to the (old) State House. Here, in the center of New England's first city and on the site of the Boston Massacre, Hays was undertaking a most ambitious and public debut. As Ellen Smith writes, he had announced his intention of playing a central role in "establishing the financial and cultural institutions that would define post-Revolutionary and 19th century Boston."[44]

In his advertising rhetoric, at any rate, Hays endeavored as well to establish credibility. In the context of the newly forming republic, in the aftermath of the crisis-ridden and mercurial business atmosphere that had been wrought by a combination of British policies and a succession of American-sponsored non-importation agreements and boycotts, and in the spirit of rationalism and level-headedness, his newspaper posting assured potential investors that his business would be conducted according to the latest methods:

A steady attention to the law, as well as mercantile affairs, has given the subscriber an opportunity of being acquainted with all the necessary transactions for such business. And as he means, reciprocal advantage with the public, he hopes, by serious application, with profound and strict integrity to merit their favor.—Great pains will be taken to procure early and the most authentic intelligence of Markets, foreign as well as those in every part of this continent within the States—Gentlemen underwriters and others, will favor the office with their preference, and any information, will be received with grateful thanks, by M. M. Hays.[45]

Hays's announcement had the ring not merely of a new business scheme but of a civic service. As the coming years of activity and the growing numbers of subscribers would prove, confidence in his ability to invest profitably and to back his word with action reflected a broader perception that he was sufficiently reliable and public-spirited as to be entrusted with a generous portion of the city's financial future. He had come a long way from his letters of 1770–1771, when he was desperately hoping to restore enough credibility to his name to restart his merchandising career. And yet the mark of those years and those letters could be seen in his Boston advertisement and its attention not only to "strict integrity" but to the prudent and "intelligent" practices that might guarantee it.

The next several years would witness Hays's expansion into several types of investment, most notably the underwriting, sale, and chartering of merchant vessels, as well as his proposal to create a fire insurance scheme and, in 1784, the establishment of a bank which continues, under a different name, to conduct business in the twenty-first century. Concurrent with these activities was his effort to establish a permanent home in Boston for himself and his family. Some of the real estate purchases and sales that Hays made suggest his broader interest in the buying and selling of distant lands. Hence, on June 24, 1784, Hays was listed as the purchaser of a piece of property at the convergence of Mill Pond, Mill Creek, and Salem Streets and, five months later, as its seller.[46] Hays made several Boston real estate purchases and sales in the coming years, and these included his participation as a shareholder, in 1784, in the purchase of land for the Boston Theater. After his having spent several years in apparently constant motion between New York and Newport, however, his move to Boston seems also to have occasioned his permanent settlement there not only as the proprietor of the office in the American Coffee-House but as the owner and inhabitant of a house on Middle (Hanover) Street, where he took up residence with a steadily increasing number not only of his own children but of two nephews and a niece, as well as their mother (his sister, Reyna Touro, whose late husband was Isaac Touro, the Newport *hazzan*).[47] The 1873 memoir of the Reverend Samuel May (the grandfather of Louisa May Alcott) included a fond and oft-quoted passage on the Hayses' warm and bustling abode. May's recollection suggested that his family's settlement in Boston had enabled Hays to acquire the standing he had so long sought. He was "a man much respected," the Unitarian minister wrote, "not only on account of his large wealth, but for his many personal virtues and the high culture and excellence of his wife, his son Judah, and his daughters."[48]

Hays's acquisition of *social* as well as economic standing was on a par, perhaps, with the attainments of the more noteworthy Newport merchants before the Revolution, most notably Aaron Lopez. As May wrote, the Hayses comprised the only "family of the despised children of the House of Israel" resident in Boston in their time, but their standing there transcended such categorization.[49] If Jews were thought to be alien, the Hayses lived on "one of the fashionable streets of the town." If they were associated with grasping habits, the Hayses' home "was the abode of hospitality," not only for the rich but for the "many indigent families who were fed pretty regularly from his table."[50] If they were thought to be withdrawn and insular, the Hayses, at least, earned a reputation for openness, even on Saturdays, "when [Hays] expected a number of friends to dine with him."[51] Hays and his family seem to have epitomized the late eighteenth-century version of "opulent" Jews—they were "literate, propertied, and . . . well-connected."[52] The difference, however, was that they also had occasion, at least in the immediate aftermath of the Revolution, to be perceived as public-spirited and virtuous in accordance not only with preexisting ideas of gentility but with republican principles. When Hays died in 1805 his long-time friend and associate Robert Treat Paine elegized these qualities of Hays's personality. In keeping perhaps with an earlier established concept of genteel cultivation, Hays's "tongue" had "charmed the social day"; his "wit" had been graced by "generous roughness" (was Paine commemorating Hays's "foreign" birth as a Portuguese-Dutch Jew?). Moses Michael Hays had been more than just a civilized and cultivated man, however. In the charitable spirit of the newly established republic, he had "watched pale want, and stored her famished cell." More important still, his "vigorous mind" had given "inspiring force to Truth and Feeling";[53] Hays was a man whose virtue grew not out of social ambition, at least in the view of men like May and Paine who commemorated him, but from his republican idealism and his eagerness to make himself useful.

The level of his involvement in Boston's burgeoning postwar commerce is made clear not only by the record of such admiring commemorations but from the pages of the city's newspapers, which ran frequent notices of his endeavors. Even as he pursued large-scale enterprises like insurance and real estate speculation, he maintained a profile as a retailer of sundry goods, including—on January 10, 1782—beef, "French Brandy, . . . West-India Rum, New-England Rum," and "a Quantity of Goods, Indigo, and about 15000 weight Ship-Bread."[54] Other notices from his early years in Boston announced his stock of such items as "Bar-Iron," "Pearl Ash," "Barcelona Handkerchiefs," "Bohea Tea," "pickled Herrings," "Florence Oil in Bottles," and "Gunpowder."[55] He would continue to engage in such trading endeavors throughout his career, but his innovation came about as he announced, often in the same pages, his objectives as a land-speculator and as a supplier of fire and nautical insurance. His notices contained news of land and appurtenances "in the town of Brimfield," "in Jamaica-Plains," and "West Boston." In August 1787, he announced the availability for purchase of "A Quantity of Rich Western Lands, in lots from 400 to 2000 acres" in an area near the "Monongechela-River" in what is currently West Virginia.[56] In this way, Hays was doing his part to help orchestrate the very growth of the nation. Any interested purchaser was advised in his notice to "set down on the land, when and as he pleased"; a deed would be made available to him from a government agent in Richmond. "The Universally acknowledged good soil, and fine climate alone," the notice announced, would make settlement worthwhile.[57] Hays advertised more land in the years to come in upstate New York (in Montgomery County), Virginia, and Georgia, and some of these lands remained in his hands for many years, as they appeared among the assets listed in his will upon his death.

Real estate speculation, particularly during this period of early national growth, was quite common, and Hays's participation in it was no mark of distinction, though it did advance his profile as a man whose business enterprises happened to coincide with, or capitalize upon, a larger national mission. His more obvious contribution to the Boston and New England economies came about as he announced and fulfilled his intention to supply fire and shipping insurance. Throughout 1784 he ran notices in the *American Herald, Independent Ledger, Salem Gazette*, and *Independent Chronicle* announcing his interest in convening a group of underwriters for "insurance against FIRE . . . [on] any Dwelling-House, Warehouse, Furniture, Merchandize, or Manufactures, in any of the New-England States."[58] The initial meeting was to be held in July, and the shares would be offered at the rate of "100 dollars." Although this particular scheme was not picked up upon his initial announcement of it, Hays was able in 1789, as the guarantor of the endeavor's viability, to spearhead the development of a collective fire insurance fund. For years to come, Boston newspapers would also run frequent advertisements for his nautical insurance business in particular. Where previous generations of the city's merchants had seen their fortunes rise and fall in accordance with their vessels' fate at sea, post–Revolutionary War Boston merchants could and did find security in the joint ventures that Hays sponsored. He may not have found as many outside investors as he initially hoped, but one historian suggests that Hays's work as an underwriter put him in the position of "carrying on for his private account the same business as is now transacted by insurance companies."[59] His insurance ledgers for the years 1790–1793 included some 122 separate accounts. Hays's ability to gain the trust of so many clients suggests that his reinvention as an upstanding and prosperous financier in the wake of his 1770 imprisonment was wholly successful.

Hays's notices concerning his underwriting of shipping ventures suggested the broad range of his capabilities. His insurance ventures were plainly laid out in the ledgers. Newspaper notices also showed the extent of his actual involvement in the shipping trade. He frequently oversaw the buying and selling of entire vessels, chartering them to interested parties, or—on occasion—looking to charter other people's vessels in order to engage far-flung trade routes. In 1796 and 1798 he offered first the *Jefferson* and then the *Washington* for sale or charter, advertising the latter as a "beautiful ship . . . [of] 230 tons burthen, four years old, constructed for sailing fast, and pierced for 20 carriage guns"[60] (his was an age of rampant privateering, not to mention a period during which British warships plied the oceans in search of American seamen they might impress into His Majesty's service).

Hays outfitted several ships over the years, so that in addition to insuring others' risks he was fairly consistently underwriting his own ventures (the insurance ledgers include several examples of this sort of "reversion"). He was also involved, in 1789, in one of New England's earliest Far Eastern trading expeditions. Between November and December of that year, notice was carried in the *Massachusetts Centinel* and in the *Independent Chronicle* of "The Good Ship Massachusetts," an eight hundred–ton vessel setting sail from Boston the coming February for Canton, with the intention of returning to New York in the spring of 1791.[61] The merchants involved at the primary level were inviting potential investors who had an interest in speculating "in the commerce with China, either by freighting on their own account, or loaning money" to participate in the venture. Hays's involvement in the enterprise extended to his being listed as the person who could be consulted, in his office at the American Coffee-House, as to the terms for investors. The voyage of the *Massachusetts* was one of several that Hays was involved in as an insurer. As had been the case with his speculation in western lands, his active participation in such speculative endeavors placed him at the forefront of Boston's financial circles and suggested his eagerness not only to build and maintain a steady and growing income but to create a noticeable profile in the public life of his adopted home.

Hays achieved his most lasting effect on the future economic life of Boston beginning in 1783, less than a year after the treaty ending the war with Britain was concluded, as he helped to draft a plan and made his own significant monetary contribution to the Massachusetts Bank (still in existence, formerly known as the Bank of Boston, then as Fleet, and in the present day owned by the Bank of America). The bank made history as the first American joint-stock bank and Massachusetts' second chartered bank.[62] Initial notice was announced on December 18, 1783, in Boston's *Continental Journal*. "The Utility of a Bank," Hays and the other sponsors announced, "exhibited on right principle," was being seriously considered and was "now ready for the patronage of those gentlemen who wish to derive the many public and private advantages which have resulted for such institutions in other countries."[63] Hays demonstrated his enthusiasm for the scheme by being its very first depositor, and an ambitious one at that, having entered over $10,000 within a month of the bank's establishment (he also withdrew significant sums in that same space of time; Hays knew what a bank was for). Where Boston's previous attempts at establishing such an institution, going back to the days of the Land Bank scheme of 1740–1741, had fallen considerably short of success, the Massachusetts Bank had come at a propitious time, and found not only governmental support but more than adequate backing from the investors whose participation was so vital to its establishment. The Bostonians had more than adequate models upon which to base their efforts, as Philadelphia's Bank of North America had been created by the Continental Congress as recently as 1781 and formally recognized by Massachusetts authorities in the following year. That bank, in turn, as the Massachusetts Bank's historian writes, had modeled itself on the Bank of England. The petitioners who sought to create the Massachusetts Bank had included among them at least four, and possibly six marine insurance brokers, including Hays.[64]

As Hays participated in and played an increasingly visible role in endeavors such as the establishment of Boston's first bank and as that city's most well known and highly patronized marine insurance broker, he was developing into an ever more important "representative" of the "Children of the House of Israel." His ability to conduct business unencumbered by the typical impediments to Jewish commerce had been occasioned by the times. New England's founders would have been taken aback at the prospect of so stalwart a Jew being not only free to conduct commerce in the City on a Hill but the object of such widespread admiration. In the course of his entire career, not a single soul seems to have uttered a word of criticism of him or to have slandered him as a Jew. On the contrary, as his career took shape, Hays seems only to have absorbed more praise and respect, often from people who were quick not only to acknowledge his Jewish background but to ascribe to it at least a modicum of credit not only for his success but for his kindness and most certainly his trustworthiness. In the obituary that marked the occasion of his death in 1805, he was described as "*fearing* no man but *loving* all."[65] As had so often been the case for Jews who met with the Christian stamp of approval during Hays's era and earlier, he was universally acknowledged as being "without guile," but also as someone who "detested hypocrisy" and "despised meanness." His participation in so many financial schemes might, in another place and time, have prompted considerable expressions of anti-Jewish prejudice, but because they occurred in conjunction with such enormous social transformations and during an era when all Americans, including those whose ethnic background marked them as natives and insiders, were adjusting to life in a new political milieu within which social differences were deemphasized in the name of egalitarianism, at least this one "guileless" Jew was not only tolerated but embraced by his gentile neighbors. It was not only his evident generosity that was remarked, although he had certainly come along when he was needed. In the wake of his time in debtor's prison, Moses Michael Hays, from his own struggle for personal redemption to his mid-career magnanimity and prosperity to his passing as one of Boston's "most valuable citizens," enacted a story that fitted precisely the sort of narrative New Englanders required as they underwent the transformations of the revolutionary era. He was the virtuous man whose religious beliefs and practices, alien though they were, paled in their importance beside his deeds and deportment in life.

No single factor was as central to Hays's ability to distinguish himself in revolutionary-era Boston as his membership and prominence within the Masonic movement. For if personal virtue and proper gentlemanly conduct were significant measures of value, and if they were to be able to substitute, ultimately, for Christian faith itself, then the Masons supplied the substance for such a transformation. Moreover, in the atmosphere of social leveling that defined the era, in which a supposed meritocracy was to take the place formerly occupied by a landed aristocracy, Masonry provided the ideal and properly fraternal social context. At the same time, however, in its development of secret rituals, its promotion of the idea of an elite, and most especially its incorporation of a sort of mysticism, Masonry also allowed and invited members to temper their rationalism with a kind of religiosity.[66] The "surface egalitarianism" of Masonic ritual, as one historian suggests, "belied its initiates' desire for authority and status."[67] Moses Michael Hays, who would prove to be one of Boston's most historically important Masons of all time (to this day, there is a lodge in that city named for him), epitomized the benefits that the movement brought to New England. In his own life, though he was of alien stock, he had managed quietly to surmount that and other challenges and gain the respect and admiration of his peers. Particularly as a Jew, he retained something of an exotic status. Overall, however, and especially as he managed his business affairs, he displayed an exemplary rationalism and consistency of temper. As a supporter of the revolutionary cause, at least in its latter days, he had been on the side of the people's advancement but, at the same time, his growing prosperity set him quite apart from the mass. New Englanders of his era would prove, despite a certain amount of social pressure from less prosperous citizens or rural districts, to be considerably less Jeffersonian than Federalist in their political and social outlook. In his simultaneous regard for republican ideals and his own cultivation of individual distinction, genteel manners, and the authority and elitism that went along with one's participation in Masonry, Moses Michael Hays dramatized New England's own dual affinities and, indeed, the lasting effects that Puritanism itself had wrought upon the political culture of the day.

Hays's involvement in Masonry preceded his time in Boston. His first appearance in connection with the movement occurred in 1768 in his former residence of New York, when he was named Deputy Inspector General of the Rite of Perfection for the West Indies and North America at the behest of his business connection and correspondent Henry Andrew Francken. In 1769 he attained the rank of New York's Master of King David's Lodge. In his correspondence from that era, including the letters in which he strived to redeem his tarnished image in the face of the Polock debacle, he seems to have internalized the Masonic ideal of friendship. In corresponding with another Mason, Hays wrote in 1769 of his eagerness to achieve a new level of trust. "I shall be singularly Happy in your Correspondence," he wrote, "more so when it Turns on the Principle of Virtue, from the Fundamentals of our noble institution."[68] That friendship was, indeed, the outgrowth of a "noble institution" in Hays's view attests to the value the movement had attained in his estimation. In the same letter, Hays asked immediately afterwards if he might "have the Pleasure of receiving [his] Jewels shortly"; the talismans of Masonic ritual were apparently of great importance to him. Within the same year, as Hays seems to have experienced a setback in his friendship with the West Indies merchant Francken, his friend and fellow Mason Dr. Samuel Stringer of Albany wrote him, encouraging him to work as he might to transcend whatever had divided him from Francken. Stringer advised Hays to "extinguish by the force of friendship the little flame I perceive kindled in your heart & Write to Mr. Francken in your former Tender Stile."[69] A year later in his correspondence with Aaron Lopez and Jacob Rivera, who were members of the Newport

Masons with whom Hays was also affiliated, Hays invoked "the faith of Korah Dathan & Abiram"—Masonry itself—as a testament to his truthfulness in confiding the story of Myer Polock's abandonment of him in the face of their collective debt.[70]

Although it did not infuse the lives of the entire colonial elite, Masonry was enormously influential among a substantial number of merchants of Hays's standing. The movement's internalization of existing tensions between the spreading of wealth and status, on the one hand, and the maintenance of a separate and elite class of citizens, on the other hand, brought it to the forefront of the new republican consciousness. Because Masonry emphasized both "exclusiveness and inclusion,"[71] it had an intrinsic appeal to men of stature and, more important, to men who sought stature. In and through it, Hays gained valuable exposure not only to the movement's ideals of friendship, cultivated citizenship, and a mystical connection to the ancient world, but to the warm acquaintanceship of specific men, many of whom were influential in the society of his day. Hays's relationships with such men as Robert Treat Paine, Paul Revere, and Henry Andrew Francken took shape in the context of his activities as a Mason, and the power and influence that he was able to wield in that capacity spilled over into his business life. Masonry not only had the effect of shoring up Hays's status as a welcome outsider in Boston, but also epitomized New England's transition state. The region as a whole had been founded by a self-selecting, "natural" aristocracy. At the same time, its earliest foundation had also coincided with or turned very quickly into the rise of certain rich and eminent men, and the relatively orderly aspect of social relationships there had the effect of separating the lower orders from men of means. The arrival of Moses Michael Hays at the moment of Masonry's greatest influence in the period following from the Revolutionary War suggested yet another convergence, as a Jewish man brought about a further elaboration of New England's dissenting legacy and its citizens' propensity to value both tradition and change.

The Masonic movement was notable for its promotion of a societal egalitarianism, but its earliest adherents in North America, the "Moderns," tended to exemplify and to display a species of elitism. As a recent historian of the movement has explained, although Masonry sought to "blunt and buffer the divisive forces of ethnicity, religion, and nationality," it could do so only by promoting yet another social demarcation—"that between gentlemen and others."[72] Particularly during the period preceding the Revolutionary War, the majority of Masons in Boston were merchants and professionals—the two groups comprised 78 percent of the total number who belonged to the order. Because religion and ethnicity were less of an object than social status, men like Hays were ideally poised to gain within the movement. In Newport, where Hays had been an active merchant for a decade before his removal to Boston, the existing lodge, King David's, had several Jewish members, having administered the rites of initiation to them during the two decades preceding the war. An advertisement from the *Newport Mercury* of June 13, 1781, announced its celebration of the annual Feast of St. John, offering admission to "all brothers, whether members of the Lodge or not."[73] Hays, who had already occupied a leadership position in the New York lodge, was listed as a Master in Newport. In a gesture that spoke directly to the Masons' apparent indifference to ethnic, national, and religious demarcations, the listing was rendered in French as well as in English. As members of the French navy were undoubtedly quartered in Newport during this final year of Revolutionary War hostilities, the men of King David's Lodge were quite unself-consciously extending the arm of friendship to Catholics in the former stronghold of Dissenting Protestantism.

If Catholics could be welcomed to the fold, then certainly the handful of virtuous Jews who had chosen Newport and, before long, would choose Boston itself might also be allowed to partake. Although a certain amount of doubt has been cast on the famous 1658 "Maconrie" certificate that some historians have used to establish the earliest Jewish presence in Newport (see Chapter 1), evidence does exist for Jewish membership in Masonic circles in England as early as 1717, where an initiation at London's Rose Tavern brought in "Several Brethren of Distinction, as well Jews as Christians."[74] A Jew was known to have designed the coat of arms for the Grand Lodge of England. In North America, Jews are known to have been welcomed into Masonry as early as 1734 in Georgia, where both the colony's founder, James Oglethorpe, and some of its first Jewish settlers, the Sheftall family, were Masons in good standing. English Masons had shown an early interest in Judaism, not so much in the spirit of ecumenicity as because Judaism supplied an otherwise missing link between modern-day Christianity and the ancient world. In particular because the

Masonic rite derived from traditional beliefs about the building of King Solomon's Temple in Jerusalem, Jewish records, such as Josephus's histories, were of natural interest to Masons.[75] The sons of Abraham, Isaac, and Jacob, therefore, could be absorbed into the movement with relative ease, provided that they were sufficiently upright in their manners and station in life to merit the fellowship of Christian men. Masonry offered Jews of means an unprecedented avenue for acceptance into the colonial elite, and it did so by championing their personal virtue. In a Calvinistic setting, acts alone could never constitute a sufficient means of distinguishing oneself, but as New Englanders adapted to changing times, they showed an increasing willingness to uphold human-centered moral uprightness (as opposed to a mysteriously conferred divine grace) as the surest sign if not of actual sanctification then of societal worth. As Ezra Stiles himself had mused in his journal, the traditional Calvinist moral preferment of a reprobate killer over an unregenerate practitioner of moral soundness was an infringement of common sense. In the newly Arminian atmosphere, the adherence of genteel Jews like Moses Michael Hays to an ironclad code of virtue and honor could no longer be ignored.

No historian has ever argued that the American Revolution resulted in any large-scale inversion of the social order, and even if an inclusive Masonry was embraced by increasing numbers of New Englanders, it did not mean that a leveling spirit had been suddenly and unequivocally triumphant. As the postrevolutionary history of Masonry, especially in Boston, would show, factional conflict arose between the more genteel sort of members and the rising ranks of a less cultivated but equally ambitious group of Masons. The war and the social vacuums and social possibilities that it had created had highlighted a long-standing division within New England society between men of relatively high birth and men who aspired to positions of power and influence under the new republican order. Masonry itself, which emphasized both a socially expansive view of who might be eligible to join the brotherhood and a tight proprietorship over its ranks, became a focal point for such internal conflicts. Moses Michael Hays, though he seems only to have prospered in the movement, exemplified Masonry's simultaneous alignment with an established gentry and its cooption by an aspirant constituency of self-made men. He came to Boston with strong Masonic credentials, quickly rose through the ranks of

Massachusetts Masonry, and seems to have stayed entirely above the fray that quite nearly split the entire movement.

Masons throughout the colonies were strongly affected by the rise, in the immediate aftermath of the Revolution, of an Ancient order whose membership succeeded in bringing about the eclipse of the Modern Masonic movement.[76] "Modern" Masons, whose ranks had been filled since the early to mid-eighteenth century by the better sort of gentlemen, had numbered among themselves such eminent men as Benjamin Franklin and George Washington. In Massachusetts, the Moderns had founded a lodge in 1733, having taken their charter from the Grand Lodge of England. As Steven Bullock suggests, its creation and early development, among other things, allowed "American gentlemen" to "[find] connection with kings and nobles," and coincided with the Anglicizing tendencies of the period.[77] Most Masons during these first few decades were at least formally educated, if not high born (Franklin being an obvious exception). Their outlook was sufficiently cosmopolitan to allow them to initiate a French Catholic prisoner of war in 1744.[78] When Moses Michael Hays arrived on the scene in the early 1780s, having come highly recommended by his brothers in New York and Rhode Island, he was easily absorbed, but he gravitated toward the nascent Ancients. The records of the Grand Lodge show that Hays visited it in the summer of 1781 and the winter of 1782, was proposed for membership in February 1782, and was "accordingly balloted for, and accepted" forthwith,[79] having first been "taken up" by the lodge president, Dr. John Warren. Initially, the members of the lodge had been duly impressed but at least slightly disoriented by Hays's arrival. Dating back to 1769 and his installment at that time in New York as "Deputy Inspector General for North America," as one Masonic historian writes, "the brethren probably thought it advisable to investigate his 'powers and authority.'"[80] Evidently, their investigation found Hays to be appropriately credentialed. Within the same year, he was elected "Master," and he served in that capacity through the first half of 1785. If Hays's Jewish background raised any eyebrows among the men who elected him, no record of such a reaction was kept. As one Mason wrote years afterwards, "if he was a Hebrew in religion, it must have sat lightly on him . . . for he found no trouble in embracing and exploiting all the degrees of all the bodies of the Rite . . . and . . . [he] was not troubled by dietetics."[81] In his home life, at least, Hays took his Judaism more seriously than his fellow Masons might have known. He was a pioneer in many respects, one of which seems to have been his uniquely "American" attitude toward religion as a private matter which ought not to intrude into one's public existence.

Hays's entry into Massachusetts Masonry coincided with the split between the Modern and Ancient movements, which effectively curtailed activity in Hays's Grand Lodge of Ancients between 1785 and 1788. The Ancients had been constituted in 1769, but it took the events of the Revolution to raise this upstart organization, which was comprised of an inordinately large contingent of mechanics and, in general, the "upper ranges of men outside the elite,"[82] to respectability. Long associated with their meeting place, the famous Green Dragon tavern where the Sons of Liberty often met during the years preceding the war, the Ancients would seek recognition by attempting to change that tavern's name to "the Mason's Arms."[83] Though they numbered among them a significant array of patriots, the Moderns—having gained their charter from English Masonry—tended with some frequency to Toryism or neutrality.[84] As agitation increased in the early 1770s, the nearly unanimously patriotic Ancients grew more vocal than ever. Their leaders included not only Paul Revere, but the martyred hero of Bunker Hill, Dr. Joseph Warren. In 1775, Revere himself had appeared at the front of a mob of Ancients who had come to taunt the Loyalist customs commissioner Benjamin Hallowell, a highly placed Modern who subsequently fled when the British left town after Bunker Hill. Hays himself had not been involved in any of these doings; he settled in Boston when the dust had already cleared from these intra-Masonic disturbances. Where the city's Masons had been bitterly divided by the events of the war, Hays somehow avoided all of the controversy. Although he was personally aligned with the Ancients, he seems to have been untainted by the split and brought his disinterested influence to bear on the negotiations that were to result, in 1792, in the merging of the factions under a single (Ancient) roof.

The Moderns' loss of influence was reified by the fact that their lodge granted its last new charters in 1780. From that point on, growth in Massachusetts Masonry was an entirely Ancient phenomenon. Even in the tumult of the Revolutionary War, the Ancients' St. Andrew's Lodge was able to bring forward and accept ninety-six new members between 1777 and 1780.[85] The triumph of the Ancients over the Moderns spoke to the increasing influence if not of the lower orders then of self-made men.

In Newport, in 1781, the force of the Ancient sensibility had been strong enough to task Hays himself with convening a group whose purpose it was to ascertain nothing less than George Washington's eligibility to be recognized as a Grand Master of North America upon his visit to that city. The group, which also included Hays's coreligionist Moses Seixas as well as three other men, found "on inquiry" that General Washington—for all of his connections to the Virginia aristocracy, not to mention his service to the new nation—was neither "a Grand Master of North America, as was supposed, nor even Master of any particular Lodge." The group was eager to avoid any controversy, but neither could it sanction conferring undue respect upon a man whose credentials were not in order.[86]

Hays's increasing prominence and respectability in Boston corresponded directly with the rise of the Ancients over the Moderns. This group of "literate, entrepreneurially active, and culturally aware" Masons had history on its side.[87] During the war itself, the Ancients succeeded in chartering nineteen new lodges. Newspaper announcements of Masonic activity from the period between 1789 and 1792 uniformly indicate Hays as the "Right Worshipfull M.M. Hays Esq. Grand Master." As early as 1787, the Ancients began to formulate their intention to "form a plan of union between the 2 Grand Lodges," and in 1792, the Grand Lodge of Ancients was able to "dictate the terms of a merger with the moderns."[88] Moses Michael Hays did not preside over this process, but he benefited immediately from its results. He experienced success and acceptance on several fronts simultaneously, and if notice was taken of his being a Jew, it did not enter the Masonic record books. His material legacy included three silver mounted truncheons which he presented to one Boston lodge and are mentioned by several Masonic chroniclers.[89] Hays's most lasting contribution as a Mason was his having presided over the granting of new charters to new lodges throughout Massachusetts and other New England states. His ability to make such inroads may have proceeded from his early attainment, during his New York days, of the highly coveted "Third Degree," an attribute which earned him no end of admiration, especially among Boston's newly empowered Ancients. The advantage Hays gained through his Masonic connections was immeasurable. His fellowship with prominent Bostonians, which brought all manner of economic and social benefits to him, was promoted by his Masonic involvement. If anything, association with him might be seen as a warrant of respectability to other Masons. In 1789, when Paul Revere wished to purchase "five or six tons of pig metal" on "three or four months credit" from a supplier in Providence, Hays prepared a letter of introduction for him and offered to be his guarantor.[90]

Like Revere himself, who was an uneducated, half-French Hugenot mechanic, Moses Michael Hays was a new kind of New Englander. If he lacked the status of a native-born Anglo Congregationalist (or, for that matter, of an arriviste Anglican Tory), he had nonetheless pursued and gained every material advantage that such pedigrees might confer. Neither he nor any other Jew who might follow in his footsteps would ever gain access to the highest echelons of prestige in Boston society, but in this respect he was hardly alone. The rise of the Ancients, like the Revolution itself, had transformed New England, and insofar as that transformation witnessed the rise of a Jewish merchant to such a height of visibility and influence, neither he nor any other "outsider" could be entirely excluded. Masonry had been the ideal instrument to bring about such a transformation. Because its membership increasingly emphasized deeds and social rectitude as opposed to adherence to religious precepts or familial pedigree, the movement provided an ideal setting in which a man like Hays, who prided himself on his attainment and cultivation of virtue, might prosper. The record of his service to the Grand Lodge abounds with evidence not only of the high regard in which he was held but of the high behavioral standard that he set. In the meeting minutes that were taken during his term as Grand Master, as two Masonic historians have it, Hays "praise[d] good work; he urge[d] caution in the admission of new members; he insist[ed] upon the secretaries keeping good records."[91] He supplied appropriate judgment when circumstances dictated, as when, for example, he reprimanded one member of his lodge in 1783 for having apparently been married to two women simultaneously. The man's crime was, in Hays's words, "highly derogatory for the laws of Morality, Society and Honor; & Diametrically opposed to the Principles of Masonry."[92]

On July 4, 1795, when the cornerstone for the new Massachusetts State House was set on Beacon Hill, the Ancients, who now dictated the terms of Massachusetts Masonry, were among the most prominent men in attendance. Paul Revere's address to the crowd, which is his only public speech on record, emphasized Massachusetts' apparent adoption of solid Masonic thinking. He admonished his listeners to "live within the compass of Good Citizens,"[93] but did not urge any even remotely sectarian practices or alignments. The controversy over which view of church and state relationships would have control in the Commonwealth had not been resolved, even by its adoption of the United States Constitution, which itself had deferred to the states' discretion on such matters. Where Masons held sway, at least, and among the sorts of new men of whom Revere was an exemplar, religious conviction and affiliation were of considerably less significance than they once had been. Hays had not triumphed in this realm because he was a Jew or, for that matter, in spite of that fact. He triumphed because he was universally acknowledged to be a virtuous and charitably minded upstanding citizen and a contributor to the greater good of society. An Arminian view of human salvation had not necessarily supplanted the old New England tradition. It had been a present and active ingredient all along in so many of their ambitious communitarian endeavors, but it took the drastic social realignments of the Revolution to bring about its temporary dominance, at least in the political realm. Before too much time passed, a powerful anti-Masonic movement would check the advance of New England secularism. Massachusetts, after all, would be the last state to end its tradition of church establishment (state sponsorship of Congregationalism was practiced until the mid-1830s). In the meantime, with men like Hays and Revere at the helm, religious affiliation was rendered secondary to fraternal affinity. Most lodges, including the Grand Lodge of Massachusetts, actually forbade sectarian religious discourse of any kind (the Newport Jews had passed a similar bylaw decades earlier in their social club, where any mention of synagogue business was grounds for an offender's having to supply wine to the entire group). It was deemed detrimental to fellowship and unity. Sectarianism was "particularly dangerous because," ironically, "[it] hindered the spread of religion and the morality it encouraged."[94]

Within this milieu, Hays was able to retain his private connections to Judaism and, moreover, to impart the Jewish tradition to his children, niece, and nephews, each of whom maintained the tie into the next generation. He was a steady and generous contributor both the New York and the Newport synagogues. In public life, however, Hays was universally known to be a faithful Jew (if one unencumbered by any concern with "dietetics"), but his public acts, at least as far as Bostonians were concerned, occurred outside the purview of his religious affiliation. He was on record as having contributed, around 1780, to Harvard College. In 1785 his name appeared on a list of contributors toward the improvement of the Boston Common. When the city of Philadelphia was devastated by a yellow fever epidemic in 1793, Hays was indicated as the person in Boston in charge of the fund that had been designated to assist in the Pennsylvania city's relief. He was also listed as one of five members of the Boston Chamber of Commerce in 1796. In 1798, Hays's name was actually put forward when a vote was being taken for senator for Suffolk County.[95] Members of the synagogue communities in New York and Newport were also aware of his philanthropic tendencies, but Bostonians who sought deeper insight into his private life as a Jew would have to have read between the lines when, in 1796, the Federal Orrery listed the marriage of Hays's daughter Sally to Samuel Myers of Petersburg, Virginia, who was a member of one of that state's most noteworthy Jewish families.[96] Year after year in the 1790s the official Boston directory relayed the circumstances of Hays's existence in a matter-of-fact way—he lived at the same address on Hanover Street in a household consisting of "2 Free white males over 16 [himself and his son Judah], 2 white males under 16, 11 white females, 2 other Free persons and no slaves."[97]

What sort of Jewish life was this? Though his estate was found to contain twenty-three Hebrew books upon his death and, as tradition has it, the family "conducted regular worship services in their house,"[98] could any one man or any one family live Jewishly in such isolation? Even as Hays had resisted all temptations to convert to Christianity or to walk away from his Judaism, the absence of a surrounding community precluded any sense of his success in Boston being equivalent to a Jewish triumph. In Samuel May's often cited reminiscence, the Hayses' Jewish "fastings and prayers" occupied comparatively less space than the author's gratitude to his hosts for their vigilance on the matter of his own childhood Christian obligations. "Every night I was required on going to bed," May wrote of his days as a Hays houseguest, "to repeat my Christian prayers and hymns to them, or else to an excellent Christian servant woman who lived with them many years."[99] Perhaps Hays and his family were eager to take care lest their neighbors perceive them as any kind of threat to the predominance of Protestant Christianity in the land of the Puritans. His hypervigilance against such an outcome notwithstanding, Hays may just as easily have so fully internalized the standards of integrity and secular virtue that he applied in his business life and in his Masonic activities that he viewed compelling the young Samuel May to say his Christian prayers under a Jewish roof as a right course of action, equivalent in some way to paying off every debt and following every proper protocol of human fellowship.

Hays's Judaism was not free of social encumbrances, and the private form that it took suggested anything but an integral Jewish "arrival" in postrevolutionary New England. It had no direct or influential effect on the larger religious context in which it took shape, any more than the fleeting presence of itinerant Jewish merchants in seventeenth-century Boston or the presence of settled Jewish merchants in eighteenth-century Newport had had upon those cities. Like the earlier Jewish "incursions" into New England culture, Hays's presence signaled a wider transformation in which cultural tendencies and tensions that were already inherent in New England culture became manifest. The battle between a view of human beings as self-actualizing and inherently redeemable and a view of them as not only corruptible but as incapable of affecting their fate (whether in the afterlife or as the inheritors of an inequitable social milieu on earth) would continue to be fought, even after the Revolution and the Constitution began the process of granting civil rights to non-Protestants. Hays's achievement of "success as both a Bostonian and as a Jew"[100] spoke more volubly to New England's adoption of gentility, virtue, and social rectitude as guiding principles upon which to build a society than it did to its transformation into a bastion of religious freedom. The two public commemorations of his death in 1805 in Boston gave voice to the development of such an atmosphere. Robert Treat Paine's "Elegiac Sonnet" made no mention of Hays's background or religious profession, but it did hint that the "rich resources" he had been afforded by his adherence to "Truth and Feeling" were sufficient to redeem both the living and the dead. Those who mourned his death could assuage their grief through "the recollection of his virtues," read the obituary that was widely printed in newspapers not only in Boston, New York, and Newport but in such outlying areas such as Newburyport and Worcester, Massachusetts; Walpole, New York; Keene, New Hampshire; and Portland, Maine. The obituary's one reference to Hays's Judaism was its announcement, in its concluding sentence, that his body was to be borne from Boston to Newport, "to be deposited in the Jewish sepulchre in that city."[101]

If Hays left any sort of Jewish legacy it was through his and Rachel's influence over their own children. Every one of them, as well as his sister's three offspring, retained their Judaism, albeit outside of Boston.[102] The only glimpse we are afforded of him as anything but the most solicitous of personages was conveyed within the family, whose tradition suggests that "stern old uncle Moses Hays"[103] had stood in the way when his nephew Judah Touro sought his (Hays's) daughter Catherine's hand in marriage, on the obvious grounds that their consanguinity, although it may have been less of an impediment among the famously insular and aristocratic Sephardim than it would have been outside the fold, made such a connection inadvisable. Neither Judah nor Catherine ever did marry, but they both held firmly throughout their lifetimes to their parents' religion. Of an even more immediate concern, however, was Hays's apparent eagerness to impart the civil religion that had served him in such good stead through his years in Boston. In a letter he wrote in 1796 to his son Judah, who was about to embark upon a voyage to France, he devoted several sentences to some secular advice whose origins lay in his own experiences as a man who had made his way in the world on the strength of his adherence to a strict behavior code. In addition to giving his son practical advice on the importance of protecting his letters of introduction and of making himself a "perfect master of the French language and of the commerce of France," he wished Judah to make his "friendships and connexions with none but persons of honour and reputation. You are now going into the world, and at a great distance from your country and connexions. . . . Be very careful and attentive to guard and keep from any reflection on your integrity and the principles of rectitude which I know are fully imbibed in you. . . . Take care what company you go into, be very careful indeed; you will find traps, snares, and allurements momently."[104] It would be many years before the Hayses or any other New England Jews would be able to let down their guard and fully enjoy their prosperity on anything other than a purely individual basis. The symbolic importance of their limited successes, which can hardly be overemphasized as indicators of New England's dynamism and its dual allegiance to communitarian and individualistic thinking, concealed the culture's reluctance to grant Jews, as members of an integral community with rights and interests of its own, anything approaching equal status.

CONCLUSION

"GONE ARE THE LIVING BUT THE DEAD REMAIN"

The Jewish Legacy in Nineteenth-Century New England

IN FEBRUARY 1790 MANUEL JOSEPHSON, president of Philadelphia's Mikveh Israel congregation, wrote to Moses Seixas of Newport about the "capricious & whimsical disposition of some of the individuals" associated with the Rhode Island synagogue. The Philadelphian reflected on the liturgical dilemmas faced by all Jews living in the New World: "As to our North American Congregations, not so much can be said . . . as in reality they have no regular system; chiefly owing (in my opinion) to the smallness of their numbers, & the frequent mutability of the members from one place to another—And as from their first establishment they had no fixed and permanent rules to go by, so they have continually remained in a state of fluctuation."[1] Like so many other Old World cultural phenomena in America, Judaism employed an improvisatory spirit as it sought to adapt its ancient rituals to a newly pluralistic social milieu. While most Jews in Europe still lived apart from gentiles and were suffered, on that basis, to follow strong communal precedent, North American Jews had, as Jonathan Sarna puts it, "achieved an unprecedented degree of 'equal footing' by the end of the eighteenth century."[2] As increasingly visible participants in rather than complete outsiders to the culture of the new nation, Jews were now taking their place within the nation's panoply of rapidly democratizing sectarian interests. At the same time, though Jews were no longer mere figments of the Protestant imagination, the idea of Jews lived on as New Englanders and other Americans verbalized their ambivalent views regarding democracy, merchant capitalism, and national identity.

Even as Jewish congregations would increase dramatically in number and size over the coming decades (by 1820 the young republic's Jewish population would grow fivefold, to approximately ten thousand), the central tenet underlying Josephson's assessment would hold. Extreme mobility, in combination with the unavailability of formal training (elsewhere in his letter, Josephson lamented the pattern by which each new Jewish arrival from the Old World, believing "it next to impossible that any knowledge can be obtained out of Europe," would chastise more thoroughly Americanized congregants for their extreme ignorance of traditional Judaism), necessitated the continual revision of American Jews' religious and communal behavior. To non-Jews, Judaic liturgy still offered an object lesson in an alien ritual practice, and divisions *among* Jews would have been difficult to detect (among other changing circumstances, as early as 1790, when the first national census was conducted, Ashkenazic Jews had begun to outnumber their Sephardic predecessors). Notwithstanding their extreme numeric inferiority, however, Jews had built actual communities in New York, Newport, Charleston, Savannah, Richmond, Lancaster, Pennsylvania, and Philadelphia by the turn of the nineteenth century, and their worship services revealed them to at least some non-Jews as modern-day practitioners of a living faith as opposed to relics of a bygone era in a distant hemisphere. In the aftermath of Philadelphia's Fourth of July parade in 1788, Benjamin Rush wrote famously about his sight of "the Rabbi of the Jews locked in the arms of two ministers of the gospel"[3] as members of that city's churches marched together into the nation's pluralistic future (in their ecumenical zeal, parade organizers had even seen to it that separate tables featuring kosher foods would be available to the Jews upon the conclusion of the actual parade). As much of the new nation, particularly under the sway of an Enlightenment-informed Democratic-Republicanism, indulged a newly laissez-faire attitude toward religious profession, Jews saw their political fortunes rise and their economic opportunities expand in unprecedented ways *outside New England.*

Newport and New England more generally were less than central to the burgeoning of a newly American Judaism. The area's long history as a Calvinistic holdout, notwithstanding the growth even there of a small Anglican (and, therefore, "cosmopolitan") interest and Rhode Island's ostensible indulgence of dissenters of every stripe, had never recommended it to practicing Jews in the first place. Jewish life in the Rhode

Island port had reached its heyday in the years preceding the Revolution, when Aaron Lopez and other scions of the transatlantic trade had established the colonies' second synagogue in the midst of an Anglicizing trend toward refinement and gentility. After the British occupation of Newport, few of the city's Jews remained to conduct trade or maintain a communal existence there. Even Lopez, who had created his fortune in Newport, left for the greener pastures of nearby Leicester, Massachusetts, where he might conduct his business more safely away from the dangers of the coast. He maintained his economic ties to Rhode Island, but his early death from drowning in 1782 helped to spell out the end of Newport's centrality to Jewish economic endeavors in the area.

Newport itself had been forever changed by the Revolution. If its economic fortunes had been on the rise before the war, a large-scale shift in postwar trading patterns had placed New England's second city on a path to a long dormant period that would precede its eventual reinvention, many decades later, as a playground for the rich whose charm and architectural glory would speak more volubly to departed grandeur than to any contemporary dynamism. Among the more significant of the city's architectural and historical landmarks was its synagogue, whose congregants had all but departed but whose mantle of exotic colonial-era refinement would provide visitors with a symbol of a faded New England cosmopolitanism. As soon as Newport's economic fortunes had begun to wane, New England's sole Jewish oasis was nearly vacated. Josephson's letter arrived at a moment when, as one historian puts it, the Newport group was "on the threshold of extinction."[4] On the eve of the Revolution, according to Ezra Stiles's reckoning, there had been twenty-five Jewish families in Newport. In 1790, only ten families (comprising "a total of seventy-six souls") remained there. Before long, the once vibrant community would be devoid of all its Jews. New England would not see another organized Jewish community until the mid-nineteenth century, when predominantly German Jewish communities would form in Boston, Hartford, and Bangor. New England natives, on the other hand, retained their prior interest in Jewish history and continued to deploy that interest as a marker of their unique and vexing preoccupations.

While a small number of actual Jews had been at least marginally involved in the development of the Puritans' theological Hebraism, neither the physical presence nor the written commentary of practicing Jews appears to have played any role in the development of the revolutionary- and Constitutional-era *republican* Hebraism that has been a subject of current research by American historians. Although until recently "political Hebraism has not been seen as pertinent to America beyond its initial seventeenth century settlement period,"[5] scholarship on this subject has attempted to show that, like their Puritan forbearers, late eighteenth-century Americans sought corroborative "proof" from the Hebrew Bible for the moral and practical experiments that they were conducting in republican democracy. None other than Thomas Paine, whose *Age of Reason* (1795) was one of the Enlightenment era's most vociferous rejections of religious faith and of the Bible itself, devoted significant portions of *Common Sense* to arguing that "biblical myth could also have a noneschatalogical function"[6] and, more specifically, that the Hebrew texts contained strong evidence of the moral and practical limitations of monarchy. With the Revolutionary War concluded, other republican Hebraists extended Paine's argument regarding the precedents in Jewish history for the rejection of monarchy. According to the group of New England pastors who form the basis for Eran Shalev's recent study of "the Mosaic Constitution," the Hebrew Bible contained ample proof texts for the establishment of a "federal arrangement" of tribes.[7] One preacher, Joseph Huntington, even remarked that America's thirteen states might be thought of as equivalent to ancient Israel's thirteen tribes, taking into account the division of Joseph's tribe into those of Efraim and Menasseh.[8]

Jews were not consulted as to the biblical efficacy of republican Hebraism. Nor were their opinions sought on the more tangible question of how the power of the emergent national government might be balanced with that of the new states. An abstract (and, naturally, stereotypical informed) Jewry helped nonetheless to inform the ongoing disputation between advocates of a stronger and a weaker central government. New England, the one-time font not only of revolutionary fervor but of Puritanical zeal, was quickly evolving into a hotbed of political Federalism. Many of the area's most prominent political leaders "identified Judaism with treasonous attachment to a cataclysmic Republicanism of natural rights and political disorder"[9] and associated the enfranchisement of Jews with the rise of French Jacobinism. In a strangely sonorous echo of earlier New Englanders' Hebraic fixation, spokesmen for Federalism indulged a primarily discursive interest in Jews that spoke more volubly to their abstract interests than to the actual presence of practicing Jews in their midst. Where Anne Hutchinson and other antinomians had associated the "precisianism" of those who would impose an excess of congregational order and pastoral authority with the legalism of "old Jewes," however, postrevolutionary Federalists equated Judaism with an excess of democracy. The Jews feared by Federalists were not the finger-wagging and imperious upholders of an obsolete covenantal faith but the rabble-rousing practitioners of a godless economic opportunism.

Despite the absence of an even remotely "Jewish" interest in New England (or anywhere else in the republic, for that matter), Federalists employed a newfound interest in the Jews in order to express their deep ambivalence about the nation's uncertain political future. This new New England Judeocentrism was decidedly post-biblical in its implications. The would-be conservators of political order and hierarchy were commenting on current affairs, as opposed to an ancient legacy, when they invoked the "influence" of Jews. Fearing lest the leveling and Francophile interests of the Jeffersonians gain the upper hand, postrevolutionary New England politicians warned against the subtle plots of seditious Jews who would like nothing better than to foment a Robespierrian reign of terror. As if to prove that the old formulation by which New Englanders might themselves be rendered as surrogate Jews for rhetorical purposes, however, a prominent anti-Federalist like Thomas Jefferson could see the ideological advantage, à la Hutchinson perhaps, to be gained from equating his *Federalist* opponents with Jews. At the height of the Adams administration Jefferson asserted in a letter to his political ally John Taylor that the New Englanders who opposed his policies "were circumscribed within such narrow limits . . . that their numbers will ever be the minority and they are marked, like the Jews, with such a perversity of character as to constitute . . . the natural divisions of our parties."[10]

A notable exception to the tendency among New England Federalists to resort to paranoid anti-Jewish rhetoric was John Adams himself, whose presidency ushered in the Alien and Sedition Acts of 1798 and who might have been happy to embrace, as opposed to reject, Jefferson's formulation of New Englanders-as-Jews. In private correspondence after the conclusion of his presidency, Adams indicated an uncharacteristically charitable attitude toward Jews. In an 1809 letter to F. A. Vanderkamp, he expressed his admiration for "the Hebrews," who had not only "done more to civilize men than any other nation," but whom "fate had ordained . . . to preserve and propagate to all mankind the doctrine of a supreme, intelligent, wise, almighty sovereign of the universe, which I believe to be the great essential principle of all morality, and consequently of all civilization."[11] Adams's albeit measured admiration for "the Hebrews" (in his letter to Vanderkamp, he had admitted to his general skepticism toward all "nations") was not merely a paean to their vaunted biblical heritage. In 1818, he wrote encouragingly to Mordecai Manuel Noah, that era's most prominent and accomplished American Jew: "I have had occasion to be acquainted with several gentlemen of your nation, and to transact business with some of them, whom I found to be men of as liberal minds, as much honor, probity, generosity and good breeding, as any I have known in any sect of any religion or philosophy."[12] Adams concluded his letter with as unequivocal statement of acceptance as might be found in any document from the period of the early republic. "I wish your nation may be admitted to all the privileges of citizens in every country of the world," he wrote Noah, who for his part represented the nation's first prominent voice for Jewish political enfranchisement.[13]

The first half of the nineteenth century would see the steady advancement of Jewish rights in nearly every state of the union. New England's Hebraic heritage, however, played a limited role in the achievement of those rights, and New England states would be among the last ones not only to recognize the citizenship of Jews but to welcome their organized presence.[14] Whether it was the result of vestigial Calvinism or, for that matter, the waning influence of the same Puritan legacy whose promoters had once displayed so fervent an interest in Judaic precedent, the odd absence of Jews from New England when other parts of the nation, including not only its large seaports but the growing population centers of the West and even the rural South, were admitting an ever-increasing Jewish influx was noteworthy. Like the Federalists of the early republic period, mid-nineteenth-century New Englanders were interested in Jews as economic beings as opposed to as the practitioners of an ancient faith. More than one mid-nineteenth-century traveler to New England noted the absence of Jews from that section of the nation, some quipping, as one German writer did in 1846, that Jews were scare there because, in trading endeavors, "no Jew on earth is a match for a Yankee."[15] The Transcendentalist preacher Theodore Parker had apparently remarked in 1864 "that New England was one of the few places in the civilized world where there were no Jews" because, as he put it, "The Yankees are too sharp for the children of Israel."[16] Even in their physical absence, Jews were enabling New Englanders to explore and promote their distinct identity on the national stage.

German Jews, who began their large-scale immigration to the United States in the aftermath of the unrest of 1848, would eventually make their way to the very same New England hinterlands where the Yankee traders had once held sway. Nineteenth-century views of Jewish peddlers in North America were often influenced by widespread belief in, or at least enchantment with, the tale of the Wandering Jew. The Christian story of Ahasverus, the cobbler of Jerusalem who mocked Jesus and was condemned to find no rest for eternity, was first published in Germany in 1602, but had its roots in several medieval European narratives. Several versions of the story were popular throughout early America and contributed to an overarching association of Jews in general, but more particularly itinerant Jews, with an intrinsic rootlessness. Whether sympathetic or contemptuous, print versions of the story found in the New England states tended to equate Jewish peddlers directly with Ahasverus and his curse. Even if Jewish peddlers themselves did not internalize the Wandering Jew motif, they lived with its implications.

As several scholars have pointed out, the Wandering Jew story bore multiple interpretations, especially within the framework of an industrializing New England. In a land whose settlers of European origin lacked any equivalent to an Old World peasant class with seemingly timeless connections to single places, geographical and economic mobility were commonplace. To be sure, the Wandering Jew stories were entirely fanciful projections of long-held stereotypes. At the same time, however, they were also projections of nineteenth-century Americans' misgivings regarding such themes as homelessness, economic change, and cultural marginalization. Accordingly, the Jewish ethnographer Rudolf Glanz suggested in the 1930s that "the Wandering Jew mirrored the thoughts of the American nation . . . about the nation itself."[17] Within an economic milieu "consisting not of orderly growth but of feverish speculation, frequent bankrupt-cies, and the disturbing evidence of failure at every turn,"[18] traveling Jewish peddlers, like the Wandering Jew himself, manifested an Otherness that came closer to home than many people imagined.

At least one classic American author, Nathaniel Hawthorne, provided his mid-nineteenth-century readers with a particularly telling case in point. Near the climactic moment of Hawthorne's 1851 tale, "Ethan Brand," the arrival on the scene of "an old German Jew" came close to upstaging the story's namesake in his great quest for "the unpardonable sin." The Jewish peddler (sometimes referred to by the narrator as "the German")—who carried on his back a diorama depicting, among other things, "cities, pub-lic edifices and ruined castles of Europe"—embodied cosmopolitanism.[19] Critics have compared him to the Wandering Jew and to Mephistopheles. His sudden appearance at the foot of the Berkshires' Mt. Greylock enhanced the story's exotic and altogether enchanted atmosphere. Here was a char-acter whose alien physique, history, and accoutrements suggested the broadest of exposures, whose worldliness rivaled even that of the story's protagonist, who had evidently gone *everywhere* in search of an answer to the eternal question that plagued him. Whether or not Hawthorne wished his story to be a commentary on such matters, however, it was the Faustian Ethan Brand who ultimately outdid even this most worldly and alien Jew at his own game. Brand's headlong plunge into the abyss of spiritual alien-ation originated in what Hawthorne had described elsewhere in the tale as homegrown Yankee Transcendentalism. For all of his predictable rep-rehensibility, the Jewish peddler fell far short of Ethan Brand's own *native-born* itinerancy, rank commercialism, and soul-killing selfishness.

Other New England authors of the nineteenth century indulged addi-tional forms of Judaic interest, including Ralph Waldo Emerson, whose recorded reaction to the sight of a Washington Allston portrait of a "Polish Jew" in 1839 expressed repulsion toward a group that he evidently thought of as "the primitive people of the Talmud."[20] Later in life, Emerson would befriend the poet Emma Lazarus, whose descent from early American Sephardic Grandees had conferred upon her a suitably noble American pedigree. On the whole, however, Emerson's references to Jews either faulted them for having invented a transcendent God who rivaled "Man" for power or, as Robert Lowenberg puts it, for being "usurers and low-minded people."[21] A more philo-Semitic perspective on the Jewish legacy on the part of a "classic" New England author of the nineteenth century came with the publication of Henry Wadsworth Longfellow's poem "At the Jewish Cemetery in Newport." Although the poem expressed a romantically informed sympathy with the persecuted Sephardim who had settled in eighteenth-century Newport, its elegiac form (it was, after all, inspired, by the poet's visit to a cemetery) confirmed the old Calvinist notion that, as far as Jews were concerned, only "the dead remain."[22] By 1852, the year of its release, the Newport burial ground had evolved into a mysterious marker of a long-departed and somehow inexplicable Jewish presence in the heart of New England. Generations of Judeocentrists, from John Cotton to Cotton Mather to Ezra Stiles, had struggled to come to terms with the existence, let alone presence, of actual Jews, and Longfellow was following in their footsteps.

The existence of the cemetery in Newport, like the lives of the old Jews who were buried in it, had an irresistibly alien quality for native New Englanders. Its very maintenance had passed into Christian hands in the 1820s when, according to Rebecca Touro, the complete absence of any of the old families had made it necessary for their descendants in New York and elsewhere "to appoint Mr. Stephen Gould as an agent in their behalf" to see to its proper upkeep.[23] The cemetery that Gould maintained and that Longfellow visited was a showcase of exotic material culture, if for no other reason than its inclusion of so many Hebrew inscriptions; thirty-six of its thirty-seven stones included at least some Hebrew lettering.[24] Still, "except for the uniqueness of inscriptions written in Hebrew and dates rendered in the Jewish ritual calendar [and] the 12 vertical tablet-like headstones," as David Gradwohl writes, the cemetery's overall look was not out of keeping with that of most other New England burial grounds of its time period. Five of the stones included the popular winged-cherub motif, and one—that of Jacob Lopez—was marked by a death's head. Whether or not Gradwohl is correct in claiming that such stones violated "the traditional Hebraic taboo against the use of graven images," the inclusion of those motifs might have struck Jews, if not Christians, as odd.[25] Longfellow, for one, didn't comment on it.

The Jews of eighteenth-century Newport were profoundly transnational in their cultural identity and, accordingly, had created a cemetery which spoke to their complex heritage, multiple allegiances, and fraught inheritance. From the standpoint of visiting "native" New Englanders, however, these long-dead Sephardim were, simply, "imports from Europe to America."[26] Perhaps the alien origin of the dead Newport Jews was so reminiscent of the New Englanders' own relatively recent "importation" from European shores that it blinded them to its central implications. In the words of N. H. Gould himself, who appears to have had more interaction with the Jews than any of his neighbors had, their religious distinctiveness had hardly set them apart from their fellow "exiles" of gentile birth. They had been "prudent, industrious, and enterprising," Gould wrote about the Jews in 1826, "elegant in their dress and deportment and perfected an extensive knowledge of the world."[27] The Newport Jews' embodiment of such *forward-looking* New England ideals, fleeting as it had been, had been all but invisible to men and women so long accustomed to imagining not only "these Hebrews" but also themselves as the progeny of ancient Israel.

While the Newport Jews (as well as their coreligionists in Boston) had hardly gone unnoticed, neither had they succeeded in establishing anything like a permanent presence in New England. For all of their fervor in *thinking* about Jews and in debating their legacy, after all, New England Puritans had never made any pretense of embracing them, let alone seeking them out. The privileged place within Puritan thought occupied by the Jewish legacy, rendered more complex by virtue of New England's transatlantic exposure and the presence of a few actual Jews from time to time, was offset by a consistent ethnic insularity that only increased in its intensity in and through the nineteenth and early twentieth centuries. For New England "natives," a permanent Jewish presence in the region was as unthinkable as the idea that Catholicism might ever gain a solid foothold there.[28] While other seaboard Jewish communities whose origins lay in the colonial or early republican periods (New York, Charleston, Philadelphia, and even Richmond, Virginia) had grown only by fits and starts, Jewish life had at least been uninterrupted in those places. New England provided an odd exception to such a pattern.

It is difficult to square such a fact with the state of affairs as we know them at the beginning of the twenty-first century, when upwards of four hundred thousand of the nation's six million Jews make their homes in the New England states, when Brandeis University and a host of other nationally known Jewish institutions inform the cultural life of the region, and when the state of Israel has for many years maintained a New England consulate in Boston. The establishment of these institutions and of so large a population for them to serve has only come about as the result of enormous demographic and cultural changes that, for better or worse, have reduced the Puritan tradition to the status of a faded and typically misunderstood memory.

NOTES

INTRODUCTION

1. Max Weber, *The Sociology of Religion* (1922; Boston: Beacon Press, 1993), 623.
2. David Gelernter, "The Jewish Roots of American Puritanism," excerpted in the *Jewish Ledger* (Springfield, Mass.), November 22, 2008, 23.
3. Arthur Hertzberg, *The Jews in America* (New York: Simon and Schuster, 1989), 33.
4. Jacob Rader Marcus's many works on early American Jewish history, including his three-volume *Colonial American Jew, 1492–1776* (Detroit: Wayne State University Press, 1970), constitute the most thoroughly researched and comprehensive studies on this subject. Since the publication of Marcus's works, Jonathan Sarna (*American Judaism* [New Haven: Yale University Press, 2004]), Hasia Diner (*The Jews of the United States, 1654–2000* [Berkeley : University of California Press, 2004]) and William Pencak (*Jews and Gentiles in Early America* [Ann Arbor: University of Michigan Press, 2005]) have produced comprehensive works that chronicle Jewish life in North America during the period preceding the American Revolution. Shalom Goldman's edited volume, *Hebrew and the Bible in America: The First Two Centuries* (Hanover, N.H.: University Press of New England, 1994), and his own *God's Sacred Tongue: Hebrew and the American Imagination* (Chapel Hill: University of North Carolina Press, 2004) comprise two rather recent treatments of Puritan Hebraism in early America.
5. Jorge Canizares-Esguerra, "Typology in the Atlantic World: Early Modern Readings of Colonization," in *Soundings in Atlantic History*, ed. Bernard Bailyn and Patricia Denault. (Cambridge: Harvard University Press, 2009), 239.
6. Ibid., 264.
7. I have borrowed and adapted this term from Richard Cogley, whose numerous works on Puritan eschatology employ it in connection with the widespread (though hardly universal) belief that the exact timing of, as well as the geographical specificities surrounding the Second Coming of Christ hinged in large part on events in the Jewish world (i.e., on Jewish dispersion, conversion, and an eventual restoration to the land of Israel). See "The Fall of the Ottoman Empire and the Restoration of Israel in the 'Judeo-Centric' Strand of Puritan Millenarianism," *Church History* 72 (June 2003), 304–32; "The Most Vile and Barbarous Nation of All the World: Giles Fletcher the Elder's *The Tartars Or, Ten Tribes, ca. 1610*," *Renaissance Quarterly* 58 (Fall 2005), 781–814; "The Ancestry of the American Indians: Thomas Thorowgood's *Iewes in America* (1650); and *Jews in America* (1660)," *English Literary History* 35 (Fall 2005), 304–30.
8. Keith Sprunger, *Trumpets from the Tower: English Puritan Printing in the Netherlands, 1600–1640* (Leiden: E. J. Brill, 1994), 70.

9. Ibid., 49.

10. Ibid.

11. Henry Mechoulan and Gerard Nahon, introduction to *The Hope of Israel—The English Translation by Moses Wall, 1652* (Oxford: Oxford University Press, 1987), 3.

12. Jane Gerber, *The Jews of Spain: The Sephardic Experience* (Ann Arbor: University of Michigan Press, 1992), 195.

13. Miriam Bodian, *Hebrews of the Portuguese Nation: Conversos and Community in Early Modern Amsterdam* (Ann Arbor: University of Michigan Press, 1997), 1.

14. Ibid., 103.

15. Gordon Schochet, "Introduction: Hebraic Roots, Calvinist Plantings, American Branches," *Hebraic Political Studies* 4 (Spring 2009), 102–3.

16. David Katz, *Philo-Semitism and the Readmission of the Jew to England, 1603–1655* (Oxford: Clarendon Press, 1982), 20–29.

17. Ibid., 73.

18. Bodian, 69–70.

19. Arend H. Huussen, "The Legal Position of the Jews in the Dutch Republic, c. 1590–1796," in *Dutch Jewry: Its History and Secular Culture (1500–2000)*, ed. Jonathan Israel and Reiner Salverda (Leiden: Brill, 2002).

20. Katz, 9.

21. Todd Endelman, *The Jews of Britain, 1656–2000* (Berkeley: University of California Press, 2002), 18.

22. Katz, 90.

23. Ibid., 177.

24. Endelman, 29.

25. One complicating factor, as religious historian Richard Cogley points out, was the question of how millions of Native American descendants of the Lost Tribes might ever be transported, physically, across the ocean to their original "home" in Israel.

26. Thomas Thorowgood, *Jewes in America, Or Probabilities that the Americans are of that Race* (London: Henry Brome, 1650), 23.

27. Richard Popkin, "Jewish Messianism and Christian Millenarianism," in *Culture and Politics from Puritanism to the Enlightenment*, ed. P. Zagorin (Berkeley: University of California Press, 1970), 77.

28. John Eliot (in Thorowgood, *Jewes in America*), 15.

29. Thorowgood, *Jewes in America*, 28.

30. Cogley, "The Fall," 327.

31. Glenn Moots, "Response: The Complications and Contributions of Early American Hebraism," *Hebrew Political Studies* 4 (Spring 2009), 159.

32. Thorowgood, *Jewes in America*, 30.

33. Canizares-Esguerra, 253.

34. Andrew Murphy, "New Israel in New England: The American Jeremiad and the Hebrew Scriptures," *Hebraic Political Studies* 4 (Spring 2009), 128.

35. William Scheick, "The Captive Exile Hasteth: Increase Mather, Meditation, and Authority," *Early American Literature* 36, no. 1 (2001), 189.

CHAPTER ONE

1. Avihu Zakai, *Exile and Kingdom: History and Apocalypse in the Puritan Migration to America* (Cambridge: Cambridge University Press, 1992), 138.

2. Sacvan Bercovitch, *Puritan Origins of the American Self* (Cambridge: Harvard University Press, 1975), 81.

3. Shira Wolosky, "Biblical Republicanism: John Cotton's 'Moses His Judicials' and American Hebraism," *Hebrew Political Studies* 4, no. 2 (Spring 2009), 117.

4. Ibid., 116.

5. James W. Jones, *The Shattered Synthesis* (New Haven: Yale University Press, 1973), ix.

6. Wolosky, 113 and 115.

7. James Byrd, *The Challenges of Roger Williams: Religious Liberty, Violent Persecution and the Bible* (Macon: Mercer University Press, 2002), 9.

8. Bernard Bailyn, *New England Merchants in the Seventeenth Century* (Cambridge: Harvard University Press, 1955), 16.

9. Andrew Delbanco, *The Puritan Ordeal* (Cambridge: Harvard University Press, 1991).

10. T. H. Breen, *Puritans and Adventurers: Change and Persistence in Early America* (Oxford: Oxford University Press, 1980), 53.

11. Philip Gura, *A Glimpse of Sion's Glory: Puritan Radicalism in New England, 1630–1660* (Middletown: Wesleyan University Press, 1984), 4.

12. Richard Archer, *Fissures in the Rock: New England in the Seventeenth Century* (Hanover, N.H.: University Press of New England, 2001), 130.

13. Ibid., 144.

14. Theodore Dwight Bozeman, *The Precisianist Strain: Disciplinarian Religion and Antinomian Backlash to 1638* (Chapel Hill: University of North Carolina Press, 2004), 25.

15. Ibid., 94.

16. *Cyclopedia of American Literature*, ed. Evert Duyckinck and George Duyckinck (New York: Scribners, 1865), 56.

17. Bozeman, *Precisianist*, 150.

18. Clifford Shipton, "The Hebraic Background of Puritanism," *Publications of the American Jewish Historical Society* (1958), 150.

19. Larzer Ziff, *Puritanism in America* (New York: Viking, 1973), 80.

20. Wolosky, 106.

21. Bozeman, *Precisianist*, 24.

22. Ziff, 54.

23. Ellen Smith, "Strangers and Sojourners: The Jews of Colonial Boston," in *The Jews of Boston*, ed. Scott-Martin Kosofsky, Jonathan Sarna, and Ellen Smith (New Haven: Yale University Press, 2005), 28.

24. Bozeman, *Precisianist*, 32.

25. Wolosky, 106.

26. Smith, 29.

27. Robert H. Pfeiffer, "The Teaching of Hebrew in Colonial America," *Jewish Quarterly Review* 45 (1954–1955), 365.

28. Ibid., 367.

29. Albert Ehrenfried, *A Chronicle of Boston Jewry from the Colonial Settlement to 1900* (Boston: Privately printed, 1963), 36–37.

30. Quoted in Edgar McManus, *Law and Liberty in Early New England: Criminal Justice and Due Process, 1620–1692* (Amherst: University of Massachusetts Press, 1993), 21.

31. Stanley Broches, *Jews in New England: Part I, Historical Study of the Jews in Massachusetts, 1650–1750* (New York: Block, 1942), 7.

32. John Murrin, "Magistrates, Sinners, and a Precarious Liberty: Trial by Jury in Seventeenth Century New England," in *Saints and Revolutionaries*, ed. David Hall, John Murrin, and Thad Tate (New York: Norton, 1984).

33. Theodore Dwight Bozeman, *To Live Ancient Lives: The Primitivist Dimension in Puritanism* (Williamsburg: Institute of Early American History, 1988), 32, 161–62.

34. Richard Cogley, *John Eliot's Mission to the Indians before King Philip's War* (Cambridge: Harvard University Press, 1999), 78.

35. Ibid., 80.

36. McManus, 37.

37. Worthington Chauncey Ford, "Moses His Judicials," *Massachusetts Historical Society Proceedings*, 2nd ser., 16 (1902), 276.

38. Ibid., 278.

39. Ibid., 276.

40. Ibid., 278.

41. Bozeman, *To Live Ancient Lives*, 171.

42. The closest we have to an original manuscript copy of John Cotton's 1641 "An Abstract of the laws of New England as they are now established," was hand copied by William Grays in 1767 and is in the collection of the Massachusetts Historical Society. Aspinwall's 1655 commentary can be found in "Two treatises on the question of the veto power of the Magistrates of the Massachusetts Bay Colony over the resolutions of the deputies to the General Court," a manuscript which is also in the possession of the Massachusetts Historical Society.

43. McManus, 10.

44. Bozeman, *To Live Ancient Lives*, 143.

45. Perry Miller, *Nature's Nation* (Cambridge: Harvard University Press, 1967), 209.

46. Ford, 279.

47. McManus, 9 and 15.

48. Ford, 280.

49. Quoted in Delbanco, 37.

50. Ford, 280.

51. Quoted in Michael Winship, *Making Heretics: Militant Protestantism and Free Grace in Massachusetts, 1630–1641* (Princeton: Princeton University Press, 2002), 84.

52. Ford, 284.

53. Bozeman, *To Live Ancient Lives*, 175.

54. Wolosky, 108.

55. Reiner Smolinski, "Israel Redivivus: The Eschatological Limits of Puritan Typology," *New England Quarterly* 63 (September 1990), 371.

56. Ibid., 382.

57. Massachusetts State Archives, Reel 15A (A180), 13. W. E. B. Du Bois Library, University of Massachusetts, Amherst.

58. Jaspar Danckaerts and Peter Sluyter, *Journal of a Voyage to New York and a Tour of Several*

of the American Colonies, 1679–1680. Translated from the Dutch and reprinted in 1869 by the Long Island Historical Society, 386–87.

59. *Records of the Governor and the company of the Massachusetts bay in New England* (Boston: W. White, 1853–1854), no page number. This passage is also quoted in several secondary works, including Ehrenfried and *The Jews of Boston* (see note 23, above).

60. Josiah Henry Benton, *Warning Out in New England* (Boston: W. B. Clarke, 1911).

61. Jacob Rader Marcus, *The Jew in the American World: A Sourcebook* (Detroit: Wayne State University Press, 1996), 27.

62. Smith, 24.

63. Jack P. Greene, *Pursuits of Happiness: The Development of Early Modern British Colonies and the Formation of American Culture* (Chapel Hill: University of North Carolina Press, 1988), 63.

64. Marcus, *Colonial American Jew*, 303.

65. David Graizbord, *Souls in Dispute: Jewish Identities in Iberia and the Jewish Diaspora, 1580–1700* (Philadelphia: University of Pennsylvania Press, 2003), 2.

66. Lois Dubin, "Port Jews of the Atlantic," *Jewish History* 20 (2006), 120.

67. Ibid., 118.

68. R. Solomon Franco, "Truth Springing Out of Earth" (London: J. Flesher, 1668), 3.

69. Samuel Silverman, *Hartford Jews* (Hartford: Connecticut Historical Society, 1970).

70. Broches, *Part I*, 13.

71. Jacob Rader Marcus, "Light on Early Connecticut Jewry," *American Jewish Archives* (June 1950), 5.

72. Ibid., 9.

73. McManus, 45.

74. Bozeman, *Precisianist* 108.

75. Quoted in Gura, 93.

76. Lee Friedman, *Jewish Pioneers and Patriots* (Philadelphia: Jewish Publication Society, 1945), 43.

77. Reproduced in Jay Mack Holbrook, *Boston Beginnings, 1630–1699* (Boston: Privately published, 1980), 876:29.

78. Perry Miller, *The New England Mind: From Colony to Province* (Cambridge: Harvard University Press, 1953), 45.

79. Photostat of the manuscript version is in possession of and provided by courtesy of the American Jewish Archives, Cincinnati, Ohio. Like the Franco document, part or all of Gideon's appeal has also been reproduced in several secondary works on early American Jewish history.

80. Smith, 26.

81. Marcus, *Early American Jewry*, vol. 1, 105.

82. Nathaniel Ward, *Massachusetts Body of Liberties* (1641) (Hanover: Hanover Historical Texts Project, 1990), 272–73.

83. Friedman, *Jewish Pioneers*. See also *Bevis Marks Records, Part 1: The Early History of the Congregation from the Beginning until 1800* (Oxford: Oxford University Press, 1940).

84. *El Libro De Los Acuerdos* (*Bevis Marks Records, 1663–1681*), vol. 1 (London: Spanish and Portuguese Synagogue, 1931), xiii.

85. McManus, 18–19.

86. Steven Waldman, *Founding Faith: How Our Founding Fathers Forged a Radical Approach to Religious Liberty* (New York: Random House, 2009), 9.

87. Thomas O'Connor, *Boston Catholics: A History of the Church and Its People* (Boston: Northeastern University Press, 1998), 89.

88. Bozeman, *Precisianist*, 312.

89. Gura, 14.

90. Ibid., 156.

91. Janice Knight, *Orthodoxies in Massachusetts: Rereading American Puritanism* (Cambridge: Harvard University Press, 1994), 5–9.

92. Bernard Bailyn, *The Peopling of North America: An Introduction* (New York: Knopf, 1986), 48.

93. Ibid., 48–49.

94. Archer, 3.

95. Ibid.

96. Roger Williams, *The Bloudy Tenent of Persecution*, in *Complete Writings of Roger Williams*, vol. 4, ed. Perry Miller (New York: Russell and Russell, 1964), 200.

97. Richard Reinitz, "The Typology Argument for Religious Toleration," *Early American Literature* 5 (Spring 1970), 124.

98. Byrd, 85.

99. Williams, *Tenent*, 283.

100. Ibid.

101. Byrd, 9.

102. Reinitz, 108.

103. Williams, *Tenent*, 3.

104. Bozeman, *To Live Ancient Lives*, 157.

105. Williams, *Tenent*, 324.

106. Ibid.

107. Ibid., 322.

108. Byrd, 39.

109. Williams, *Tenent*, 95.

110. Ibid., 170–71.

111. Ibid., 171.

112. Ibid., 38.

113. Byrd, 56.

114. Ibid., 57.

115. Hugh Peter, "A Word for the Armie; and Two Words for the Kingdome" (London: Giles Calvert, 1647), 11.

116. Patricia Bonomi, *Under the Cope of Heaven: Religion, Society, and Politics in Colonial America* (Oxford: Oxford University Press, 1986), 219.

117. Quoted in Irving Preston Richman, *Rhode Island: A Study in Separatism* (Providence: Preston and Rounds, 1905), 126.

118. Broches, Part I, 11.

119. Holly Snyder, "A Sense of Place: Jews, Identity and Social Status in Colonial British America, 1654–1831" (Ph.D. diss.: Brandeis University, 2000), 57.

120. Leo Hershkowitz makes the case that the frequently cited date of 1654 as the

earliest permanent Jewish settlement in North America (when the first Jews are said to have landed in what was then New Amsterdam) is not quite accurate. Nearly all of the storied twenty-three Jews who would have landed in the Dutch outpost at that time stayed for a very short period of time. Hershkowitz also suggests that they may have been preceded by two other Jewish merchants, one of whom—Asser Levy, of Vilna—appears in official records as the only long-term seventeenth-century Jewish resident who can be proven to have made his first landfall in the city in 1654. See "New Amsterdam's Twenty-Three Jews: Myth or Reality?" in *Hebrew and the Bible in America*, ed. Shalom Goldman (Hanover, N.H.: Brandeis University Press, 1993), 171–83.

121. Morris Aaron Gutstein, *The Story of the Jews of Newport* (New York: Bloch, 1936), 37.

122. Ibid., 343. Gould's claim was that an elderly relative of his had inherited the original document in the mid-eighteenth century and that by the time it had fallen into his hands, it was so threadbare that it required recopying. In its English usage, the Gould certificate sounds like any number of entries in the congregational rule books, or *acuerdos*, kept by Portuguese Jews throughout the Atlantic world. On the other hand, as Masonry itself was not fully developed until the early decades of the eighteenth century, the document constitutes dubious stand-alone "proof" of a mid-seventeenth-century Jewish presence in Newport.

123. Ibid., 37–38.

124. William Pencak, *Jews and Gentiles in Early America*, 83.

125. Snyder, "A Sense of Place," 61.

126. Ibid., 62.

127. Stanley Chyet, *Lopez of Newport* (Detroit: Wayne State University Press, 1970), 35. For his part, David Brown was the brother of Saul Brown (Brown was merely a translation of their original name, Pardo), who was an early minister to the Jewish congregation in New York. Their grandfather, who had been born in Salonica, became a rabbi in Amsterdam, as did their father.

128. Pencak, *Jews and Gentiles*, 85.

129. Ibid., 87.

130. Gutstein, 43.

131. Pencak, *Jews and Gentiles*, 87.

132. Marcus, *Colonial American Jew*, 435; see also *Records of the Colony of Rhode Island* (1688), 243.

133. Marcus, *Colonial American Jew*, 794.

134. Ibid., 624.

135. Gutstein, 44.

136. Holly Snyder, "Rules, Rights, and Redemption: The Negotiation of Jewish Status in British Atlantic Port Towns, 1740–1831," *Jewish History* 20 (2006), 153.

137. Eli Faber, *A Time for Planting: The First Migration, 1654–1820* (Baltimore: Johns Hopkins University Press, 1995), 37.

138. Bailyn, *Peopling*, 112–13.

139. Faber, 26.

140. Max Kohler, *Proceedings of the American Jewish Historical Society* 2 (1894), 84–85.

141. Graizbord, 2–3.

142. Joseph Conforti, *Imagining New England: Explorations of Regional Identity from the Pilgrims to the Mid-Twentieth Century* (Chapel Hill: University of North Carolina Press, 2001), 7.

143. Michael Winship, "Contesting Control of Orthodoxy among the Godly: William Pynchon Reconsidered," *William and Mary Quarterly*, 3rd ser., 54 (1997), 821.

144. Snyder, "A Sense of Place," xii.

CHAPTER TWO

1. *Boston News-Letter*, March 11, 1706. *America's Historical Newspapers*, http://infoweb. newsbank.com.

2. Jacob Marcus, *Colonial American Jew*, 771.

3. Ibid.

4. See Eli Faber, *A Time for Planting*, and also Wim Klooster, *Illicit Riches* (Leiden: KITLV Press, 1998). Other sources mention this "wave" of Jewish immigration from Curaçao to Newport, including Thomas William Bicknell in *The History of Rhode Island and Providence Plantations*, vol. 2 (New York: American Historical Society, 1920), 629, and George Alexander Kohut in *Proceedings of the American Jewish Historical Society* 6 (1897), 63.

5. Ezra Stiles copy of John Mumford's 1712 hand-drawn map, in the collection of the Massachusetts Historical Society (Ezra Stiles Papers).

6. Andrew Delbanco and Alan Heimert, *The Puritans in America: A Narrative Anthology* (Cambridge: Harvard University Press, 1985), 277.

7. Larzer Ziff, *Puritanism in America*, 253.

8. Ibid., 253–54.

9. Delbanco and Heimert, 278.

10. Francis Bremer, *The Puritan Experiment: New England Society from Bradford to Edwards* (Hanover, N.H.: University Press of New England, 1995), 208.

11. Mark Peterson, "Theopolis Americana: The City-State of Boston, the Republic of Letters, and the Protestant International," in *Soundings in Atlantic History*, ed. Bernard Bailyn and Patricia Denault (Cambridge: Harvard University Press, 2009), 331.

12. Joseph Conforti, *Imagining New England*, 65.

13. Samuel Sewall, *Phaenomena quoedam apocalyptica ad aspectum Novi orbis configurata: Or, some few lines towards a description of the New heaven as it makes to those who stand on the New earth* (London: Benjamin Eliot, 1727), 37.

14. Ibid., 36.

15. Ibid.

16. Broches, Part 1, 14.

17. Marcus, *Colonial American Jew*, 771.

18. *Calendar of State Papers, Domestic Series of the Reign of William and Mary* (preserved in the Public Record Office [Great Britain]), ed. Cecil Headlam, 496.

19. Ibid.

20. Samuel Sewall, *The Diary of Samuel Sewall*, Massachusetts Historical Society, 5th ser., 6 (1878).

21. Stephen Birmingham, *The Grandees: America's Sephardic Elite* (New York: Harper and Row, 1971), 52.

22. Ibid.

23. Arnold Witnitzer, *The minute book of congregations Zur Israel of Recife and Magen Abraham of Mauricia, Brazil* (London: Maurice Jacobs, 1953), 3.

24. *Sephardim in America: Studies in Culture and History*, ed. Martin A. Cohen and Abraham Peck (Tuscaloosa: University of Alabama Press, 1993), 58.

25. Witnitzer, 15.

26. Ibid.

27. Birmingham, 52.

28. Sewall, *Phaenomena*, 37.

29. *Bevis Marks Records*, 24.

30. The members of New York's Shearith Israel evidently coped with a similar phenomenon. Young boys in that congregation were so rambunctious that they required seating in a single corner of the synagogue "where they could be watched by the Hazzan." See Doris Groshen Daniels, "Colonial Jewry: Religion, Domestic, and Social Relations," in *American Jewish History: The Colonial and Early National Periods*, ed. Jeffrey Gurock (New York: American Jewish Historical Society, 1998), 309.

31. *Bevis Marks Records*, 79.

32. Jehoshuah Da Silva, *Thirteen Articles of the Creed* (Amsterdam and London: Judita de Mosen Enriques Valentin, 1688). Privately translated from the Portuguese by Simone Gugliotta.

33. Sewall, *Phaenomena*, 37.

34. Samuel Willard, *The fountain opened: or, The great Gospel priviledge of having Christ exhibited to sinfull men: Wherein is also proved that there shall be a national calling of the Jews: From Zech. XIII* (Boston: Green and Allen, 1700), 3.

35. Ibid.

36. Eve LaPlante, *Salem Witch Judge: The Life and Repentance of Samuel Sewall* (New York: Harper One, 2008), 200.

37. Ibid., 182.

38. Ibid., 183.

39. Michael Winship, *Seers of God: Puritan Providentialism in the Restoration and Early Eighteenth Century* (Baltimore: Johns Hopkins University Press, 2000), 5.

40. Ibid., 6.

41. Bremer, 218.

42. Perry Miller, *The New England Mind*, 167.

43. Ibid.

44. James W. Jones, *The Shattered Synthesis*, 34.

45. Dana Nelson, "Economies of Morality and Power: Reading 'Race' in Two Colonial Contexts," in *A Mixed Race: Ethnicity in Early America*, ed. Frank Shuffleton (Oxford: Oxford University Press, 1993), 26.

46. Ibid., 216–17.

47. Marcus, *Colonial American Jew*, 1136.

48. Cotton Mather, *Diary of Cotton Mather, 1681–1724*, ed. Worthington Chauncey Ford (New York: Ungar, 1957), 200.

49. Arthur Hertzberg, *The Jews in America*, 39.

50. Quoted in Shalom Goldman, *God's Sacred Tongue*, 29.

51. Peterson, 345, and Librarything.com.

52. John Stuart Erwin, *The Millennialism of Cotton Mather: An Historical and Theological Analysis* (New York: E. Mellen Press, 1990), 137.

53. Ibid.

54. Louis Feldman, "The Influence of Josephus on Cotton Mather's Biblia Americana," in *Hebrew and the Bible in America*, ed. Shalom Goldman,140.

55. Reiner Smolinski, "Israel Redivivus," 382.

56. Erwin, 141.

57. Delbanco, *Puritan Ordeal*, 226.

58. Cotton Mather, *Diary*, 300.

59. Ibid.

60. Cotton Mather, *The Faith of the Fathers, Or, The articles of the true religion* (Boston: Green and Allen, 1699), 13.

61. Ibid., 3.

62. Ibid., 20.

63. Thomas Kidd, *The Protestant Interest: New England after Puritanism* (New Haven: Yale University Press, 2004), 148.

64. Sacvan Bercovitch, *Puritan Origins of the American Self*, 53.

65. Cotton Mather, *Faith of the Fathers*, 24.

66. Feldman, 126.

67. Lee Max Friedman, *Pilgrims in a New Land* (New York: Jewish Publication Society, 1948), 77.

68. Feldman, 128.

69. Cotton Mather, *Biblia Americana*. All citations refer to the appendix following Mather's treatment of the Book of Acts. On microfilm in the collection of the Massachusetts Historical Society (Reel 6). Mather's Bibilia is currently being edited under the direction of Reiner Smolinski, published by Mohr Siebeck and Baker Academic (vol. 1: Genesis, 2010).

70. Ibid.

71. Ibid.

72. Conforti, 57.

73. Cotton Mather, *Biblia*.

74. Ibid.

75. Ibid.

76. Ibid.

77. Delbanco, *Puritan Ordeal*, 115.

78. Ibid., 224.

79. See for example T. H. Breen, "War, Taxes, and Political Brokers: The Ordeal of Massachusetts Bay, 1675–1692," in *Puritans and Adventurers: Change and Persistence in Early America*, ed. T.H. Breen (Oxford: Oxford University Press, 1980), 81–105.

80. Cotton Mather, *Biblia*.

81. Samuel Sewall, *Diary*, 80.

82. Marcus, *Colonial American Jew*, 771.

83. Winship, *Seers*, 6.

84. *Proceedings of the Massachusetts Historical Society* 44 (1911), 686.

85. Ibid.

86. Samuel Sewall, Diary, 95.

CHAPTER THREE

1. G. B. Warden, Boston, 1689–1776 (Boston: Little, Brown, 1970), 81.

2. Francis Bremer, The Puritan Experiment, 197–98.

3. William Pencak argues that Shute, having gained his position as governor thanks to the efforts of his kinsman John Shute (the Viscount Barrington), whose leadership of the Dissenting group in Parliament made him indispensable to the Massachusetts Puritans' efforts to maintain their long-standing ecclesiastical autonomy, was an essential ally both for advocates of continued autonomy for Massachusetts and for the Harvard authorities who presided over Monis's conversion and appointment. When an attempt was made on Governor Shute's life on December 31, 1722, prompting him to leave the Bay in secret, Harvard's situation grew more precarious. See Pencak's War, Politics, and Revolution in Provincial Massachusetts (Boston: Northeastern University Press, 1981).

4. Warden, 86.

5. Cotton Mather, Faith Encouraged: A Brief Relation of a Strange Impression from Heaven, on the Minds of Some Jewish Children at the City of Berlin (Boston: J. Allen, 1718), 16.

6. Benjamin Franklin, "Dogood Paper Number Four," New England Courant, May 14, 1722.

7. Shalom Goldman, God's Sacred Tongue, 45.

8. Joseph Conforti, Imagining New England, 72.

9. Michael Winship, Seers of God, 87.

10. Ibid., 89.

11. D. W. Meinig, The Shaping of America: A Geographical Perspective on 500 Years of History, vol. 1, Atlantic America, 1492–1800 (New Haven: Yale University Press, 1986), 105.

12. Yasuhide Kawashima, Puritan Justice and the Indian (Middletown: Wesleyan University Press, 1986), 112.

13. New England Courant, February 12–19. 1722. America's Historical Newspapers, http://infoweb.newsbank.com. The Courant's inclusion of such inflammatory articles as this one led to its publisher, James Franklin, needing to place his soon-to-be-famous brother, Benjamin, temporarily in charge of the paper.

14. Mather, Faith Encouraged, 12.

15. George Foote Moore, Proceedings of the Massachusetts Historical Society 52 (1919), 285.

16. Eisig Silberschlag, "Judah Monis in Light of an Unpublished Manuscript," Proceedings of the American Academy for Jewish Research (1980), 496–97.

17. Moore, 285.

18. George Alexander Kohut, "Judah Monis, M.A., the First Hebrew Instructor at Harvard University," American Journal of Languages and Literature 14.4 (1898), 218.

19. Moore, 287.

20. American Jewish Historical Society, Samuel Oppenheim collection (P-255), Box 8. New York City.

21. New England Courant, April 2, 1722. America's Historical Newspapers.

22. *Inhabitants and Estates of the Town of Boston*, and *The Crooked and Narrow Streets of the Town of Boston*, 1630–1822, compiled by Annie Haven Thwing, electronic resource accessible at the Massachusetts Historical Society (Boston: Lauriat, 1925).

23. Quoted in Moore, 290.

24. Robert H. Pfeiffer, "The Teaching of Hebrew," 366.

25. Ibid., 378.

26. Ibid., 366.

27. Silberschlag, 497.

28. Monis probably did not receive the M.A. from Harvard until his conversion had already taken place. In his article on Monis's gravestone, David Gradwohl argues convincingly that references to the grammarian's having been a 1720 graduate of Harvard proceed from an unfortunate misprint, and that the bulk of evidence points to his having been included as a member of the College's class of 1723: Gradwohl, "Judah Monis's Puzzling Gravestone as a Key to His Enigmatic Personality," *Markers, the Journal of the Association for Gravestone Studies* 21 (2005), 74.

29. Quoted in *Biographical Sketches of Those who Attended Harvard University, in Cambridge, Massachusetts*, ed. Clifford Shipton (Cambridge: Harvard University Press, 1933–1975), vol. 7 (1723), 640.

30. Quoted ibid.

31. Ibid.

32. Ibid.

33. Ibid., 641.

34. Arthur Hertzberg, *The Jews in America*, 43.

35. Silberschlag, 495–96.

36. Gradwohl, "Judah Monis's Puzzling Gravestone," 70, 91.

37. Hannah Adams, *The History of the Jews* (Boston: John Eliot, 1812), 312.

38. The complete text of the inscription, as transcribed by David Gradwohl, reads as follows:

> A native branch of Jacob see!
> Which, once from off its olive brok,
> Regrafted, from the living tree   Rom. XI. 17–24
> Of the reviving sap partook.
> From teeming Zion's fertile womb   Isai. LXVI. 8.
> As dewy drops in early morn,   Psal. CX. 3.
> Or rising bodies from the tomb,   Iohn V. 28, 29
> Be Isr'el's nation born!   Isai. LXVI. 8.

39. Frederick Greenspahn, "The Beginnings of Judaic Studies in American Universities," *Modern Judaism* 20.2 (2000), 210.

40. Kohut, "Judah Monis," 218.

41. Ibid., 219. As Jonathan Sarna points out, Kohut may have been influenced in this assessment by the late nineteenth-century case of Russian Semitist Daniel Chwolson, who famously quipped that he had converted to Christianity because "it is better to be a professor at Petersburg than a melamed in Eishishok." As Chwolson remained a lifelong friend to Jews despite his apostasy, Kohut and other turn-of-the-

century Jewish American historians who wrote about Monis were applying ample, if anachronistic, evidence for their claims that Jewish converts to Christianity were, if not conflicted, then halfhearted in their abandonment of their old faith. E-mail message to author, October 22, 2009.

42. Milton Klein, "A Jew at Harvard in the 18th Century," *Proceedings of the Massachusetts Historical Society* 97 (1985), 136–37.

43. *New England Courant*, April 2, 1722. *America's Historical Newspapers.*

44. Quoted in Lee Freidman, "Judah Monis, First Instructor in Hebrew," *Publications of the American Jewish Historical Society* 22 (1914), 3.

45. Quoted ibid.

46. Benjamin Colman, *Moses A Witness unto Our Lord Jesus* (Boston: Printed by Samuel Kneeland for Daniel Henchman, 1722), 10–11.

47. Ibid.

48. Ibid., 25.

49. Ibid., i–ii.

50. Theodore Dwight Bozeman, *The Precisianist Strain*, 7.

51. Increase Mather, preface to Colman, 10–11, ii.

52. Colman, 8–9.

53. Ibid., 9.

54. Ibid., 15.

55. Ibid., 25.

56. Ibid.

57. Mather, preface to Colman, ii–iii.

58. Shipton, *Biographical Sketches*, 641. The Mathers' championing of Monis's cause, despite such reservations, may have been motivated by their squabbling with Harvard's new leadership, which they deemed excessively liberal.

59. Mather, preface to Colman, iii.

60. Cotton Mather, *Faith Encouraged*, 7–8.

61. Ibid., 7.

62. Ibid., 8.

63. Correspondence of Bishop Kennett (Robert Wodrow) with Benjamin Colman, reprinted in *Proceedings of the Massachusetts Historical Society* 53 (1920), 79.

64. Ibid., 80.

65. Ibid.

66. Klein, 136–37.

67. Judah Monis, Preface to *The Truth, The Whole Truth, and Nothing But the Truth* (Boston: Printed by Samuel Kneeland for Daniel Henchman, 1722), i.

68. Ibid., 4.

69. Moore, 306.

70. Moore and Gradwohl both argue this point.

71. Moore, 303.

72. Monis, *The Truth*, 7.

73. Ibid., 17.

74. Ibid., 4–5.

75. Cotton Mather, *Diary 1709–1724*, ed. Clifford Shipton et al., *Collections of the Massachusetts Historical Society, Seventh Series* (Boston: Massachusetts Historical Society, 1892), 741.

76. Monis made a similar claim for the *Nomenclatura Hebraica*, a handwritten lexicon he produced to accompany the grammar, which was intended "for advancing of those who are Desirous to obtain the Knowledge of the Hebrew Tongue in of which may be that great help to understand not only the Sacred oracles in their original, but even any Jewish author." See Silberschlag, 493.

77. Judah Monis, *Hebrew Grammar* (hand-copied 1727 version of Monis's text belonging to John Cotton [1712–1789], in the collection of the Massachusetts Historical Society).

78. Quoted in Hertzberg, 44.

79. Shipton, *Biographical Sketches*, 643.

80. Ibid.

81. Moore, 296.

82. Thomas Siegel, "Professor Stephen Sewall and the Transformation of Hebrew at Harvard," in *Hebrew and the Bible in America*, ed. Shalom Goldman, 239. Sewall was later to disgrace himself in a more dramatic fashion than Monis ever did, as Harvard relieved him of all duties in 1785 because of his drinking problem.

83. Ibid.

84. Shipton, *Biographical Sketches*, 640.

85. Judah Monis, *A Grammar of the Hebrew Tongue* (Boston: J. Green, 1735), Preface.

86. Goldman, *God's Sacred Tongue*, 38.

87. Monis, *A Grammar of the Hebrew Tongue*, Preface.

88. Ibid.

89. Monis, *Hebrew Grammar* (John Cotton copy), 56.

90. Cotton Mather, *Diary*, 743.

91. Monis, *A Grammar of the Hebrew Tongue*, 92.

92. Ibid.

93. Lee Friedman, *Judah Monis: First Instructor in Hebrew at Harvard* (Cambridge: Harvard University Press, 1914), 35.

94. Goldman, *God's Sacred Tongue*, 37. As William Pencak points out (Seminar commentary, delivered at the Massachusetts Historical Society, November 5, 2009), fifty pounds had also been the exact amount that Harvard had "offered" Increase Mather in 1701 when it wished (successfully) for him to resign the presidency.

95. Friedman, "Judah Monis," 35–36.

96. Jon Butler, *Becoming America: The Revolution before 1776* (Cambridge: Harvard University Press, 2000), 94.

97. Massachusetts Judicial Court records, Massachusetts Historical Society.

98. Friedman, "Judah Monis," 16.

99. Ibid.

100. Ibid.

101. *Vital Records of Cambridge to the Year 1850*, ed. Thomas Williams Baldwin (Boston: Wright and Potter, 1915), 441.

102. Edward Augustus Holyoke, in *The Holyoke Diaries, 1706–1856* (Salem: Essex Institute, 1911), 35.

103. *Boston Weekly Newsletter*, November 20, 1760. *America's Historical Newspapers.*

104. Friedman, "Judah Monis," 17.

105. *Massachusetts Gazette and Boston Newsletter*, January 5, 1764. *America's Historical Newspapers.*

106. Adams's judgment on such matters, as William Pencak points out (Seminar commentary, MHS, November 5, 2009), may very well have followed from her doctrinaire New England Federalism, which—in the period of the early Republic—would have stipulated strong anti-Jewish prejudices. In the new, post-Washingtonian political regime, Jews were largely suspected of having "gone over" to Jefferson in sympathy with his support of the French Revolution and its enfranchisement of French Jews. See Conclusion, pp. 240–241.

107. *Records of the Church of Christ at Cambridge in New England, 1632–1830*, ed. Stephen Paschall Sharples (Boston: Eben Putnam, 1906), 210.

108. Ibid., 207.

CHAPTER FOUR

1. Richard Bushman, *From Puritan to Yankee: Character and the Social Order in Connecticut, 1690–1765* (Cambridge: Harvard University Press, 1967).

2. Jonathan Edwards, *A Treatise to Distinguish Religious Affections, in Three Parts* (Philadelphia: James Crissy, 1821), 94.

3. See Shalom Goldman, *God's Sacred Tongue*, 74–88, for an extended treatment of Edwards's Hebraism.

4. Timothy Hall, *Contested Boundaries: Itineracy and the Reshaping of the Colonial American Religious World* (Durham: Duke University Press, 1994), 2.

5. Thomas Kidd, *The Protestant Interest: New England after Puritanism* (New Haven: Yale University Press, 2004).

6. Hall, 21.

7. An attendant mystery here is that the earliest extant grave marker in that burial ground dates only to 1761. Preliminary archaeological surveys suggest the strong possibility of earlier unmarked graves, but to date no firm evidence for the date or exact location of these sites exists. Indeed, Sewall's single diary reference constitutes the strongest hint of such graves existing, since it is the only written evidence of any Jewish burials taking place in Newport before the 1760s. See David Gradwohl, *Like Tablets of the Law Thrown Down: The Colonial Jewish Burying Ground in Newport, Rhode Island* (Ames, Iowa: Sigler Printing, 2007).

8. Morris Gutstein, *The Story of the Jews of Newport*, 63.

9. Ezra Stiles's hand-drawn copy of this map indicates a "Jews Street" and an adjacent "Jews Alley," both presumably dating to the time of the map's original issue in 1712. The map is in the Ezra Stiles Papers in the collection of the Massachusetts Historical Society.

10. Leon Huhner, "The Jews in New England (Other Than Rhode Island) Prior to 1800," *Publications of the American Jewish Historical Society* 11 (1922), 12.

11. Gutstein, 55.

12. Jacob Marcus, *Early American Jewry: The Jews of New York, New England, and Canada, 1649–1794* (New York: Jewish Publication Society of America, 1961), 198.

13. *Commerce of Rhode Island, 1726–1800*, vol. 1 (Boston: Massachusetts Historical Society, 1915).

14. American Jewish Historical Society, Jacques Judah Lyons Collection (New York: American Jewish Historical Society, 1920; hereafter Lyons Collection), vol. 1, 151.

15. Marcus, *Colonial American Jew*, 318.

16. Jonathan Sarna, *American Judaism*, 30.

17. Hall, 4.

18. Ibid., 33.

19. Kidd, *Protestant Interest*, 12.

20. See T. H. Breen, "An Empire of Goods: The Anglicization of Colonial America, 1690–1776," *Journal of British Studies* 25 (1986), 467–99, and John Murrin, "Anglicizing an American Colony: The Transformation of Provincial Massachusetts" (Ph.D. diss., Yale University, 1966).

21. Joseph Conforti, *Imagining New England*, 74.

22. Ibid.

23. Hall, 5.

24. Ibid., 6.

25. Marcus, *Colonial American Jew*, 875.

26. Transcription of Lopez's letter in the Samuel Oppenheim Papers.

27. Lyons Collection, vol. 2, 177.

28. Marcus, *Colonial American Jew*, 876.

29. Lyons Collection, vol. 2, 177.

30. Ibid.

31. Ibid., 178.

32. Ibid., 179.

33. Irwin Rhodes, *References to Jews in the Newport Mercury, 1758–1786* (Cincinnati: American Jewish Archives, 1961), 4.

34. Isaac Mendez Belisario, *A sermon occasioned by the death of His late Majesty: preached on Saturday the 29th of November, 1760, in the synagogue of the Portuguese Jews in London* (London: Brotherton, 1761), 15.

35. Seebert Goldowsky, "Brown University and the Jews," *Rhode Island Jewish Historical Studies* 16 (1958), 87.

36. Belisario, 16.

37. Elisha Williams, quoted in Patricia Bonomi, *Under the Cope of Heaven*, 156.

38. Marcus, *Colonial American Jew*, 319.

39. Gutstein, 98–99.

40. *Newport Mercury*, December 5, 1763. America's Historical Newspapers, http://infoweb.newsbank.com.

41. Hall, 85.

42. Ibid., 77.

43. Ibid., 85.

44. Gilbert Tennent, *The Dangers of an Unconverted Ministry* (Philadelphia, 1741), reprinted

in *The Great Awakening: Documents on the Revival of Religion, 1740–1745*, ed. Richard Bushman (Chapel Hill: University of North Carolina Press, 1989), 73.

45. Ibid., 73–74.

46. Marcus, *Colonial American Jew*, 945.

47. This rift between New England merchants occurred when the entrepreneurial aspirations of over a thousand middling New England traders seeking a means to gain capital on extended credit were quashed by English colonial authorities, who had gained the backing of Boston's more "opulent" merchants in a press to maintain a tighter monopoly on the New England trade. See, for example, Margaret Newell, "A Revolution in Economic Thought: Currency and Development in Eighteenth Century Massachusetts," in *Entrepreneurs: The Boston Business Community, 1700–1850*, ed. Conrad Edick Wright and Katheryn Viens (Boston: Massachusetts Historical Society, 1997), 1–22.

48. Holly Snyder, "Reconstructing the Lives of Newport's Hidden Jews," in *The Jews of Rhode Island*, ed. George Goodwin and Ellen Smith (Hanover, N.H.: University Press of New England, 2004), 27.

49. Ibid., 31.

50. Ibid.

51. Lyons Collection, vol. 2, 182.

52. William Pencak, *Jews and Gentiles*, 90.

53. Ibid.

54. Ibid. See Chapter 6 of this book.

55. New Englanders had already gained a wide reputation for habitually suing one another. See review essay by John Murrin in *History and Theory* 2, no. 1 (1972), 226–75.

56. Marcus, *Colonial American Jew*, 611.

57. Lyons Collection, vol. 2, 210.

58. Quoted in Huhner. Though Lopez had no public critics, Stiles came closest in his private writings, and before his friend's death, to condemning him. For all of his genuine interest in their religious traditions and practices, Stiles couldn't help but harbor contempt for Lopez's apparently small-minded rejection of Christ.

59. Marcus, *Colonial American Jew*, 642.

60. Lyons Collection, vol. 2, 457.

61. *Commerce of Rhode Island*, vol. 1, 162.

62. Ibid.

63. Ibid., 18.

64. Snyder, "A Sense of Place," 135.

65. Virginia Bever Platt, "And Don't Forget the Guinea Voyage: The Slave Trade of Aaron Lopez of Newport," *William and Mary Quarterly*, 3rd ser., 32 (October 1975), 601–18.

66. Virginia Bever Platt, "Tar, Staves, and New England Rum: The Trade of Aaron Lopez of Newport, Rhode Island with Colonial North Carolina," *North Carolina Historical Review* 48 (1971), 16–18.

67. For a thorough refutation of efforts by latter-day anti-Semites to suggest that Jews like Lopez profited inordinately from the slave trade, or that the slave trade was a

"Jewish conspiracy," see Eli Faber, *Jews, Slaves, and the Slave Trade: Setting the Record Straight* (New York: New York University Press, 1998).

68. Snyder, "A Sense of Place," 136.

69. *Commerce of Rhode Island*, vol. 1, 415.

70. Ibid.

71. Snyder, "Reconstructing."

72. Pencak, *Jews and Gentiles*, 94.

73. Richard Bushman, *The Refinement of America: Persons, Houses, Cities* (New York: Vintage, 1993), 170.

74. Ibid.

75. Conforti, 68.

76. David de Sola Pool, *Touro Synagogue of Congregation Jeshuat Israel, Newport, Rhode Island: Founded 1658, dedicated 1763, designated as a national historic site, 1946* (Newport: Society of Friends of Touro National Historic Shrine, 1946), 14.

77. Nancy Halverson Schloss, "Peter Harrison, the Touro Synagogue, and the Wren City Church," *Winterthur Portfolio* 18 (1973), 187–200.

78. Marcus, *Colonial American Jew*, 642.

79. Bushman, *Refinement*, 174.

80. Lyons Collection, vol. 2, 454.

81. Pool, *Touro Synagogue*, 8.

82. Lyons Collection, vol. 2, 454.

83. Pool, *Touro Synagogue*, 11.

84. Bushman, *Refinement*, 176.

85. Conforti, 73.

86. Sarna, *American Judaism*, 30.

87. *Commerce of Rhode Island*, vol. 1, 694.

88. Ibid., vol. 2, 51.

89. Ibid., 58.

90. Ibid., 68.

91. Samuel Oppenheim Papers.

92. Ibid.

93. Marcus, *Colonial American Jew*, 976–77.

94. Ibid.

95. *Newport Mercury*, November 28, 1765, America's Historical Newspapers.

96. Eli Faber, *A Time for Planting*, 92.

97. Kidd, *Protestant Interest*, 14.

CHAPTER FIVE

1. The Thanksgiving had been declared in light of Britain's recent repeal of the Stamp Act.

2. Edmund Morgan, *The Gentle Puritan: 1727–1795* (New Haven: Yale University Press, 1974), 134.

3. Ezra Stiles, sermon notes for 1765–1770. Ezra Stiles Papers, Massachusetts Historical Society.

4. Ibid.

5. Christopher Grasso, *A Speaking Aristocracy: Transforming Public Discourse in Eighteenth-Century Connecticut* (Chapel Hill: University of North Carolina Press, 1999), 233.

6. Benjamin Carp, *Rebels Rising: Cities and the American Revolution* (Oxford: Oxford University Press, 2007), 99.

7. Jonathan Sarna, *American Judaism*, 282.

8. Ibid.

9. Shalom Goldman, *God's Sacred Tongue*, 56.

10. Stiles complained in his diary about Touro's pronunciation of Hebrew, which he deemed less skillful than that of Haim Carigal, the visiting rabbi from Hebron whose time in Newport is the primary focus of this chapter (see below). As Laura Leibman points out, however, the fact that Touro needed to have his pronunciation corrected from time to time as he read from the Torah was no commentary on his skill level as a reader of Hebrew; since Torah readers do not have the benefit of any vowel markers in their texts, the pronunciation of the most expert readers is subject to regular correction in the course of a service. Laura Leibman, "From Holy Land to New England Canaan: Rabbi Haim Carigal and Sephardic Itinerant Preaching in the Eighteenth Century," *Early American Literature* 44 (Spring 2009), 88–89.

11. Arthur Chiel, "Ezra Stiles and the Jews," in *Hebrew and the Bible in America: The First Two Centuries*, ed. Shalom Goldman, 157.

12. Ibid.

13. George Alexander Kohut, *Ezra Stiles and the Jews: Selected Passages from His Literary Diary concerning Jews and Judaism* (New York: P. Cowan, 1902), 18.

14. As one scholar points out, this early in Stiles's career, the minister's acquaintance with Hebrew was scant; it would not be long, however, before the Newport Jews would educate him to the proper distinction between the article in Hebrew and the article in Arabic. Ibid., 18.

15. Ezra Stiles, *The Literary Diary of Ezra Stiles*, vol. 1 (New York: Scribners, 1901), 6n.

16. Chiel, "Ezra Stiles and the Jews," 157.

17. Stiles, *Literary Diary*, vol. 1, 159.

18. Ezra Stiles, *Extracts from the itineraries and other miscellanies of Ezra Stiles, D.D., LL.D., 1755–1794: with a Selection from His Correspondence* (New Haven: Yale University Press, 1916), 53.

19. Ibid.

20. Stiles, sermon notes 1765–1770.

21. Ibid.

22. Ibid.

23. For a broader discussion of future revolutionaries' rhetorical invocation of the British king as the guarantor of their liberties, see Pauline Maier, *From Resistance to Revolution* (New York: Vintage Press, 1972), especially 100–103.

24. Stiles, sermon notes 1765–1770.

25. Carp, 99.

26. Elaine Crane, *A Dependent People: Newport, Rhode Island in the Revolutionary Era* (New York: Fordham University Press, 1985), 48.

27. Ibid., 107.

28. Goldman, *God's Sacred Tongue*, 55.
29. Grasso, 237.
30. Goldman, *God's Sacred Tongue*, 59.
31. Ezra Stiles, sermon notes 1765–1770.
32. *Literary Diary*, vol. 1, 5.
33. Ibid., 10.
34. Ibid.
35. Ibid., 422.
36. Ibid., 20.
37. Ibid., 19.
38. Jonathan Sarna, "The Impact of the American Revolution on American Jews," in *Jews and the Founding of the Republic*, ed. Benny Kraut and Jonathan Sarna (New York: M. Weiner, 1985), 153.
39. *Literary Diary*, vol. 1, 5.
40. Ibid., 41.
41. Ibid., 91.
42. Ibid.
43. Ibid., 151.
44. Ibid.
45. Ibid., 220.
46. Ibid., 317.
47. Goldman, *God's Sacred Tongue*, 60.
48. Morgan, 134.
49. Ibid., 121.
50. Abraham Redwood, *Laws of the Redwood Library Corporation and A Catalogue of the Redwood Library and Athenaeum* (Newport: Samuel Hart, 1821), 3–4.
51. Ibid., 3.
52. Grasso, 240.
53. Matt Goldfish, *Judaism in the Theology of Sir Isaac Newton* (Dordrecht, the Netherlands: Kluwer, 1998), 33.
54. Holly Snyder, "A Sense of Place," 11.
55. Holly Snyder, "English Markets, Jewish Merchants, and Atlantic Endeavors: Jews and the Making of British Transatlantic Commercial Culture, 1650–1800," in *Atlantic Diasporas: Jews, Conversos, and Crypto-Jews in the Age of Mercantilism*, ed. Richard Kagan and Philip Morgan (Baltimore: Johns Hopkins University Press, 2009).
56. See Crane, *A Dependent People*, and Snyder, "A Sense of Place."
57. Ezra Stiles, sermon notes for 1757–1765.
58. Ibid.
59. Morgan, 168.
60. Grasso, 236.
61. W. Willner, "Ezra Stiles and the Jews," *Publications of the American Jewish Historical Society*, no. 8 (1902), 121.
62. Grasso, 265.
63. *Literary Diary*, vol. 1, 376–77.

64. Arthur Chiel, "The Mystery of the Rabbi's Lost Portrait," *Judaism* 22, no. 4 (Fall 1973), 484.

65. Stiles's and Carigal's correspondence in Hebrew (along with Stiles's own translated English versions of each letter) is housed in the Ezra Stiles Papers at the Beinecke Library at Yale University. They are used with permission.

66. *Literary Diary*, vol. 1, 370.

67. Letter from Haim Carigal to Ezra Stiles, May 29, 1773. Stiles Papers, Beinecke Library.

68. *Literary Diary*, vol. 1, 389.

69. Ibid., 357.

70. Ibid.

71. Letter from Ezra Stiles to Haim Carigal, July 19, 1773. Stiles Papers, Beinecke Library.

72. Ibid.

73. Ibid.

74. Ibid.

75. Ibid.

76. Ibid.

77. David de Sola Pool, *Portraits Etched in Stone: Early Jewish Settlers, 1682–1831* (New York: Columbia University Press, 1952), 483.

78. Ibid.

79. Letter from Benjamin Gale to Ezra Stiles, June 29, 1773. Ezra Stiles Papers, Beinecke Library.

80. Stiles, *Literary Diary*, vol. 1, 386–87.

81. As Laura Leibman points out, Carigal actually delivered his sermon in Ladino, the Spanish-Hebrew dialect of most Sephardim: "From Holy Land to New England Canaan," 71.

82. Ibid., 79.

83. *Literary Diary*, vol. 1, 393.

84. Haim Carigal, *A sermon preached at the Synagogue in Newport, Rhode-Island, 1773* (New York: Jewish Publication Society of America, 1975), 14.

85. See Grasso.

86. *Literary Diary*, vol. 1, 393.

87. Ibid.

88. Carigal, *Sermon*, 3.

89. Leibman, 84.

90. Ibid.

91. Carigal, *Sermon*, 7.

92. *Literary Diary*, vol. 1, 378.

93. Ibid., 392.

94. Ibid.

95. Ibid., 399.

96. Grasso, 238.

97. *Literary Diary*, vol. 1, 151.

98. William Pencak, *Jews and Gentiles*, 105.

99. Crane, 133. By most historians' estimates, approximately half of the Newport Jews can be classified as having been loyal, even if they only became so gradually, to the American cause. At least two Newport Jews are documented as having served in the Continental Army.

100. Ibid., 120.

101. Ibid., 160.

102. Alexander Guttman, "Ezra Stiles, Newport Jewry, and a Question of Jewish Law," *American Jewish Archives* 34 (April 1982), 100.

103. Ibid.

104. Ibid., 99.

105. Pencak, *Jews and Gentiles*, 97.

106. Ibid., 98.

107. Ibid., 188.

108. Ibid., 106.

109. Ezra Stiles Papers, Massachusetts Historical Society.

110. Ibid.

111. Grasso, 253.

112. *Literary Diary*, vol. 1, 114.

113. Ibid.

114. Ibid.

115. Morgan, 144.

116. *Literary Diary*, vol. 1, 115.

117. Ibid.

118. Morgan, 176.

119. Ibid.

120. *Literary Diary*, vol. 1, 400.

121. Ibid.

122. Letter from Haim Carigal to Ezra Stiles, September 14, 1775. Ezra Stiles Papers, Beinecke Library.

123. Ibid.

124. Letter from Ezra Stiles to Haim Carigal, May 1774. Ezra Stiles Papers, Beinecke Library.

125. Ibid.

126. Ibid.

127. Letter from Haim Carigal to Ezra Stiles, September 14, 1775. Ezra Stiles Papers, Beinecke Library.

128. Letter from Ezra Stiles to Haim Carigal. July 7, 1775. Ezra Stiles Papers, Beinecke Library.

129. Chiel, "Mystery," 483.

130. Ibid.

131. Grasso, 236.

132. Robert Blair St. George, *Conversing by Signs: Poetics of Implication in New England Culture* (Chapel Hill: University of North Carolina Press, 1998), 368.

133. *Literary Diary*, vol. 1, 131.

134. Ibid.

135. Grasso, 230.

136. *Literary Diary*, vol. 1, 354.

137. Ibid.

138. Ibid.

139. Chiel, "Mystery," 485–86.

140. King had evidently gotten his dates wrong, as the entirety of Carigal's sojourn in Newport had occurred in 1773; or he had been asked to depict the rabbi as he might have appeared *before* he arrived in Rhode Island.

CHAPTER SIX

1. Letter from Moses Michael Hays to Jacob Rod Rivera and Aaron Lopez. December 18, 1770. Moses Michael Hays Papers, Correspondence from 1768–1771, Massachusetts Historical Society.

2. Ibid.

3. Letter from Moses Michael Hays to Samson Mears, December 3, 1770. Massachusetts Historical Society.

4. Ibid.

5. Letter from Moses Michael Hays to Myer and Jacob Polock, December 31, 1770. Massachusetts Historical Society.

6. Ibid.

7. Letter from Moses Michael Hays to Solomon Simpson, December 10, 1770. Massachusetts Historical Society.

8. Ibid.

9. Letter from Moses Michael Hays to Mssrs. Evers and Backe, December 11, 1770. Massachusetts Historical Society.

10. Ibid.

11. Ibid.

12. Jon Butler, *Becoming America*, 243.

13. Ibid.

14. Ellen Smith, "Jews of Boston," 28.

15. Ibid.

16. Ibid., 34.

17. Ibid., 35.

18. Ibid.

19. Harold Korn, "The Receipt Books of Judah and Moses Michael Hays, Commencing January 12, 1763 and Ending July 18, 1776," *Publications of the American Jewish Historical Society* 28 (1922), 223–30.

20. Ibid., 225–26.

21. Letter from Jonas Philips to Moses Michael Hays, September 14, 1769. Massachusetts Historical Society.

22. Letter from Moses Michael Hays to Jacob Pinto, August 10, 1769. Massachusetts Historical Society.

23. Stephen Birmingham, *The Grandees*, 140.

24. Letter from Moses Michael Hays to Samson Mears, December 3, 1770. Massachusetts Historical Society.

25. Letter from Moses Michael Hays to Myer and Jacob Polock, December 31, 1770. Massachusetts Historical Society.

26. Ibid.

27. Letter from Moses Michael Hays to Samuel Hart, August 14, 1769. Massachusetts Historical Society.

28. Letter from Moses Michael Hays to Jacob Rod Rivera and Aaron Lopez, December 18, 1770. Massachusetts Historical Society.

29. The New-York Journal, June 14, 21, and, 1770. America's Historical Newspapers, http://infoweb.newsbank.com.

30. Newport Mercury, May 20, September 30, and October 14, 1771. America's Historical Newspapers.

31. Ibid., July 27, 1772.

32. Commerce of Rhode Island, vol. 2, 211.

33. Letter from Moses Michael Hays to Mssrs. Harford and Powell, May 12, 1769. Massachusetts Historical Society.

34. Lee Max Friedman, "Mr. Hays Speaks Out," Menorah Journal 27 (1939), 79.

35. Richard B. Morris, "The Role of the Jews in the American Revolution in Historical Perspective," in American Jewish History: The Colonial and Early National Periods, 1654–1840, ed. Jeffrey Gurock (London: Routledge, 1998), 58.

36. Friedman, "Mr. Hays," 79.

37. Ibid., 80–81.

38. Ibid., 82.

39. Newport Mercury, June 3, 1776, America's Historical Newspapers.

40. Perhaps he went to Boston in order to avoid other Jews, as he could be freer there to make the most of his trade connections to Jews in other locales without having to compete directly with them. William Pencak notes a similar pattern in connection with Jews who settled in the Pennsylvania towns of Easton, Reading, and Lancaster during the eighteenth century, presumably in order to avoid having to compete directly with one another for the same markers. See Jews and Gentiles in Early America.

41. Richard Bushman, The King and the People in Provincial Massachusetts (Chapel Hill: University of North Carolina Press, 1992), 213.

42. Ibid., 241.

43. Independent Ledger (Boston), December 24, 1781. America's Historical Newspapers.

44. Smith, 36.

45. Independent Ledger, December 24, 1781.

46. Annie Haven Thwing, Inhabitants and Estates of the town of Boston and Crooked and Narrow Streets of Boston. New England Historic Genealogical Society and Massachusetts Historical Society (electronic resource).

47. Smith, 38.

48. Samuel Joseph May, Memoir of Samuel Joseph May (Boston: BiblioLife, 2009), 15.

49. Ibid.

50. Ibid., 16.

51. Ibid.

52. Morris, 50.

53. Robert Treat Paine, "Elegiac Sonnet Inscribed to the Memory of M. M. Hays, Esq.," in *The Works in Verse and Prose* (Boston: Belcher, 1812), 292.

54. *New England Chronicle*, January 10, 1782, America's Historical Newspapers.

55. *New England Chronicle*, July 6, 1782, America's Historical Newspapers.

56. *Independent Chronicle*, August 9, 1787, America's Historical Newspapers.

57. Ibid.

58. *American Herald*, June 21 and 28, 1784, *Independent Ledger*, June 21 and 28, 1784, *Salem Gazette*, June 22 and 29, 1784, and *Independent Chronicle*, June 24, 1784. America's Historical Newspapers.

59. Sereno D. Nickerson, "Moses Michael Hays," *New England Freemason* 11 (1878), 71.

60. *Federal Orrery*, July 4 and 7, 1796, and *Massachusetts Messenger*, March 16, 1798. America's Historical Newspapers.

61. *Massachusetts Centinel*, November 28, December 12, and December 28, 1789, and *Independent Chronicle* December 10, 1789 and January 9, 1790. America's Historical Newspapers.

62. Smith, 36.

63. *Continental Journal* (Boston), December 18, 1783. America's Historical Newspapers.

64. N. S. B. Gras, *The Massachusetts First National Bank in Boston* (Boston: Harvard University Press, 1937), 21.

65. *Boston Gazette*, May 3, 1805, *Independent Chronicle*, May 13, 1805, *Newburyport Herald*, May 14, 1805, *New York Herald*, May 22, 1805, *New England Palladium*, May 14, 1805. America's Historical Newspapers.

66. Steven Bullock, *Revolutionary Brotherhood: Freemasonry and the Transformation of the American Social Order* (Chapel Hill: University of North Carolina Press, 1996).

67. Butler, 179.

68. Letter from Moses Michael Hays to Samuel Stringer, July 3, 1769. Massachusetts Historical Society.

69. Letter from Samuel Stringer to Moses Michael Hays, July, 1769. Massachusetts Historical Society.

70. Letter from Moses Michael Hays to Jacob Rod Rivera and Aaron Lopez, December 31, 1770. Massachusetts Historical Society.

71. Bullock, 4.

72. Ibid., 79.

73. *Newport Mercury*, June 13, 1781. America's Historical Newspapers.

74. Harry Smith and Jacob Hugo Tatsch, *Moses Michael Hays: Merchant-Citizen-Freemason, 1739–1805* (Boston: M. M. Hays Lodge, 1937).

75. Bullock, 23.

76. Ibid., 85.

77. Ibid.

78. Ibid., 59.

79. Nickerson, 51.

80. Ibid.

81. James Hodge Codding, "The Career of Moses Michael Hays," in *Jubilee Year of the Supreme Council of Grand Inspectors* (Boston: Supreme Council for Northern Jurisdiction, 1918), 99.

82. Bullock, 96.

83. Ibid., 98.

84. Ibid., 90.

85. Ibid., 113.

86. *Washington's Masonic Correspondence*, ed. Julius Friedrich Sachse (New York: Press of the New Era Printing Company, 1915), 12.

87. Bullock, 85.

88. Ibid.

89. Nickerson, 77.

90. Jacob Marcus, *American Jewry: Documents, Primarily Hitherto Unpublished Manuscripts* (Cincinnati: Hebrew Union College Press, 1959), 46.

91. Smith and Tatsch, 58.

92. Ibid.

93. Bullock, 152.

94. Ibid., 167.

95. Lee Max Friedman, *Jewish Pioneers and Patriots* (New York: Macmillan, 1942), 391.

96. *Federal Orrery*, September 22, 1796. *America's Historical Newspapers*.

97. *Boston Directory* (Boston: Manning and Lowry, 1796), 54.

98. Smith, 39.

99. May, 15.

100. Smith, 39.

101. *Newburyport Herald, Massachusetts Spy* (Worcester), *Farm Weekly News* (Walpole), *New Hampshire Sentinel* (Keene), and *Eastern Argus* (Portland), May 14, 18, 18, 18, and 24, respectively, 1805. *America's Historical Newspapers*.

102. Judah Touro, a nephew of Hays who had grown up in the family's household in Boston, went on to attain notable stature as one of the greatest American philanthropists of his era and, for many, was the public face of nineteenth-century American Judaism. Touro eventually settled in New Orleans, but the Newport synagogue was later named in his memory as well as that of its first hazzan, his father Isaac.

103. Birmingham, 140.

104. Smith and Tatsch, 41.

CONCLUSION

1. Lyons Collection, vol. 2, 185, 188.

2. Jonathan Sarna, *American Judaism*, 38.

3. Quoted in Arthur Hertzberg, *The Jews in America*, 69.

4. Ira Rosenwaike, "An Estimate and Analysis of the Jewish Population of the United States in 1790," *Publications of the American Jewish Historical Society* 50 (September 1960), 25.

5. Eran Shalev, "The Perfect Republic: The Mosaic Constitution in Revolutionary New England, 1775–1788," *New England Quarterly* 82 (June 2009), 239.

6. Nathan Perl-Rosenthal, "The 'Divine Right of Republics': Hebraic Republicanism and the Debate over Kingless Government in Revolutionary America," *William and Mary Quarterly* 66 (July 2009), 264.

7. Shalev, 252.

8. Ibid., 254.

9. Frederic Cople Jaher, *Scapegoats*, 135. Federalists had previously gone on record as supportive of Jewish liberty, as in Pennsylvania a Federalist caucus had passed a state constitution that enfranchised Jews who, under the 1776 version, had been restricted from voting.

10. John Diggins, *John Adams* (New York: Times Books, 2003), 160.

11. February 16, 1809 letter reprinted in *Publications of the American Jewish Historical Society* 4 (1895), 220.

12. Mordecai Manuel Noah, *Travels in England, France, Spain and the Barbary States in the Years 1813, 1814 and 1815* (New York: Kirk and Mercein, 1819), Appendix, xxvi.

13. Ibid.

14. Massachusetts' support of a state church and continued use of a test oath prevented Jewish enfranchisement until the 1830s. New Hampshire maintained its prohibition of Jewish voting rights until 1871.

15. Rudolf Glanz, *Studies in Judaica Americana* (New York: KTAV, 1970), 333.

16. Ibid.

17. Ibid., 116.

18. Rowena Olegario, *A Culture of Credit: Embedding Trust and Transparency in American Business* (Cambridge: Harvard University Press, 2006), 173.

19. Nathaniel Hawthorne, *The Works of Nathaniel Hawthorne*, vol. 3 (New York: Houghton Mifflin, 1883), 490.

20. Gerd Korman, "Jews as a Changing People of the Talmud: An American Exploration," *Modern Judaism* 21 (2001), 36.

21. Robert Loewenberg, *An American Idol: Emerson and the "Jewish Idea"* (Lanham, Md.: University Press of America, 1984), 34.

22. Henry Wadsworth Longfellow, "At the Jewish Cemetery in Newport," in *The Complete Writings of Henry Wadsworth Longfellow*, vol. 3 (New York: Houghton Mifflin, 1908), 191.

23. Lyons Collection, vol. 2, 435.

24. David Gradwohl, *Tablets*, 45.

25. Ibid.

26. Ibid., 54.

27. N. H. Gould, in *Worcester Magazine and Historical Journal*, 1826.

28. As indeed it did; as early as 1860 more Catholics lived in New England than in any other region of the nation. See Stephen Nissenbaum, "New England," in *All Over the Map: Rethinking American Regions*, ed. Edward Ayers and Peter Onuf (Baltimore: Johns Hopkins University Press, 1996), 39. A handful of salutary "Jewish" events did still take place in the region both before and after the Civil War. German Jewish synagogues were established in Boston, Hartford, and even Bangor, Maine, in the

1840s. In 1854, the death of Judah Touro, a nephew of Moses Michael Hays and antebellum America's greatest philanthropist, occasioned a noteworthy public burial in the Newport cemetery which time, as Longfellow had so recently written, seemed altogether to have forgotten. The year 1881 saw the reopening of the Newport (now called Touro) synagogue as a shrine not only to America's Jews but to the very idea of religious freedom. But even then, the repopulation of the synagogue was a fleeting event, and many of the Jews who came to the reopening had had to make pilgrimages there from other distant cities and American regions.

INDEX